Richard II

edited by Andrew Worrall

with additional material by John Seely and Ken Elliott

Series Editor: John Seely

Don Gressw

Heinemann

Heinemann Educational Publishers
Halley Court, Jordan Hill, Oxford OX2 8EJ
A division of Reed Educational and Professional Publishing Ltd

OXFORD BLANTYRE CHICAGO PORTSMOUTH (NH) USA
MELBOURNE AUKLAND IBADAN GABORONE

First published in the *Heinemann Advanced Shakespeare* series
2000

06 05 04 03 02 01 00
10 9 8 7 6 5 4 3 2 1

ISBN 0 435 193066

Cover design by Miller Craig and Cocking
Cover illustration by Nigel Casseldine

Typeset by TechType

Printed and bound in the United Kingdom by Biddles Ltd,
www.biddles.co.uk

CONTENTS

How to use this book

This edition of *Richard II* has been prepared to provide
you with several different kinds of information and guidance.

The introduction

Before the text of the play there is:
* a summary of the plot
* a brief explanation of Shakespeare's texts.

The text and commentary

On each right-hand page you will find the text of the play. On
the facing left-hand pages there are three types of support
material:
* a summary of the action
* detailed explanations of difficult words, phrases and longer
  sections of text
* suggestions of points you might find it useful to think
  about as you read the play.

End-of-act activities

After each act there is a set of activities. These can be tackled as
you read the play. Many students, however, may want to leave
these until they undertake a second reading. They consist of a
number of different activities, including:

Keeping track: straightforward questions directing your
attention to precisely what happens in each act.

Characters: questions that help to guide your study of the
changing perspectives of the characters.

Drama: practical drama activities to help you focus on key
characters, relationships and situations.

Close study: a detailed exploration of the act, scene by scene and
in some cases, line by line.

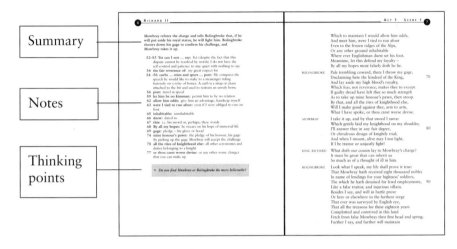

Themes and imagery: brief guidance on important themes to look for in the imagery of the play.

Key scene: a focus on an important scene in the act. This section applies the thinking you have done in the CLOSE STUDY to a key scene within the act and encourages you to think about how the scene fits in to the structure of the play as a whole.

Writing: progressive activities throughout the book help you to develop essay writing skills.

Explorations

At the end of the book there are a variety of different items designed to draw together your thoughts and insights about the play as a whole:

- how to approach thinking about the whole play
- work on character
- work on themes and issues
- work on the language of the play
- guidance on how to tackle practical drama activities
- advice on preparing for an examination
- advice on essay writing
- practice essay questions
- glossary of technical terms.

The story of the play

Act 1
It is the year 1398. **Richard II, King of England**, listens to the accusations made by his cousin, **Henry Bolingbroke, Duke of Herford,** against **Thomas Mowbray, Duke of Norfolk**. Bolingbroke charges Mowbray with treason, with stealing money that should have been paid to the King's army, and with conspiring to murder the Duke of Gloucester, who was the uncle of both Richard and Henry. Mowbray denies the charges. Both men demand trial by combat, a duel to the death, since they claim that God will give victory to whichever of them is telling the truth. Richard attempts to reconcile them. When they refuse, he appoints a date for their combat.

The widowed **Duchess of Gloucester** is convinced of Mowbray's guilt and infuriated that Bolingbroke's father, **John of Gaunt, Duke of Lancaster**, will not take action. Gaunt believes that the King is responsible for Gloucester's death and that only God can avenge.

When all assemble for the trial by combat, Richard stops the fight as it is about to begin and banishes both Bolingbroke and Mowbray, the latter for life. When Gaunt intervenes the King reduces Bolingbroke's exile from ten years to six. Father and son part sadly.

Richard and his other cousin, the **Duke of Aumerle**, are amused by Bolingbroke's downfall. The King turns his attention to raising an army to put down a rebellion in Ireland but is interrupted by news that John of Gaunt is on his deathbed and wishes to see him.

Act 2
Gaunt is with his brother the **Duke of York** (father of Aumerle) who says that Richard is influenced by flatterers and will not listen to the dying man's wise advice. Gaunt is appalled that Richard has wasted his resources and betrayed the country. The King will not listen to him and becomes angry. As soon as Gaunt

dies Richard seizes his possessions to help pay for his Irish army. York complains bitterly at this injustice but is ignored. The **Earl of Northumberland** discloses to **Ross** and **Willoughby** that Bolingbroke, with an army, is planning to return from exile to claim his inheritance.

Richard's wife, **Queen Isabel**, reveals her grief at Richard's absence in Ireland and her premonition of disaster. She soon learns of Bolingbroke's return and the treachery of Northumberland and other noblemen. York promises to support Richard but it is clear that, since Richard is in Ireland, there is no army to defend his crown.

In Gloucestershire Bolingbroke and Northumberland meet their allies, including Northumberland's son, **Harry Percy**, but are confronted by the Duke of York. However, York is sympathetic to Bolingbroke and has no army with which to fight him.

Richard is still in Ireland and the **Earl of Salisbury** speaks of his fear that Richard will fall from power: his Welsh supporters believe him already dead and will not stay to fight.

Act 3

Bolingbroke reaches Bristol where he executes two of Richard's favourites, **Bushy** and **Green**.

Richard arrives in Wales. Initially he believes that God will save him from Bolingbroke's rebellion, but hearing of the departure of his Welsh army, that Bolingbroke has gained huge support across the country, and of the death of his favourites, he despairs and will not be comforted. Aumerle suggests that they can rely on the support of his father, York, but when Richard learns that he also has joined Bolingbroke he decides to retreat to Flint Castle.

Bolingbroke arrives at Flint to find the King already there. He sends Northumberland to negotiate on his behalf. Richard appears on the castle battlements with every semblance of power but he knows that Bolingbroke can now do whatever he chooses.

The Queen, staying at the Duke of York's house, hears a gardener commenting on the King's downfall. He laments that

Richard has not exercised the same care for England as the gardener has for his garden.

Act 4

Bolingbroke holds court in Westminster Hall, London. He asks one of Richard's favourites, **Bagot**, to tell what he knows of the death of the Duke of Gloucester. Bagot accuses Aumerle of conspiring with Richard. Aumerle refutes the charge. Other lords echo the accusation, though the **Duke of Surrey** supports Aumerle. It is agreed to bring the Duke of Norfolk home from exile in order to hear his evidence, but the **Bishop of Carlisle** reports that Norfolk has died.

York enters with the news that Richard has agreed to abdicate in favour of Bolingbroke. Carlisle is appalled that God's anointed King should be replaced in this way and prophesies that the result will be civil war. Northumberland arrests the Bishop for treason. Bolingbroke commands Richard be sent for to make a public abdication.

Richard holds centre stage. He teases Bolingbroke, inviting him to seize the crown that he holds before him. Eventually he makes his abdication speech but Northumberland then demands that he read out a list of his crimes against the state. Richard objects and reveals his grief and despair. Bolingbroke has him conveyed to the Tower of London and appoints the date for his own coronation.

After Bolingbroke has left, the **Abbot of Westminster** reveals that there is a plot, involving Carlisle and Aumerle, to restore Richard to the throne.

Act 5

The Queen meets Richard on the road to the Tower. She is surprised that he seems so resigned to his fate. Northumberland enters to say that Richard is now to be imprisoned in Pomfret Castle in Yorkshire and the Queen must go to a French convent. They part from each other with great tenderness.

The Duke of York is giving his wife an account of Bolingbroke and Richard's entry into London when his son, Aumerle, enters.

The Duke sees a document tucked in Aumerle's clothing and demands to read it. When he realises that it is evidence of the conspiracy against Bolingbroke (now King Henry IV) he sets off to reveal all to the King. The Duchess cannot stop her husband so tells her son to take York's horse and confess all to the King before York can reach him.

The King is at Windsor Castle, complaining of the delinquent behaviour of his son, when Aumerle bursts in and demands a private audience. Aumerle asks for forgiveness which the King grants, even before he has heard what had been planned. York arrives and tries to persuade the King to execute his son for treason. The Duchess of York enters and demands that the King pardon Aumerle, not understanding that he has already done so. Bolingbroke commands the death of the other conspirators.

Sir Piers Exton reveals that he has heard the King wish for the death of Richard. Sir Piers believes that the wish was intended as his command.

Richard is imprisoned in Pomfret and meditates on the nature of his life and mortality. He is visited by a former groom whose attempts to comfort Richard are undermined by his description of Bolingbroke's heroic ride to his coronation on Richard's favourite horse. Exton arrives with his servants and attacks Richard. Though Richard kills some of the men, Exton overcomes him. Exton realises the horror of his act.

At Windsor King Henry is hearing of the defeat of the rebels when Exton enters with the body of Richard. The King admits that he wished for the death of Richard but is now appalled by the murder. He banishes Exton and declares that he will make a pilgrimage to the Holy Land in order to expiate his guilt.

Background

Richard II is one of eight Shakespeare plays which chronicle English history from shortly before the end of Richard's reign in 1399 to the accession of Henry VII, in 1485. His story is that of

the competing noble families of Lancaster and York. It begins
with the deposition of the last Plantagenet king and ends with
the first Tudor monarch, grandfather of Queen Elizabeth I.

When Shakespeare wrote *Richard II*, probably in 1595, he had
already written three plays about the reign of Henry VI and
Richard III. He almost certainly contributed to an earlier,
anonymous play, *King Edward III*, which is concerned with
episodes from the life of Richard's grandfather and his immediate
predecessor as king. Shakespeare completed the story between
1596 and 1599 by writing two plays about Henry IV (the
Bolingbroke of this play) and *Henry V*.

Shakespeare's purpose was not merely to write popular history.
When the play was first published in 1597 it was under the title
of *The Tragedie of King Richard the Second*: a recognition that
this was first and foremost a theatrical structure which was
intended to have a particular emotional impact. What history
Shakespeare knew he carefully crafted into a dramatic and poetic
work, and as we study the play we shall concentrate on those
elements that give it tragic force. However, in order to make
sense of some of the incident of the play it will be helpful to
know something of English history and the way an Elizabethan
audience may have understood it.

The historical background

Shakespeare's audience would have known stories of Richard II's
father, the Black Prince, and his grandfather, Edward III, who
had reigned from 1327 to 1377. Their victory against the
French at the Battle of Crécy was an English legend. Edward's
court seemed to represent the ideal of medieval chivalry. It was
he who had invented the Order of the Garter and *Edward III*
seeks to demonstrate that the knightly code of honour was a
peculiarly English virtue. Edward had many children and
grandchildren, some of whom become key characters or points of
reference in *Richard II*.

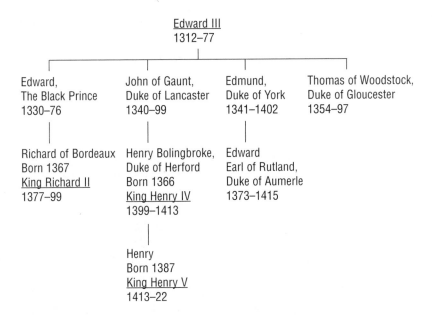

The Black Prince and John of Gaunt had battled for power during the last years of Edward's reign. The Black Prince died before his father, so when the King died the ten-year-old Richard succeeded Edward III. At the age of sixteen Richard showed great courage in confronting Wat Tyler during the Peasants' Revolt. During his reign he struggled constantly with his uncles. He was a patron of artists such as the poet Chaucer and the architects who built Westminster Abbey and Canterbury Cathedral. However, he was implicated in the death of Gloucester in 1397 and it is with the consequences of this act that Shakespeare begins his play.

Sources
Shakespeare's main source for the material of *Richard II* is Raphael Holinshed's *Chronicles of England, Scotland and Ireland* (1586–7). He probably used other chronicles by Hall and Froisart, *Woodstock* (an anonymous Elizabethan play), and a narrative poem by Samuel Daniel, one of his contemporaries. Of most interest is how the

playwright takes these detailed and complex accounts of events that span more than two years and shapes them dramatically. He telescopes events and distorts the chronology, creates key minor characters and puts words into the mouths of major historical figures who, in the sources, are either silent or speak in formal and undifferentiated ways.

The contemporary background

In Shakespeare's England the writing of history was a potentially dangerous activity. Strict political censorship controlled the theatre and the printed word, so writers were often obliged to clothe their criticisms of the Queen and her ministers in fictional or historical dress. Even when no specific political comment was intended, Shakespeare and his contemporaries used foreign or historically remote settings. No play that Shakespeare wrote has a local and contemporary setting.

The two tetralogies (groups of four) history plays which we are concerned with now did, however, have a strong contemporary relevance. First, they show how Elizabeth came to inherit the crown of England and Wales. She could trace her lineage back to Edward III. The line had been broken by the criminal deposition of Richard II but, after the misery of civil conflict, restored through Henry Tudor. Her right to be monarch and her pursuit of peace are thus affirmed through the plays.

Secondly, they present a glorified view of monarchy which Elizabeth and her court encouraged. The monarch is God's representative on Earth, anointed by Him to rule by 'divine right' over the 'demi-paradise' which is England. All power flows from the monarch and the nobles are kept in check by their oaths of allegiance and by their honourable observance of the chivalric code. This is a world in which everyone knows his place. He has a duty to those above him and responsibility for those below. It is a masculine world where women are often considered of little account (though they are to be treated well) and emotional honesty is less important than knightly justice. It is a view of the world as an ordered mechanism.

However, the play does concern itself with the deposition of a rightful sovereign. This was a dangerous subject. Elizabeth had been on the throne for 36 years but for 30 of those years Mary, Queen of Scots, whom she had first imprisoned and then executed, had threatened her. She had been, throughout, in conflict with neighbouring countries and, because she was not married, the succession to her throne was not secure. When *Richard II* was published in Elizabeth's lifetime, in the Quarto editions of 1597 and 1598, the scene in which Richard abdicates (Act 4, scene 1, lines 154–319) was omitted. When the powerful Earl of Essex rebelled in 1601 he arranged for a public performance of a play called *Richard II*. This was probably Shakespeare's play and it was given despite the misgivings of the actors, who were doubtless terrified of the possible consequences. Elizabeth is recorded as knowing that there was a popular identification of herself with Richard and Bolingbroke with Essex.

Richard II had, for its original audience, contemporary overtones which we cannot ignore, and which enrich our own appreciation of it.

The text of Shakespeare's plays

Shakespeare's work is generally treated with such immense respect that it may seem strange to admit that we cannot be certain exactly what he wrote. The reasons for this mystery lie in the circumstances of the theatre and publishing in the sixteenth and seventeenth centuries.

Shakespeare was a professional actor and shareholder in a company of actors, the Lord Chamberlain's Men, for whom he wrote his plays. Since copyright and performing rights did not exist before the eighteenth century, there was always the risk that if a play were successful other companies would perform it and reap the financial rewards. To avoid this problem, acting companies guarded the handwritten copy of a completed work. It was the company's most valuable resource and kept by the prompter: each actor was given only his own lines and his cues. None of these manuscripts survives to the present day.

This lack of printed texts seems strange to modern readers but, like the work of other playwrights of his time, Shakespeare's plays existed essentially as oral, not written, texts. His concern was with what they looked and sounded like on the stage, not what they looked like on the page.

However, there was money to be made from printed plays and during his lifetime nearly half of Shakespeare's plays were printed in what are known as quartos: paperback editions of single plays. Some of these are pirated editions based on the memories of actors and audience. Others are much more accurate and may have been authorised by Shakespeare or the sharers in his company, perhaps to capitalise on a popular success which was about to go out of repertory or to forestall a pirate edition. None, however, seems to have been supervised by the playwright and all differ, often considerably, from the key text of Shakespeare's plays, the *First Folio*.

The *First Folio*, published in 1623, is a collected edition of almost all Shakespeare's plays. It was edited by John Hemming and Henry Condell, two sharers in the Lord Chamberlain's Men, using 'good' quartos, prompt copies and other company papers to provide an accurate text as a fitting memorial to their partner. They did not start the editing process until after Shakespeare died and apparently based their editorial decisions on what had happened in the theatre. We cannot be certain how far the *First Folio* represents what Shakespeare's ultimate intentions might have been.

Even if Shakespeare had approved the text which went to the printer, it was the custom for writers to leave much of the detail of spelling and punctuation to the printer or to a scribe who made a fair copy from the playwright's rough drafts. The scribe and printer thus introduced their own interpretation and inaccuracies into the text. The *First Folio* was reprinted three times in the seventeenth century and each edition corrected some inaccuracies and introduced new errors.

A modern editor tries to provide a text which is easy to read and close to Shakespeare's presumed intentions. To do this the editor may modernise spelling and change punctuation, add stage directions and scene divisions and make important decisions about which of several readings in quarto and folio editions is most acceptable.

If you are able to compare this edition of the play with other editions you are likely to find many minor variations between them, as well as occasional major differences which could change your view of a character or situation.

The text of *Richard II*

Richard II was first printed in a Quarto of 1597. It is likely that this was produced from Shakespeare's manuscript and appears to be very accurate, though it lacks, as mentioned above, the deposition scene. The publication was successful and reprinted twice in 1598. Further quarto editions were produced following the death of Elizabeth and the coronation of James I. These include versions of the deposition scene. The play was included in the *First Folio*.

This edition of the play is based on the First Quarto. Where significant alterations have been made, usually on the basis of corrections in the other quartos or the *First Folio*, this is noted in the Commentary.

KING RICHARD II

CHARACTERS

KING RICHARD THE SECOND
JOHN OF GAUNT, DUKE OF LANCASTER ⎤
EDMUND OF LANGLEY, DUKE OF YORK ⎦ *uncles to the king*
HENRY BOLINGBROKE, DUKE OF HERFORD, *son of John of Gaunt; afterwards King Henry IV*
THOMAS MOWBRAY, DUKE OF NORFOLK
DUKE OF AUMERLE, *son of Duke of York*
DUKE OF SURREY
EARL OF SALISBURY
LORD BERKELEY
SIR JOHN BUSHY ⎤
SIR WILLIAM BAGOT ⎬ *King Richard's servants*
SIR HENRY GREEN ⎦
EARL OF NORTHUMBERLAND
HENRY PERCY, *his son*
LORD ROSS
LORD WILLOUGHBY
LORD FITZWATER
BISHOP OF CARLISLE
ABBOT OF WESTMINSTER
LORD MARSHAL
SIR STEPHEN SCROOP
SIR PIERS EXTON
WELSH CAPTAIN
QUEEN ISABEL, *King Richard's wife*
DUCHESS OF GLOUCESTER
DUCHESS OF YORK
Ladies attending the Queen
Gardeners, Keeper of the prison, Groom of the stable to King Richard
Lords, Heralds, Officers, Soldiers, Attendants

SCENE: *England and Wales*

Richard II, King of England, presides over his court. His uncle,
John of Gaunt, is present, accompanied by his son, Henry
Bolingbroke, Duke of Herford. Bolingbroke has accused Thomas
Mowbray, Duke of Norfolk, of treason. Bolingbroke and Mowbray
greet the king.

1 **time-honoured**: The Duke of Lancaster had been born in Ghent
   (Gaunt) and was fifty-eight in 1398 (see 'The Story of the Play')
2 **band**: bond; binding agreement
3 **Herford**: Henry Bolingbroke, Duke of Herford. His title is
   pronounced with two syllables throughout the play
4 **boisterous late appeal**: violent, recent accusation
5 **leisure**: the lack of freedom from other occupations
7 **liege**: lord; one who is owed loyalty
9 **If he appeal**: If he accuses
   on ancient malice: because of a long-standing hatred
11 **ground**: evidence
12 **sift him**: examine him closely
13 **apparent**: obvious
14 **inveterate**: ancient
15 **our**: my; the royal plural used by monarchs when speaking
   formally
16 **frowning brow to brow**: in head-to-head confrontation
18 **high-stomached**: very stubborn and courageous
   ire: anger
22 **Each day still better other's happiness**: may each day be better
   than the last
23 **hap**: fortune
24 **Add an immortal title to your crown**: follow your earthly
   kingship with heavenly life

- *What is the dramatic impact of Richard's opening
  speeches?*

Act one

Scene 1

Enter KING RICHARD, JOHN OF GAUNT, *with other* NOBLES *and* ATTENDANTS

KING RICHARD   Old John of Gaunt, time-honoured Lancaster,
Hast thou according to thy oath and band
Brought hither Henry Herford, thy bold son,
Here to make good the boisterous late appeal,
Which then our leisure would not let us hear,
Against the Duke of Norfolk, Thomas Mowbray?

JOHN OF GAUNT I have, my liege.

KING RICHARD   Tell me moreover, hast thou sounded him
If he appeal the Duke on ancient malice,
Or worthily as a good subject should   10
On some known ground of treachery in him?

JOHN OF GAUNT As near as I could sift him on that argument,
On some apparent danger seen in him
Aimed at your highness, no inveterate malice.

KING RICHARD   Then call them to our presence;

[*Exit* ATTENDANT

                 face to face,
And frowning brow to brow, ourselves will hear
The accuser and the accused freely speak.
High-stomached are they both and full of ire,
In rage deaf as the sea, hasty as fire.

Enter BOLINGBROKE *and* MOWBRAY

BOLINGBROKE   Many years of happy days befall   20
My gracious sovereign, my most loving liege.

MOWBRAY   Each day still better other's happiness
Until the heavens, envying earth's good hap,
Add an immortal title to your crown.

Bolingbroke charges Mowbray with treason and asks to be able to prove the truth of what he says in single combat. Mowbray refutes the charge and tells Bolingbroke that, if he will put aside his royal status, he will fight him.

25 **but:** only
26 **As well appeareth by the cause you come:** as is perfectly obvious from the nature of the dispute you bring before me
27 **appeal:** accuse
32 **Tendering:** having care and concern for
33 **misbegotten:** unlawful; illegitimate
34 **appellant:** requesting judgement
36 **mark my greeting well:** listen carefully to my speech
37 **make good:** prove
38 **divine:** immortal
39 **miscreant:** villain; wrong-doer. The word has connotations of heresy and infidelity
40 **Too good ... to live:** i.e. he does not have the noble nature appropriate to his rank and breeding
41 **fair and crystal:** beautiful and clear
43 **note:** mark of disgrace
46 **right-drawn:** rightfully drawn in a just cause
47 **Let not my cold words here accuse my zeal:** do not let the apparent calmness of my words suggest I lack enthusiasm to prove my loyalty
48 **a woman's war:** a war of words
49 **eager:** sharp
50 **Can arbitrate this cause betwixt us twain:** can decide this argument between the two of us
52–53 **Yet can I not ... say:** Yet (despite the fact that this dispute cannot be resolved by words) I do not have the self-control and patience to stay quiet with nothing to say
54 **the fair reverence of:** my great respect for
54–56 **curbs ... reins and spurs ... post:** He compares the speech he would like to make to a messenger riding furiously on a relay of horses. A curb is a strap or chain attached to the bit and used to restrain an unruly horse
56 **post:** travel at speed
59 **let him be no kinsman:** permit him to be no relation

KING RICHARD	We thank you both, yet one but flatters us,
	As well appeareth by the cause you come,
	Namely, to appeal each other of high treason.
	Cousin of Herford, what dost thou object
	Against the Duke of Norfolk, Thomas Mowbray?

BOLINGBROKE	First, heaven be the record to my speech,	30
	In the devotion of a subject's love,
	Tendering the precious safety of my prince,
	And free from other misbegotten hate,
	Come I appellant to this princely presence.
	Now Thomas Mowbray do I turn to thee,
	And mark my greeting well; for what I speak
	My body shall make good upon this earth,
	Or my divine soul answer it in heaven.
	Thou art a traitor and a miscreant,
	Too good to be so, and too bad to live,	40
	Since the more fair and crystal is the sky,
	The uglier seem the clouds that in it fly.
	Once more, the more to aggravate the note,
	With a foul traitor's name stuff I thy throat,
	And wish – so please my sovereign – ere I move,
	What my tongue speaks my right-drawn sword may
	prove.

MOWBRAY	Let not my cold words here accuse my zeal.
	'Tis not the trial of a woman's war,
	The bitter clamour of two eager tongues,
	Can arbitrate this cause betwixt us twain.	50
	The blood is hot that must be cooled for this.
	Yet can I not of such tame patience boast
	As to be hushed, and naught at all to say.
	First the fair reverence of your highness curbs me
	From giving reins and spurs to my free speech,
	Which else would post until it had returned
	These terms of treason doubled down his throat.
	Setting aside his high blood's royalty,
	And let him be no kinsman to my liege,
	I do defy him, and I spit at him,	60
	Call him a slanderous coward, and a villain,

Bolingbroke throws down his gage to confirm his challenge, and Mowbray takes it up. Richard asks for details of the charge against Mowbray. Bolingbroke tells him that while Mowbray was governor of Calais he defrauded the army.

62 **allow him odds:** give him an advantage; handicap myself
63 **were I tied to run afoot:** even if I were obliged to run on foot
65 **inhabitable:** uninhabitable
66 **durst:** dared to
67 **this:** i.e. his sword or, perhaps, these words
68 **By all my hopes:** he swears on his hope of immortal life
69 **gage:** pledge – his glove or hood
74 **mine honour's pawn:** the pledge of his honour, his gage. By picking up the gage Mowbray will accept the challenge
75 **all the rites of knighthood else:** all other ceremonies and duties belonging to a knight
77 **or thou canst worse devise:** or any other worse charges that you can make up
80–81 **in any fair degree ... trial:** in any appropriate manner according to the laws of chivalry
82 **light:** alight
85–86 **inherit us ... him:** give me even a passing thought that he may have done wrong
87 **Look what:** that which
88 **eight thousand nobles:** a noble was a gold coin. There were three nobles to a pound so this sum would have a purchasing power equivalent to several millions today
89 **In name of lendings:** as advances in pay
90 **Lewd employments:** improper or wicked uses
93 **Or here:** either here
95 **these eighteen years:** in the eighteen years since the hated Poll Tax of 1380, which led to Wat Tyler's Peasants' Revolt
96 **Complotted:** plotted with others
97 **Fetch ... head and spring:** i.e. they flow from Mowbray like a river

• *Do you find Mowbray or Bolingbroke the more believable?*

Which to maintain I would allow him odds,
And meet him, were I tied to run afoot
Even to the frozen ridges of the Alps,
Or any other ground inhabitable
Where ever Englishman durst set his foot.
Meantime, let this defend my loyalty –
By all my hopes most falsely doth he lie.

BOLINGBROKE   Pale trembling coward, there I throw my gage,
Disclaiming here the kindred of the King,   70
And lay aside my high blood's royalty,
Which fear, not reverence, makes thee to except.
If guilty dread have left thee so much strength
As to take up mine honour's pawn, then stoop.
By that, and all the rites of knighthood else,
Will I make good against thee, arm to arm,
What I have spoke, or thou canst worse devise.

MOWBRAY   I take it up, and by that sword I swear
Which gently laid my knighthood on my shoulder,
I'll answer thee in any fair degree,   80
Or chivalrous design of knightly trial;
And when I mount, alive may I not light,
If I be traitor or unjustly fight!

KING RICHARD   What doth our cousin lay to Mowbray's charge?
It must be great that can inherit us
So much as of a thought of ill in him.

BOLINGBROKE   Look what I speak, my life shall prove it true:
That Mowbray hath received eight thousand nobles
In name of lendings for your highness' soldiers,
The which he hath detained for lewd employments,   90
Like a false traitor, and injurious villain.
Besides I say, and will in battle prove
Or here or elsewhere to the furthest verge
That ever was surveyed by English eye,
That all the treasons for these eighteen years
Complotted and contrived in this land
Fetch from false Mowbray their first head and spring.
Further I say, and further will maintain

Bolingbroke accuses Mowbray of plotting the death of Thomas, Duke of Gloucester, another of King Richard's uncles. Richard asks Mowbray to defend himself, assuring him of his impartiality despite his relationship to Bolingbroke. Mowbray says that three-quarters of the money he is accused of taking was given to the army and the rest was the settlement of a personal debt. He says that he had nothing to do with Gloucester's death, though he refers vaguely to his neglect of duty.

100 **the Duke of Gloucester's death:** Thomas of Woodstock had died at Calais in the previous year while in the custody of Mowbray. It was widely believed that Mowbray had killed him on Richard's orders

101 **Suggest his soon-believing adversaries:** incite Gloucester's easily convinced enemies

104 **sacrificing Abel's, cries:** In Genesis Chapter 4 Abel and his brother Cain make sacrifices to God. When God prefers Abel's offering Cain kills him. God condemns Cain, telling him that 'the voice of thy brother's blood crieth unto me from the ground'. Bolingbroke's use of the image is perhaps intended to suggest Richard's guilt in respect of his uncle's death

107 **the glorious worth of my descent:** the glory and honour of my ancestry

109 **pitch:** the highest point of a falcon's flight, before it swooped upon its prey

113 **slander of his blood:** disgrace to his family

118 **my sceptre's awe:** the reverence and fear symbolised by the sceptre, the jewelled rod carried by the monarch

119 **sacred blood:** holy blood – because the king is considered to be God's annointed representative on earth

120–121 **nothing privilege ... soul:** give him no advantage or prevent me from being impartial and unbending in my honest heart

124–5 **as low as ... liest:** Mowbray develops a common proverbial expression: 'you lie in your throat' (see also line 44, above)

126 **receipt I had for Calais:** money I received while at Calais

130 **Upon remainder of a dear account:** for the balance of a large sum of money

131 **Since last ... queen:** Mowbray had negotiated the marriage of Richard and Isabel, daughter of Charles VI. The word fetch means *to go in quest of*

132–134 **For Gloucester's death ... case:** The meaning – either to kill Gloucester as Richard had instructed or to protect him – is obscure and may depend on how, and to whom, these words are said. Mowbray may be subtly reminding Richard of his part in his uncle's death

Upon his bad life to make all this good,
That he did plot the Duke of Gloucester's death,   100
Suggest his soon-believing adversaries,
And consequently like a traitor coward,
Sluiced out his innocent soul through streams of
    blood,
Which blood, like sacrificing Abel's, cries
Even from the tongueless caverns of the earth
To me for justice and rough chastisement.
And by the glorious worth of my descent,
This arm shall do it, or this life be spent.

KING RICHARD   How high a pitch his resolution soars.
Thomas of Norfolk, what sayst thou to this?   110

MOWBRAY   O let my sovereign turn away his face,
And bid his ears a little while be deaf,
Till I have told this slander of his blood,
How God and good men hate so foul a liar.

KING RICHARD   Mowbray, impartial are our eyes and ears.
Were he my brother, nay, my kingdom's heir,
As he is but my father's brother's son,
Now by my sceptre's awe I make a vow,
Such neighbour nearness to our sacred blood
Should nothing privilege him, nor partialize   120
The unstooping firmness of my upright soul.
He is our subject, Mowbray, so art thou.
Free speech and fearless I to thee allow.

MOWBRAY   Then Bolingbroke as low as to thy heart
Through the false passage of thy throat thou liest.
Three parts of that receipt I had for Calais
Disbursed I duly to his highness' soldiers;
The other part reserved I by consent,
For that my sovereign liege was in my debt
Upon remainder of a dear account   130
Since last I went to France to fetch his queen.
Now swallow down that lie. For Gloucester's death,
I slew him not, but to my own disgrace
Neglected my sworn duty in that case.

Mowbray apologises for once having conspired against John of Gaunt. He then throws down his gage as a counter-challenge to Bolingbroke. Richard orders Gaunt to help him to make peace between the two challengers. Mowbray says that to refuse combat would shame him.

139–141 But ere I last … had it: Mowbray claims to have confessed and asked forgiveness both from John of Gaunt and from God prior to attending Mass; he asks to be viewed as a good and penitent Christian

142 appealed: of which I am accused

143 rancour: bitterness

144 recreant: coward

145 in myself: with my own body; in personal combat

146 interchangeably: in return

147 overweening: arrogant; presumptuous

149 Even in the … bosom: to the extent of spilling the blood from the chambers of his heart. At this point Bolingbroke must pick up Mowbray's gage (see line 161, below)

150 In haste whereof: in order quickly to prove myself loyal

151 trial day: appointed time to prove in battle which of us is right

153 choler: bile. The four humours (blood, choler, phlegm and black choler) were believed to be responsible for physical and mental well-being. Choler caused anger. In order to remain in 'good humour', excesses could be purged by medicine or, in the case of blood, by 'letting' with a leech or razor

160 become: suit

163 Obedience bids … again: the obedience which you should show me as your father requires that I do not have to ask you again

164 We bid, there is no boot: since I, the King, ask you there is no alternative for it

166 but not my shame: you shall not command me to bring shame upon myself (by rejecting the challenge)

167–168 but my fair … grave: my name will live on after my death – as an inscription on my grave stone (and in my reputation)

• *Why might Richard be eager to make peace between the two noblemen?*

For you my noble lord of Lancaster,
The honourable father to my foe,
Once did I lay an ambush for your life,
A trespass that doth vex my grieved soul.
But ere I last received the sacrament,
I did confess it, and exactly begged   140
Your grace's pardon; and I hope I had it.
This is my fault. As for the rest appealed,
It issues from the rancour of a villain,
A recreant and most degenerate traitor,
Which in myself I boldly will defend,
And interchangeably hurl down my gage
Upon this overweening traitor's foot,
To prove myself a loyal gentleman,
Even in the best blood chambered in his bosom.
In haste whereof most heartily I pray   150
Your highness to assign our trial day.

KING RICHARD   Wrath-kindled gentlemen, be ruled by me,
Let's purge this choler without letting blood.
This we prescribe, though no physician;
Deep malice makes too deep incision.
Forget, forgive, conclude, and be agreed.
Our doctors say this is no month to bleed.
Good uncle, let this end where it begun.
We'll calm the Duke of Norfolk, you your son.

JOHN OF GAUNT   To be a make-peace shall become my age.   160
Throw down, my son, the Duke of Norfolk's gage.

KING RICHARD   And Norfolk, throw down his.
                                    When, Harry, when?

JOHN OF GAUNT   Obedience bids I should not bid again.

KING RICHARD   Norfolk, throw down we bid, there is no boot.

MOWBRAY   Myself I throw, dread sovereign, at thy foot.
My life thou shalt command, but not my shame;
The one my duty owes, but my fair name,
Despite of death that lives upon my grave,
To dark dishonour's use thou shalt not have.

Neither Mowbray nor Bolingbroke will give up the fight. Each claims he will be dishonoured if he makes peace with the other. King Richard fixes the date for Mowbray and Bolingbroke to meet at Coventry for a joust to the death.

170 **impeached:** discredited; accused
170 **baffled:** disgraced; specifically, the public punishment of a perjured knight
171 **venomed:** poisoned
172 **balm:** healing ointment
174–175 **lions ... spots:** even a leopard would cower before the lion, lord of the animal kingdom. The lion is the heraldic symbol of the English crown whereas a leopard was that of the Mowbray family. The spots of the leopard are symbolic of constancy, since the animal cannot change his spots, but also spots here perhaps refer to stains of dishonour
177 **mortal times:** earthly life
182 **in one:** together and united
186 **throw up your gage:** telling Bolingbroke to give up Mowbray's gage. This is the Quarto reading: the Folio has 'throw down'
188 **crest-fallen:** humbled. A knight wore a crest, often of feathers, on his helmet and this reference further emphasises the nobility of the antagonists
190 **outdared dastard:** skulking coward who lacks my daring
191 **feeble wrong:** referring to Mowbray and the 'wrongness' of his denials
192 **sound so base a parle:** referring to trumpets blowing to call for peace talks during a battle, which, Bolingbroke suggests, would in this case be dishonourable
192–195 **my teeth ... face:** I would bite off my own tongue – that organ which is a slave to one's cowardice and change of mind – and spit it in Mowbray's shameful and dishonourable face. To bite (out) one's tongue in order to remain silent was proverbial
SD [*Exit* **JOHN OF GAUNT**]: This stage direction is in the Folio only and may have been thought necessary because Gaunt begins the next scene
196 **sue:** beg
199 **Saint Lambert's Day:** 17 September
202 **atone:** reconcile literally, 'at one'
203 **design the victor's chivalry:** designate the victor through chivalrous combat – since such an honourable fight would demonstrate God's judgment: only the man of honour could win

I am disgraced, impeached, and baffled here,   170
Pierced to the soul with slander's venomed spear,
The which no balm can cure but his heart-blood
Which breathed this poison.

KING RICHARD   Rage must be withstood.
Give me his gage; lions make leopards tame.

MOWBRAY   Yea, but not change his spots. Take but my shame,
And I resign my gage. My dear dear lord,
The purest treasure mortal times afford
Is spotless reputation; that away,
Men are but gilded loam, or painted clay.
A jewel in a ten-times barred-up chest   180
Is a bold spirit in a loyal breast.
Mine honour is my life, both grow in one
Take honour from me, and my life is done.
Then, dear my liege, mine honour let me try;
In that I live, and for that will I die.

KING RICHARD   Cousin, throw up your gage; do you begin.

BOLINGBROKE   O God defend my soul from such deep sin.
Shall I seem crest-fallen in my father's sight?
Or with pale beggar-fear impeach my height
Before this outdared dastard? Ere my tongue   190
Shall wound my honour with such feeble wrong,
Or sound so base a parle, my teeth shall tear
The slavish motive of recanting fear,
And spit it bleeding in his high disgrace
Where shame doth harbour, even in Mowbray's face.

                    [*Exit* JOHN OF GAUNT

KING RICHARD   We were not born to sue, but to command,
Which since we cannot do to make you friends,
Be ready as your lives shall answer it,
At Coventry upon Saint Lambert's Day.
There shall your swords and lances arbitrate   200
The swelling difference of your settled hate.
Since we cannot atone you, we shall see
Justice design the victor's chivalry.

205 home alarms: troubles at home, as opposed to the troubles in Ireland described in Act 1 Scene 4

John of Gaunt meets his widowed sister-in-law, the Duchess of Gloucester. He makes it clear that he believes Richard to have been responsible for Gloucester's death but that only God can deliver justice. The Duchess is scornful of Gaunt's attitude, and urges him to avenge his brother's death for the sake of his family ties.

SD Duchess of Gloucester: the widow of Thomas of Woodstock, Duke of Gloucester
1 the part ... blood: my blood relationship to Woodstock: both were sons of Edward III
2 solicit me: urge me to do something
4 those hands: Richard's
8 hot vengeance: referring to Psalm 11 'In the Lord put I my trust ... Upon the wicked he shall rain snares, fire and brimstone.' It suggests 'fire' to the Duchess in line 10
9 brotherhood: the fact that you were brothers
12 as seven vials ... blood: like seven relics of his holy blood
vials: small glass bottles
14–15 Some of those ... cut: some of the seven sons are dead by natural causes or the operations of the Fates (who determine the length of a person's life)
23 mettle: stuff; spirit; courage
self mould: same birth and upbringing

> • *Are Richard's final words in scene 1 a sign of strength or weakness?*
> • *What is revealed here that modifies our understanding of the events of scene 1?*

Lord Marshal, command our officers-at-arms
Be ready to direct these home alarms.

[*Exeunt*

Scene 2

Enter JOHN OF GAUNT *with the* DUCHESS OF
GLOUCESTER

JOHN OF GAUNT Alas, the part I had in Woodstock's blood
Doth more solicit me than your exclaims
To stir against the butchers of his life.
But since correction lieth in those hands
Which made the fault that we cannot correct,
Put we our quarrel to the will of heaven;
Who, when they see the hours ripe on earth,
Will rain hot vengeance on offenders' heads.

DUCHESS OF GLOUCESTER Finds brotherhood in thee no sharper spur?
Hath love in thy old blood no living fire?   10
Edward's seven sons, whereof thyself art one,
Were as seven vials of his sacred blood,
Or seven fair branches springing from one root.
Some of those seven are dried by nature's course,
Some of those branches by the destinies cut;
But Thomas my dear lord, my life, my Gloucester,
One vial full of Edward's sacred blood,
One flourishing branch of his most royal root,
Is cracked, and all the precious liquor spilt,
Is hacked down, and his summer leaves all faded.   20
By envy's hand, and murder's bloody axe.
Ah Gaunt, his blood was thine, that bed, that womb,
That mettle, that self mould, that fashioned thee
Made him a man; and though thou livest and
    breathest,
Yet art thou slain in him. Thou dost consent
In some large measure to thy father's death

The Duchess of Gloucester says that if John of Gaunt does nothing he undermines his own security. Gaunt maintains that only God can act because the guilty man is God's deputy on earth, an anointed king. Gaunt tells the Duchess to pray to God. She wishes Bolingbroke success in the joust with Mowbray.

31 **Thou showest ... life:** you show that your own life is undefended

33 **mean men:** ordinary (as opposed to noble) men

37–38 **God's substitute:** His deputy: King Richard

47 **sit:** 'set' in some editions

49 **if misfortune ... career:** if the first charge of the horses should not result in the death of Mowbray

51 **courser:** war horse

52 **lists:** place of combat

53 **caitiff recreant:** captive coward

54 **thy sometimes brother's wife:** the wife of him who was once your brother

58 **boundeth:** bounces (like a ball). This description of the Duchess's grief is apparent in the way she stops and starts before finally exiting at the end of the scene

• *How do you react to the Duchess of Gloucester? Do you consider her account of events to be reliable?*

In that thou seest thy wretched brother die,
Who was the model of thy father's life.
Call it not patience, Gaunt, it is despair.
In suffering thus thy brother to be slaughtered,   30
Thou showest the naked pathway to thy life,
Teaching stern murder how to butcher thee.
That which in mean men we entitle patience
Is pale cold cowardice in noble breasts.
What shall I say? To safeguard thine own life
The best way is to venge my Gloucester's death.

JOHN OF GAUNT God's is the quarrel – for God's substitute,
His deputy anointed in his sight,
Hath caused his death; the which if wrongfully,
Let heaven revenge, for I may never lift   40
An angry arm against his minister.

DUCHESS OF GLOUCESTER Where then, alas, may I complain myself?

JOHN OF GAUNT To God the widow's champion and defence.

DUCHESS OF GLOUCESTER Why then I will. Farewell old Gaunt.
Thou goest to Coventry, there to behold
Our cousin Herford and fell Mowbray fight.
O sit my husband's wrongs on Herford's spear
That it may enter butcher Mowbray's breast.
Or if misfortune miss the first career,
Be Mowbray's sins so heavy in his bosom   50
That they may break his foaming courser's back
And throw the rider headlong in the lists,
A caitiff recreant to my cousin Herford.
Farewell old Gaunt, thy sometimes brother's wife,
With her companion grief, must end her life.

JOHN OF GAUNT Sister farewell, I must to Coventry.
As much good stay with thee as go with me.

DUCHESS OF GLOUCESTER Yet one word more. Grief boundeth where
        it falls,
Not with the empty hollowness, but weight.
I take my leave before I have begun,   60
For sorrow ends not when it seemeth done.

The grief-stricken Duchess has difficulty taking leave of
Gaunt but finally asks him to send his brother, the Duke of
York, to visit her. Then she changes her mind: her house is so
desolate with grief she would rather York did not visit her
there. She will, she says, go home to die.

66 **Pleshey:** her country home near Felsted, Essex
68 **empty lodgings and unfurnished walls:** empty rooms and
   walls bare of the tapestry hangings (which would always
   adorn the home of a rich family when they were in
   residence)
69 **Unpeopled offices:** no servants at their duties
71 **commend me:** greet him from me

The day of the joust at Coventry has arrived. It is a formal,
highly ritualised occasion, organised by the Lord Marshal
and presided over by the King.

2 **at all points ... in:** [armed] from head to foot and waits
   impatiently to enter the field of battle (the *lists*)
4 **Stays but:** waits only for
9 **orderly:** according to the rules
10 **swear him ... cause:** make him take an oath that his reason
   for fighting is just and true

> • *In what ways does the mood of the play change between the
> end of scene 2 and the beginning of scene 3?*

Commend me to thy brother Edmund York.
Lo this is all. Nay yet depart not so,
Though this be all, do not so quickly go.
I shall remember more. Bid him – ah, what? –
With all good speed at Pleshey visit me.
Alack and what shall good old York there see
But empty lodgings and unfurnished walls,
Unpeopled offices, untrodden stones?
And what hear there for welcome but my groans?   70
Therefore commend me. Let him not come there
To seek out sorrow that dwells everywhere.
Desolate, desolate will I hence and die.
The last leave of thee takes my weeping eye.

[*Exeunt*

Scene 3

Enter the LORD MARSHAL *and the* DUKE OF AUMERLE

LORD MARSHAL   My Lord Aumerle, is Harry Herford armed?

AUMERLE   Yea, at all points, and longs to enter in.

LORD MARSHAL   The Duke of Norfolk, sprightfully and bold,
Stays but the summons of the appellant's trumpet.

AUMERLE   Why then, the champions are prepared, and stay
For nothing but his majesty's approach.

The trumpets sound and the KING *enters with his
nobles. When they are set, enter* MOWBRAY, *in arms
defendant, and a* HERALD

KING RICHARD   Marshal, demand of yonder champion
The cause of his arrival here in arms;
Ask him his name, and orderly proceed
To swear him in the justice of his cause.   10

LORD MARSHAL   [*to* MOWBRAY]In God's name and the King's, say
   who thou art,

Mowbray and Bolingbroke appear in the lists, fully armed.
They announce their names and the nature of their quarrel.

14 on thy knighthood and thy oath: as required by the oath
you swore when you were knighted and by your oath of
allegiance to the king

18 defend: forbid

20 my succeeding: the Folio has 'his' but the parallel
construction in lines 24 and 40 suggests this less likely to
be correct

21 appeals me: accuses me

28 plated in habiliments of war: wearing armour

30 Depose him in: have him take an oath as to

43 touch the lists: enter into or interfere with the field of
battle

> • *What features of dialogue and language are most*
> *noticeable at the start of scene 3? What is their dramatic*
> *impact?*

And why thou comest thus knightly clad in arms,
Against what man thou comest, and what thy quarrel.
Speak truly on thy knighthood and thy oath,
And so defend thee heaven and thy valour.

MOWBRAY   My name is Thomas Mowbray Duke of Norfolk,
Who hither come engaged by my oath –
Which God defend a knight should violate –
Both to defend my loyalty and truth
To God, my King, and my succeeding issue,   20
Against the Duke of Herford that appeals me;
And by the grace of God, and this mine arm,
To prove him, in defending of myself,
A traitor to my God, my King, and me.
And as I truly fight, defend me heaven.

The trumpets sound. Enter BOLINGBROKE, *appellant,
in armour, and a* HERALD

KING RICHARD   Marshal, ask yonder knight in arms
Both who he is, and why he cometh hither
Thus plated in habiliments of war;
And formally according to our law,
Depose him in the justice of his cause.   30

LORD MARSHAL   What is thy name? And wherefore comest thou
hither
Before King Richard in his royal lists?
Against whom comest thou? And what's thy quarrel?
Speak like a true knight, so defend thee heaven.

BOLINGBROKE   Harry of Herford, Lancaster, and Derby
Am I, who ready here do stand in arms
To prove by God's grace, and my body's valour
In lists, on Thomas Mowbray Duke of Norfolk,
That he is a traitor foul and dangerous
To God of heaven, King Richard, and to me.   40
And as I truly fight, defend me heaven.

LORD MARSHAL   On pain of death, no person be so bold
Or daring-hardy as to touch the lists,

Bolingbroke greets the King. Richard tells him that he would
be sorry for his death but will not be able to avenge it.
Bolingbroke says that he is confident of victory but formally
takes his leave of the Lord Marshal and his cousin, Aumerle.
He greets his father, John of Gaunt, and asks for his
blessing.

45 **these fair designs:** this right and appropriate enterprise
(see Act 1 scene 1 lines 80–81)
51 **several:** various
55 **as:** insofar as
59–60 **let no noble ... For me:** may no one of noble birth
make the mistake of shedding a tear for me – the
implication being that only an ignoble knight could be hurt
by someone as dishonourable as Mowbray
66 **lusty:** strong and courageous
   cheerly: cheerfully
67–68 **Lo, as at English feasts ... sweet:** just as at a great
banquet, where it is customary to eat the daintiest
confectionery last in order to make the ending sweet, so I
greet you again. (These lines are addressed to his father,
John of Gaunt, to whom he now turns.)
69 **earthly author of my blood:** mortal father (as opposed to
God, his heavenly father)
70 **regenerate:** born again; recreated
71 **two-fold:** the vigour of both father and son
72 **above my head:** from heaven
73 **proof:** protection, such as comes through being tried and
tested in battle
75 **waxen coat:** armour. The image derives from the word
'steel' in the previous line where Bolingbroke imagines his
lance point being fired to make it doubly hard, piercing the
armour as if it were soft wax, and the wax being used to
polish – *furbish* (line 76) – his own reputation
77 **haviour:** behaviour

• *What is the effect of the rhyming couplets at this point in
the action?*

Except the Marshal, and such officers
Appointed to direct these fair designs.

BOLINGBROKE Lord Marshal, let me kiss my sovereign's hand,
And bow my knee before his majesty;
For Mowbray and myself are like two men
That vow a long and weary pilgrimage.
Then let us take a ceremonious leave,   50
And loving farewell of our several friends.

LORD MARSHAL The appellant in all duty greets your highness,
And craves to kiss your hand, and take his leave.

KING RICHARD We will descend and fold him in our arms.
Cousin of Herford, as thy cause is right,
So be thy fortune in this royal fight.
Farewell, my blood, which if today thou shed,
Lament we may, but not revenge thee dead.

BOLINGBROKE O let no noble eye profane a tear
For me, if I be gored with Mowbray's spear.   60
As confident as is the falcon's flight
Against a bird, do I with Mowbray fight.

[*To* LORD MARSHAL] My loving lord, I take my
    leave of you;

Of you, my noble cousin, Lord Aumerle;
Not sick, although I have to do with death,
But lusty, young, and cheerly drawing breath.
Lo, as at English feasts, so I regreet
The daintiest last, to make the end most sweet.

[*To* JOHN OF GAUNT]

O thou, the earthly author of my blood,
Whose youthful spirit in me regenerate   70
Doth with a two-fold vigour lift me up
To reach at victory above my head,
Add proof unto mine armour with thy prayers
And with thy blessings steel my lance's point
That it may enter Mowbray's waxen coat,
And furbish new the name of John o' Gaunt,
Even in the lusty haviour of his son.

Gaunt fervently wishes Bolingbroke success. Mowbray
proclaims his own innocence. Richard bids him farewell,
affirming his belief in Mowbray's goodness. Heralds
announce the beginning of the fight.

81 **amazing:** the word had stronger connotations then and
specifically meant to stun, to be put out of one's wits, by a
blow to the head
casque: helmet
82 **adverse pernicious:** hostile, destructive
84 **Mine innocence ... thrive.:** I shall depend upon my
innocence and St George (the patron saint of England) for
my success
85 **However God ... lot:** Mowbray suggests that whether he
lives or dies may be either according to the will of God or
simply a matter of luck
90 **uncontrolled enfranchisement:** free liberty. Though
tautologous, the assonance and rhythm of Mowbray's
words provide emphasis and gravity while *golden* and
dancing vividly suggest the joy with which he says that he
approaches the fight
95 **As gentle ... jest:** as calmly and as cheerfully as if I were
going to attend an entertainment
96 **Truth hath a quiet breast:** truth fears nothing
(proverbial)
97 **securely:** confidently. The adverb modifies *couched* in the
next line
98 **couched:** lodged. The metaphor is used in its technical
sense of lowering a lance into the position of attack during
a joust
102 **Strong as a tower in hope:** compare 'For thou hast been
... a strong tower from the enemy' (Psalm 61 verse 3)
112 **approve:** prove

> • *What contrast is there between Bolingbroke and Mowbray*
> *as they prepare to fight?*

JOHN OF GAUNT	God in thy good cause make thee prosperous.
	Be swift like lightning in the execution,
	And let thy blows, doubly redoubled, 80
	Fall like amazing thunder on the casque.
	Of thy adverse pernicious enemy.
	Rouse up thy youthful blood, be valiant, and live.
BOLINGBROKE	Mine innocence and Saint George to thrive.
MOWBRAY	However God or fortune cast my lot,
	There lives or dies true to King Richard's throne,
	A loyal, just, and upright gentleman.
	Never did captive with a freer heart
	Cast off his chains of bondage, and embrace
	His golden uncontrolled enfranchisement 90
	More than my dancing soul doth celebrate
	This feast of battle with mine adversary.
	Most mighty liege, and my companion peers,
	Take from my mouth the wish of happy years.
	As gentle and as jound as to jest
	Go I to fight. Truth hath a quiet breast.
KING RICHARD	Farewell, my lord, securely I espy
	Virtue with valour couched in thine eye.
	Order the trial, Marshal, and begin.
LORD MARSHAL	Harry of Herford, Lancaster, and Derby, 100
	Receive thy lance, and God defend the right.
BOLINGBROKE	Strong as a tower in hope, I cry 'Amen.'
LORD MARSHAL	Go bear this lance to Thomas Duke of Norfolk.
FIRST HERALD	Harry of Herford, Lancaster, and Derby
	Stands here for God, his sovereign, and himself,
	On pain to be found false and recreant,
	To prove the Duke of Norfolk, Thomas Mowbray,
	A traitor to his God, his king, and him,
	And dares him to set forward to the fight.
SECOND HERALD	Here standeth Thomas Mowbray Duke of Norfolk, 110
	On pain to be found false and recreant,
	Both to defend himself, and to approve
	Henry of Herford, Lancaster, and Derby

Trumpets sound at the start of the joust. Before the combatants can meet, however, Richard stops the proceedings. Richard announces that he and his council have decided that, in order to avoid spilt blood and the threat of civil war, the combatants are both to be exiled from England. Bolingbroke is forbidden to return for ten years.

115 **with a free desire:** of his own free will
118 **warder:** baton; a truncheon or staff used to signal the beginning and end of a joust
122 **While we return:** Until I tell
SD **flourish:** fanfare – to mark the passage of time while the King and his advisers confer
124 **list:** hear
125 **For that:** in order that
127 **for:** since
      dire aspect: dreadful sight
129–133 **And for … sleep:** These lines are not in the Folio and are absent from some modern editions. It is possible that Shakespeare intended to use either these lines or lines 134–138 but not both passages. The central image of each is one of England in a state of innocent peace which is in danger of being disturbed by civil war
140 **upon pain of life:** at risk to your life – upon pain of death
142 **regreet:** greet again
143 **stranger:** alien, foreign

> * *What is the dramatic effect of Richard's interruption of the combat?*
> * *What is your immediate reaction to Richard's sentence and his justification for it? Is he being fair? Do you agree with his judgement?*

To God, his sovereign, and to him disloyal,
Courageously, and with a free desire,
Attending but the signal to begin.

LORD MARSHAL   Sound trumpets, and set forward combatants.

[*A charge sounded*

Stay, the King hath thrown his warder down.

KING RICHARD   Let them lay by their helmets and their spears,
And both return back to their chairs again.   120

[*To his* LORDS]

Withdraw with us, and let the trumpets sound
While we return these dukes what we decree.

[*A long flourish*

[*To* BOLINGBROKE *and* MOWBRAY] Draw near,
And list what with our council we have done.
For that our kingdom's earth should not be soiled
With that dear blood which it hath fostered;
And for our eyes do hate the dire aspect
Of civil wounds ploughed up with neighbours'
   sword;
And for we think the eagle-winged pride
Of sky-aspiring and ambitious thoughts   130
With rival-hating envy set on you
To wake our peace, which in our country's cradle
Draws the sweet infant-breath of gentle sleep;
Which so roused up with boisterous untuned
   drums,
With harsh-resounding trumpets' dreadful bray,
And grating shock of wrathful iron arms,
Might from our quiet confines fright fair peace,
And make us wade even in our kindred's blood;
Therefore we banish you our territories.
You cousin Herford, upon pain of life   140
Till twice five summers have enriched our fields,
Shall not regreet our fair dominions,
But tread the stranger paths of banishment.

Richard banishes Mowbray for life. Mowbray is clearly astonished. He is appalled at the prospect of living where he is unable to speak English. He is, he says, too old to learn a new language.

145 That sun ... me: See also the use made of this proverb by Gaunt (lines 275–276 below). Bolingbroke may have in mind Matthew Chapter 5 verse 45: 'your Father ... maketh his sun to rise on the evil and the good'

148 doom: judgement, punishment and fate

150 sly: stealthy
determine: define; put an end to

151 dear: hard; severe; costly

154 heavy sentence: Mowbray puns on Richard's *hopeless word*

155 all unlooked for: entirely unexpected

156 A dearer merit ... maim: [I had expected] a more costly reward, not such an injury. Mowbray puns reproachfully on Richard's words in line 151

157 common air: as opposed to the 'court air' surrounding the king

161 my tongue's use ... more: my tongue is no more use to me. *Tongue* means not only his physical ability to speak but also his native language

162 viol: an instrument with between three and six strings; it has frets like a guitar but is played with a bow

163 Or: either
cunning: skilful – both in the way it is made and played. This is the same distinction as applied to tongue in line 161 above

167 portcullised: a portcullis was a grating lowered vertically into the doorway of a castle to defend it from attack

170 to fawn upon: to beg the favour of
a nurse: the person responsible for teaching a baby its first words

174 It boots ... compassionate: it is of no use to be sorry for yourself and beg for pity

175 plaining: complaining

179 royal sword: the hilt, on which Mowbray and Bolingbroke lay their hands, forms a cross and thus represents both the King's spiritual and his temporal power

- *In what way is Mowbray's reaction to his banishment both moving and surprising?*

BOLINGBROKE	Your will be done. This must my comfort be,
	That sun that warms you here shall shine on me,
	And those his golden beams to you here lent
	Shall point on me, and gild my banishment.

KING RICHARD	Norfolk, for thee remains a heavier doom,
	Which I with some unwillingness pronounce.
	The sly slow hours shall not determinate 150
	The dateless limit of thy dear exile.
	The hopeless word of 'never to return'
	Breathe I against thee, upon pain of life.

MOWBRAY	A heavy sentence, my most sovereign liege,
	And all unlooked for from your highness' mouth.
	A dearer merit, not so deep a maim
	As to be cast forth in the common air,
	Have I deserved at your highness' hands.
	The language I have learnt these forty years,
	My native English, now I must forgo, 160
	And now my tongue's use is to me no more
	Than an unstringed viol or a harp,
	Or like a cunning instrument cased up –
	Or being open, put into his hands
	That knows no touch to tune the harmony.
	Within my mouth you have engaoled my tongue,
	Doubly portcullised with my teeth and lips,
	And dull unfeeling barren ignorance
	Is made my gaoler to attend on me.
	I am too old to fawn upon a nurse, 170
	Too far in years to be a pupil now.
	What is thy sentence then but speechless death,
	Which robs my tongue from breathing native
	breath?

KING RICHARD	It boots thee not to be compassionate.
	After our sentence plaining comes too late.

MOWBRAY	Then thus I turn me from my country's light,
	To dwell in solemn shades of endless night.

KING RICHARD	Return again, and take an oath with thee.
	Lay on our royal sword your banished hands;

Richard commands Bolingbroke and Mowbray to swear an oath that they will not meet or conspire together in exile. Bolingbroke tells Mowbray to confess his guilt. He refuses, and as he leaves he hints that Bolingbroke will soon cause Richard harm. Richard sees that Gaunt is weeping. He reduces the exile of his son to six years.

181 **Our part ... banish:** we release you from the duty you owe to us as your earthly ruler

186 **regreet:** greet [each other] again (see lines 67 and 142, above)

187 **lowering:** angry, dark, threatening – commonly used of both weather and people

188 **advised:** deliberate

193 **so far ... enemy:** this is as much as I have to say to my enemy. (Some editions have *fare* for *far*, which is the reading of Q and F.)

196 **sepulchre:** tomb, and used here as a metaphor for the body as a chamber for the soul

200 **clogging:** obstructing; encumbering

202 **book of life:** a reference to Revelation chapter 3 verse 5 where it is eternal life which is being described

206–207 **Now no way ... way:** now I can go anywhere – except England the world is open to me. *Stray* can imply both geographical and moral wandering

208 **glasses:** the word means both the eye itself (which is full of tears) and the eyes as mirrors which reflect Gaunt's feelings

209 **aspect:** (accented on second syllable) appearance

210 **banished years:** years spent in banishment

> • *Why does Richard make Mowbray and Bolingbroke take an oath? What is the dramatic significance of Mowbray's final words to Bolingbroke?*

	Swear by the duty that you owe to God –	180
	Our part therein we banish with yourselves –	
	To keep the oath that we administer:	
	You never shall, so help you truth and God,	
	Embrace each other's love in banishment,	
	Nor never look upon each other's face,	
	Nor never write, regreet, nor reconcile	
	This lowering tempest of your home-bred hate.	
	Nor never by advised purpose meet	
	To plot, contrive, or complot any ill	
	'Gainst us, our state, our subjects, or our land.	190

BOLINGBROKE   I swear.

MOWBRAY   And I, to keep all this.

BOLINGBROKE   Norfolk, so far as to mine enemy:
By this time, had the King permitted us,
One of our souls had wandered in the air,
Banished this frail sepulchre of our flesh,
As now our flesh is banished from this land.
Confess thy reasons ere thou fly the realm;
Since thou hast far to go, bear not along
The clogging burden of a guilty soul.   200

MOWBRAY   No Bolingbroke, if ever I were traitor,
My name be blotted from the book of life,
And I from heaven banished as from hence.
But what thou art, God, thou, and I do know,
And all too soon, I fear, the King shall rue.
Farewell, my liege. Now no way can I stray –
Save back to England all the world's my way.
                                                    [Exit

KING RICHARD   Uncle, even in the glasses of thine eyes
I see thy grieved heart. Thy sad aspect
Hath from the number of his banished years   210
Plucked four away. [To BOLINGBROKE] Six frozen
    winters spent,
Return with welcome home from banishment.

Bolingbroke notes how easy it is for a king to make such a sweeping decision. Gaunt thanks Richard but says that he will not live long enough to see his son return: even the King cannot extend his life. Richard reminds him that, as one of his council, he was a party to the sentence of exile. Gaunt tells the King that he was forced to act as a judge rather than as a father.

214 **lagging:** lingering
    wanton: ungoverned; idle
218 **vantage:** advantage
220 **Can change ... about:** can travel through their months and seasons (times). The image of the moon suggests the comparison, developed in the next four lines, between the little lamp or candle which is a man's life and the night which will finally swallow it up
222 **extinct with:** extinguished by
223 **taper:** thin wax candle
224 **blindfold death:** In Greek mythology Atropos, one of the three Fates, cuts the thread of life with a pair of scissors and, to make her actions impartial, is blindfolded
230 **his pilgrimage:** time's passage
231–232 **Thy word is current ... breath:** your words are a currency which you could use to purchase my death from time but, once I am dead, even your entire kingdom would be insufficient to buy back my life
234 **Whereto ... gave:** you participated in making the judgement
235 **lour:** look sullen; frown
236 **Things sweet ... sour:** food which is sweet on the tongue may upset the stomach – a proverb
240 **To smooth:** to take no notice of
241 **A partial slander:** the criticism that I had not been impartial
243 **I looked when:** I hoped and expected that
244 **to make:** in making

> • *Is Richard's remission of part of Bolingbroke's sentence a sign of strength or weakness?*

BOLINGBROKE   How long a time lies in one little word.
               Four lagging winters and four wanton springs
               End in a word – such is the breath of kings.

JOHN OF GAUNT I thank my liege that in regard of me
               He shortens four years of my son's exile,
               But little vantage shall I reap thereby;
               For ere the six years that he hath to spend
               Can change their moons, and bring their times
                 about,   220
               My oil-dried lamp and time-bewasted light
               Shall be extinct with age and endless night;
               My inch taper will be burnt and done,
               And blindfold death not let me see my son.

KING RICHARD   Why uncle, thou hast many years to live.

JOHN OF GAUNT But not a minute, King, that thou canst give.
               Shorten my days thou canst with sullen sorrow,
               And pluck nights from me, but not lend a morrow.
               Thou canst help time to furrow me with age,
               But stop no wrinkle in his pilgrimage.   230
               Thy word is current with him for my death,
               But dead, thy kingdom cannot buy my breath.

KING RICHARD   Thy son is banished upon good advice
               Whereto thy tongue a party-verdict gave.
               Why at our justice seemest thou then to lour?

JOHN OF GAUNT Things sweet to taste prove in digestion sour.
               You urged me as a judge, but I had rather
               You would have bid me argue like a father.
               O had it been a stranger, not my child,
               To smooth his fault I should have been more mild.   240
               A partial slander sought I to avoid,
               And in the sentence my own life destroyed.
               Alas, I looked when some of you should say
               I was too strict, to make mine own away.
               But you gave leave to my unwilling tongue
               Against my will to do myself this wrong.

KING RICHARD   Cousin farewell – and uncle, bid him so.

King Richard leaves. Bolingbroke bids farewell to his cousin Aumerle and the Lord Marshal. Gaunt and his son attempt to find comforting words with which to part from each other. Gaunt suggests that the exile will only make his son's home seem all the more valuable when he returns to it. Bolingbroke says that he will just be reminded of all that he has lost.

249–250 what presence ... show: since I can't be with you, tell me where you are by letter

252 As far as land ... me: beside you as far as I can until we reach the sea

253 hoard thy words: stay silent; keep your thoughts to yourself

255 too few: i.e. words

256–257 When the tongue's ... heart: at a time when the tongue's duty should be to spend freely in expressing my great sadness

257 dolour: sorrow; distress. Note the pun on *dolour/dollar*

264 enforced: pronounced 'enforcéd'

266 foil: setting – the metal which enhances the effect of a jewel. Gaunt develops the image in Act 2 scene 1 line 46

269–270 what a deal ... love: how very far I travel from all that I value

271–274 Must I not ... grief?: a master craftsman started by serving a long apprenticeship, at the end of which he gained his freedom and became a journeyman. He journeyed from place to place until he could afford to set up as master. Bolingbroke imagines himself never returning to England, in which case grief will remain his master

275–276 All places ... havens: see line 145 above, and note

278 There is no virtue like necessity: proverbial

- *Bolingbroke fails to reply to Aumerle and the Lord Marshal. What reasons, other than the one he gives, could there be for this?*
- *What is the dramatic effect of the couplets used by Bolingbroke and Gaunt?*

Six years we banish him, and he shall go.

[*Flourish. Exit* KING RICHARD *with his train*

AUMERLE   Cousin farewell, what presence must not know,
                 From where you do remain let paper show.   250

LORD MARSHAL   My lord, no leave take I, for I will ride
                 As far as land will let me by your side.

JOHN OF GAUNT   O to what purpose dost thou hoard thy words,
                 That thou returnest no greeting to thy friends?

BOLINGBROKE   I have too few to take my leave of you,
                 When the tongue's office should be prodigal
                 To breath the abundant dolour of the heart.

JOHN OF GAUNT   Thy grief is but thy absence for a time.

BOLINGBROKE   Joy absent, grief is present for that time.

JOHN OF GAUNT   What is six winters? They are quickly gone.   260

BOLINGBROKE   To men in joy, but grief makes one hour ten.

JOHN OF GAUNT   Call it a travel that thou takest for pleasure.

BOLINGBROKE   My heart will sigh when I miscall it so,
                 Which finds it an enforced pilgrimage.

JOHN OF GAUNT   The sullen passage of thy weary steps
                 Esteem as foil wherein thou art to set
                 The precious jewel of thy home return.

BOLINGBROKE   Nay rather, every tedious stride I make
                 Will but remember me what a deal of world
                 I wander from the jewels that I love.   270
                 Must I not serve a long apprenticehood
                 To foreign passages, and in the end,
                 Having my freedom, boast of nothing else
                 But that I was a journeyman to grief?

JOHN OF GAUNT   All places that the eye of heaven visits
                 Are to a wise man ports and happy havens.
                 Teach thy necessity to reason thus:
                 There is no virtue like necessity.
                 Think not the King did banish thee,
                 But thou the King. Woe doth the heavier sit   280

Gaunt tells Bolingbroke that he must make the best of his
banishment by having the right attitude of mind.
Bolingbroke retorts that he cannot imagine himself into a
state of happiness. He prepares to leave the country declaring
that he will always remember that he is an Englishman.

281 **faintly:** weakly; half-heartedly
282 **purchase:** acquire – perhaps in battle
284 **Devouring pestilence:** the plague, which was thought,
    erroneously, to be airborne. The Black Death had killed a
    third of the British population during the reign of Richard's
    grandfather, Edward III. Plague regularly closed the
    theatres of Elizabethan London
286 **Look what:** whatever it is that
289 **the presence strewed:** the king's presence chamber, the
    floor of which would be covered with fresh rushes or hay
291 **measure:** stately dance
292 **gnarling:** snarling
293 **sets it light:** treats it lightly, as unimportant
295 **Caucasus:** a mountain range in Russia/Georgia and a
    traditional symbol of extreme cold
299 **fantastic:** imaginary
300 **apprehension:** knowledge
302 **Fell:** cruel. In this compact image Bolingbroke recognises
    that a wound to the skin can either harm or, when caused
    by a surgeon who lances a festering boil, cure
304 **bring:** accompany

> • *Bolingbroke finds his father's words of little comfort. Can
> you summarise Gaunt's argument in one short phrase?*

Where it perceives it is but faintly borne.
Go, say I sent thee forth to purchase honour,
And not the King exiled thee; or suppose
Devouring pestilence hangs in our air,
And thou art flying to a fresher clime.
Look what thy soul holds dear, imagine it
To lie that way thou goest, not whence thou comest.
Suppose the singing birds musicians,
The grass whereon thou treadest the presence
   strewed,
The flowers fair ladies, and thy steps no more   290
Than a delightful measure or a dance;
For gnarling sorrow hath less power to bite
The man that mocks at it and sets it light.

BOLLINGBROKE O who can hold a fire in his hand
By thinking on the frosty Caucasus?
Or cloy the hungry edge of appetite
By bare imagination of a feast?
Or wallow naked in December snow
By thinking on fantastic summer's heat?
O no, the apprehension of the good   300
Gives but the greater feeling to the worse.
Fell sorrow's tooth doth never rankle more
Than when he bites, but lanceth not the sore.

JOHN OF GAUNT Come, come, my son, I'll bring thee on thy way.
Had I thy youth and cause, I would not stay.

BOLINGBROKE Then England's ground, farewell; sweet soil, adieu,
My mother and my nurse that bears me yet.
Where'er I wander, boast of this I can,
Though banished, yet a trueborn Englishman.
                                [*Exeunt*

King Richard and his friends meet Aumerle who reports on Bolingbroke's departure. Aumerle jokes that he shed no tears for the banished Duke and says that his parting from Bolingbroke was barely civil. Richard says that Bolingbroke is unlikely to wish to see him again even when his exile is over. He notes, however, that as Bolingbroke rode away he took time to greet and show courtesy to the common people.

1 **We did observe:** compare line 24, below, where it is Bolingbroke's *courtship to the common people* which he has observed. Richard's tone should therefore be appropriate and the emphasis he places on *high* in the next line inspires Aumerle's subsequent puns and sarcasm

8 **Awaked the sleeping rheum:** caused our eyes to water

9 **hollow:** emotionless

12–15 **And, for my … grave:** and, since my heart forbade my tongue from misusing 'farewell' (by wishing Bolingbroke well), my heart also taught me how to pretend to be so grief-stricken that I could not speak, my words apparently overcome by sorrow

13 **the word:** i.e. farewell – in its literal sense

16 **Marry:** by the Virgin Mary – a mild oath

20 **cousin, cousin:** 'cousin's cousin' in some editions. Either reading could be correct since Richard, Aumerle and Bolingbroke were each other's cousins, but this reading gives a greater edge to Richard's irony in reminding Aumerle of his place

23 **Ourself and Bushy:** this line is clearly incomplete and often amended to *Ourself and Bushy, Bagot here and Greene* in order that (with line 53, below) the three favourites are introduced

26 **familiar:** inappropriately intimate

29 **underbearing of his fortune:** endurance of his bad luck

30 **As 'twere … him:** as if to take their affections into exile with him. Richard seems to be thinking both of the affection the people have for Bolingbroke and the love they should have for their king

- *How does the beginning of scene 4 establish another change of atmosphere?*
- *How does Richard's speech modify our understanding of Bolingbroke and his intentions?*

Scene 4

Enter the KING *with* BAGOT *and* GREEN *at one door, and the* LORD AUMERLE *at another*

KING RICHARD   We did observe. Cousin Aumerle,
How far brought you high Herford on his way?

AUMERLE   I brought high Herford, if you call him so,
But to the next highway, and there I left him.

KING RICHARD   And say, what store of parting tears were shed?

AUMERLE   Faith none for me, except the north-east wind,
Which then blew bitterly against our faces,
Awaked the sleeping rheum, and so by chance
Did grace our hollow parting with a tear.

KING RICHARD   What said our cousin when you parted with him?   10

AUMERLE   'Farewell' –
And for my heart disdained that my tongue
Should so profane the word, that taught me craft
To counterfeit oppression of such grief
That words seemed buried in my sorrow's grave.
Marry would the word 'farewell' have lengthened
    hours
And added years to his short banishment,
He should have had a volume of farewells;
But since it would not, he had none of me.

KING RICHARD   He is our cousin, cousin, but 'tis doubt,   20
When time shall call him home from banishment,
Whether our kinsmen come to see his friends.
Ourself and Bushy
Observed his courtship to the common people,
How he did seem to dive into their hearts
With humble and familiar courtesy;
What reverence he did throw away on slaves,
Wooing poor craftsmen with the craft of smiles
And patient underbearing of his fortune,
As 'twere to banish their affects with him.   30

Greene reminds Richard of a rebellion which has broken out in Ireland. Richard says that he will lead an army to suppress the revolt but that in order to do so he must raise money by selling the right to collect rents and taxes. He knows that he has been extravagant. Bushy enters with the news that John of Gaunt is on his death bed. Richard considers that Gaunt's wealth will pay for an army.

31 oyster-wench: oysters were then cheap and plentiful and those who sold them were poor

32 a brace of draymen: two carters

33 had the tribute of his supple knee: he bowed to them. *Supple* implies that this was a well-practised gesture

35–36 As were our England ... hope: as if England would revert to him, its rightful owner, on our death, and he represents our subjects' greatest hope after us. *Reversion* is a legal term describing the right to inherit in the future following someone's death

38 stand out: make a stand; resist

39 Expedient manage: rapid arrangements

40 leisure: delay

43 for: because

45 farm our royal realm: sell, for a fixed amount, the right to collect taxes, rents, customs duties and all other income. The King was thus provided with a predictable income and the King's favourites were able to exploit their new powers (see Act 2 scene 1 line 256, below)

48–50 blank charters ... gold: bills with the King's seal, on which his representatives could write in the names of the rich and the money they must pay the crown

52 make Ireland presently: set off for Ireland immediately ('presently': in the present moment)

61 lining: the contents, with a pun on linings for the soldiers' coats

Off goes his bonnet to an oyster-wench;
A brace of draymen bid God speed him well,
And had the tribute of his supple knee,
With 'Thanks, my countrymen, my loving friends',
As were our England in reversion his,
And he our subjects' next degree in hope.

GREEN   Well, he is gone; and with him go these thoughts.
Now for the rebels which stand out in Ireland,
Expedient manage must be made my liege,
Ere further leisure yield them further means   40
For their advantage, and your highness' loss.

KING RICHARD   We will ourself in person to this war;
And, for our coffers with too great a court
And liberal largess are grown somewhat light,
We are enforced to farm our royal realm,
The revenue whereof shall furnish us
For our affairs in hand. If that come short,
Our substitutes at home shall have blank charters,
Whereto, when they shall know what men are rich,
They shall subscribe them for large sums of gold,   50
And send them after to supply our wants;
For we will make Ireland presently.

Enter BUSHY

Bushy, what news?
BUSHY   Old John of Gaunt is grievous sick my lord,
Suddenly taken, and hath sent post-haste
To entreat your majesty to visit him.
KING RICHARD   Where lies he?
BUSHY   At Ely House.
KING RICHARD   Now put it, God, in the physician's mind
To help him to his grave immediately.   60
The lining of his coffers shall make coats
To deck our soldiers for these Irish wars.
Come gentlemen, let's all go visit him.
Pray God we may make haste and come too late.
ALL   Amen.   [*Exeunt*

ACTIVITIES

Keeping track

Scene 1

1 Why has Bolingbroke accused Thomas Mowbray of treason?
2 What reason has Mowbray for being concerned that Richard might not be impartial?
3 What is Mowbray's defence to Bolingbroke's charge?
4 How does Richard attempt to end the dispute?

Scene 2

1 Why, apart from the fact of her husband's death, is the Duchess of Gloucester so angry?
2 What is Gaunt's reason for not revenging himself upon Richard?

Scene 3

1 There is a big build-up to the mortal combat between Bolingbroke and Mowbray. List at least six elements of the ritual leading up to the fight.
2 Why does Richard say that he stops the fight?
3 What sentences are passed on Bolingbroke and Mowbray?
4 In what different ways do the two men respond to their sentences?

Scene 4

1 How does Aumerle react to the departure of Bolingbroke?
2 What has Richard noticed about the manner of Bolingbroke's departure?
3 What immediate problem does Richard now face and how does he propose to deal with it?

Characters

As you study a play, your perspectives on the characters will change. Keep notes of your reactions and the evidence on which they are based. These questions will help you to do this. There is a similar section at the end of each Act.

King Richard

- A key attribute of Richard's character is his love of acting. He enjoys holding centre stage. What else would the actor playing Richard need to know about his character? Imagine you are the actor and compile a list of questions which you would want to put to the playwright in order to perform the part well.
- Imagine that Richard is telling his wife what he thinks of the people who surround him and how he intends to treat them. What do you think he might say?
- You are the court historian, charged with presenting the king's actions in the best possible light. How might you write the official explanation of the events in Act 1? Make notes on this.

Bolingbroke

- Assess the evidence of Bolingbroke's behaviour in Act 1; why does the crowd behave towards him in the way that Richard reports in scene 4 lines 32–36?
- Look closely at Bolingbroke's speeches and actions in Act 1; how would you assess his personal code of behaviour?

John of Gaunt

- Using only the information in the play, compose an obituary for John of Gaunt.
- What do you think are the strengths and weaknesses of Gaunt's view of the world as it is portrayed by Shakespeare? Make notes which summarise both sides of the argument.

Aumerle

- Aumerle has not yet played a significant part in the play but note what he has said and done so far.

Mowbray

- Review what you know about Mowbray. To what extent do you think he can be trusted? How far do you sympathise with him as he goes into exile?

Themes

There are a number of ideas which seem to dominate Shakespeare's thinking as he constructed this play.

1 **Kingship** *Such is the breath of kings,* says Bolingbroke when he is spared four years of banishment. What is the extent and limitation of Richard's power, as it is portrayed in Act 1? What is your initial assessment of his qualities as a king?

2 **Chivalry** The play is concerned entirely with the behaviour of the nobility. Their code of conduct sometimes seems very remote from contemporary behaviour. They throw down challenges and use formal and ritualistic language. On the basis of what you have observed in Act 1, what seem to be the principles on which their behaviour is based?

3 **Family and inheritance** Almost all the principal characters are related to each other. Mowbray doubts whether he can receive fair judgement because of this. Richard is King because of the laws of inheritance, which ensure that he takes precedence over his uncles because he was the oldest son of an oldest son. In what other ways does family connection influence the events of Act 1?

Drama

1 Although Act 1 takes place in four different locations it flows rapidly between each and makes full use of the Elizabethan stage with its inner and upper acting areas. Using a diagram of a theatre such as The Globe, mark the principal entrances, exits and movements of scene 3. Make sure that you take account of the end of scene 2 and the beginning of scene 4. Remember that, apart from the inner stage, action could not be curtained off from the audience and nor could lighting be used to mark out acting areas.

2 Divide into two groups. One contains Mowbray and his legal team; the other is Bolingbroke and his team. Using the information at your disposal from Act 1, prepare the case for and against Mowbray. Act out the case as if in a modern court of law. Counsel should make opening and closing speeches and Mowbray and Bolingbroke should be cross-examined.

3 Freeze the action: Act 1 scene 3 line 212
   • Read the scene up to this point.
   • Cast the parts of Richard, Aumerle, the Lord Marshal, Mowbray, Bolingbroke, Gaunt and a number of other members of the court.
   • Position the characters as at Act 1 scene 3 line 212 and stop the action of the play.
   • Interrogate each character in turn to find out what they are feeling and thinking at this key moment.

There is more about freezing the action on page 274.

Close Study

Act 1 scene 2 lines 1–44

This scene is a striking dramatic contrast to the rest of Act 1. The Duchess of Gloucester's voice is the only female one we hear in this Act. This is the only intimate scene since the Act is otherwise played out in public and we are conscious of characters speaking for political as well as personal effect.

- Make sure you understand the family relationships between the characters in this scene and Thomas of Woodstock. Gaunt gives two reasons why he might revenge Woodstock's death. What are they? Why is Gaunt unwilling to take action against his brother's murderers?
- How does the Duchess seek to persuade Gaunt to take revenge?
- According to Gaunt, in what ways does God limit and determine human actions? In what ways does he picture God as actively intervening in human affairs?
- The Duchess uses two extended metaphors to describe the family of Edward III: the family as a tree and as sharing one blood. How does she develop and manipulate the image in her attempt to persuade Gaunt?
- Give examples of other rhetorical devices the Duchess uses in this section. (Look, for example, at the rhythm of her speech and note ways in which repetition and alliteration add emphasis.)
- What might have struck an Elizabethan audience as being unusual about the roles and attitudes assumed by Gaunt and the Duchess in this scene?

Key Scene

Act 1 scene 3 lines 118–248

Keying it in

- This is a moment of anticlimax. What, briefly, are the dramatic events in this scene which have led up to the King's interruption of the fight?

The scene itself

1 Lines 118–139

Why does Richard stop the duel and banish the combatants? There are two possible answers to this question: the one publicly stated by Richard, and his unspoken reasons.

- Summarise the official reasons which he announces in these lines.
- What other reasons might Richard have for stopping the duel? To help you, consider what the consequences would be if either Bolingbroke or Mowbray killed the other.

2 Lines 140–153
- What further advantage does Richard secure by banishing both men?
- Why does he give Mowbray a heavier sentence?

3 Lines 154–177
- Why is the sentence 'all unlooked for'?
- Mowbray is appalled that he will no longer be able to speak his 'native English'. What reasons does he give for this being his greatest loss?
- In the context of the play, and of Shakespeare and his time, why might Mowbray's regret at losing his language have seemed particularly significant to the playwright?

4 Lines 178–207
- Why does Richard make Bolingbroke and Mowbray take the oath?
- From the final words of the men to each other, how far are we able to make a clearer judgement of whether or not Mowbray is guilty?
- What basis does Mowbray have for prophesying that Bolingbroke will be a threat to Richard?

5 Lines 208–248
This is an example of more play-acting from Richard as he contrives to reduce Bolingbroke's sentence.
- In what different ways do Gaunt and his son react to this?
- In what way does Gaunt get the better of Richard here?
- What, do you think, is the tone of Richard's final couplet?

Overview
This is a play which advocates language. Action is subordinate to poetry, and the word of the king has real power – *'such is the breath of kings'*, says Bolingbroke (line 215). Mowbray's speech (lines 154–173) is an important statement of the primacy of language. Similarly, the king appears to be a kind of actor, very conscious of the effect of his words and behaviour and appearing to stage-manage events. Richard acts as though he is in control, and he certainly seems to get his own way here, but how might he be creating problems for himself in the future?

Writing

1   **Personal letter**. Richard may appear to be a thoroughly charmless character. Suppose that he justifies himself in a private letter to a friend. From his standpoint, review the events of Act 1 and allow him to explain his actions and why he had to behave in the way that he did.

2   **Character study**. What motivates the characters in this play? Choose three of the leading characters and discuss the ways in which they seem to be motivated by similar considerations.

3   **Family history**. At the end of scene 2 the Duchess of Gloucester speaks of going away to die. Imagine that her last act is to write a short history of recent events in the family of the late Edward III. She wishes to explain to future generations why things have gone so badly and perhaps to provide some advice on what should happen now. Write her account.

4   **Letters of farewell**. On the eve of their departure from England Bolingbroke writes to his father and Mowbray writes to his friend, Aumerle. Compose the contrasting letters they might each have sent.

John of Gaunt is dying. He tells his brother, the Duke of York, that he wishes to see the King in order to offer him advice. The words of the dying are presumed to have particular power. The brothers agree that Richard listens only to flattery, not to serious counsel. York says that Richard is concerned only with luxury and fashion.

2 **In wholesome counsel:** in beneficial advice. It was proverbial wisdom that the last words of the dying held special importance and should be obeyed
   unstaid: unstable; flighty and capricious
10 **glose:** talk smoothly and deceptively; flatter
11 **More are men's ... before:** Greater attention is paid to the manner of a person's death than to the way he has lived his life
12 **close:** cadence; the ending of a musical phrase. The rhyming couplets here reflect the idea of a musical ending and, perhaps, Gaunt's approaching death
13 **As the last ... last:** just as a taste of something sweet is most lasting if tasted at the end (of a meal)
16 **sad tale:** solemn advice
19 **Lascivious metres:** songs and poems inciting lust and luxury
21 **proud Italy:** Italy was synonymous in Shakespeare's time with corruption, frivolity and immorality. York uses *proud* ironically and his entire speech is a variation on the traditional complaint against earthly vanity
22 **tardy-apish:** following the fashions long after they have become dated
24 **where:** wherever
25 **So it be ... vile:** as long as it's new it doesn't matter how disgusting it is

> • *What evidence is there in the play so far to substantiate the view of Richard that is expressed here by York and Gaunt?*

Act two

Scene 1

Enter JOHN OF GAUNT *sick, with the* DUKE OF YORK
and others

JOHN OF GAUNT	Will the King come, that I may breathe my last
	In wholesome counsel to his unstaid youth?
YORK	Vex not yourself, nor strive not with your breath,
	For all in vain comes counsel to his ear.
JOHN OF GAUNT	O but they say the tongues of dying men
	Enforce attention like deep harmony.
	Where words are scarce they are seldom spent in
	vain,
	For they breathe truth that breathe their words in
	pain.
	He that no more must say is listened more
	Than they whom youth and ease have taught to
	glose;
	More are men's ends marked than their lives before.
	The setting sun, and music at the close,
	As the last taste of sweets, is sweetest last,
	Writ in remembrance more than things long past.
	Though Richard my life's counsel would not hear,
	My death's sad tale may yet undeaf his ear.
YORK	No, it is stopped with other, flattering sounds,
	As praises, of whose taste the wise are fond,
	Lascivious metres, to whose venom sound
	The open ear of youth doth always listen,
	Report of fashions in proud Italy,
	Whose manners still our tardy-apish nation
	Limps after in base imitation.
	Where doth the world thrust forth a vanity –
	So it be new, there's no respect how vile –
	That is not quickly buzzed into his ears?

10

20

Gaunt prophesies that the King's burst of vain and extravagant behaviour will prove destructive. He contrasts the glorious history of England with Richard's destruction of it by his financial policy.

28 where will ... regard: where desire challenges the understanding provided by reason

30–32 breath ... expiring: a series of puns or quibbles on *breath.* Gaunt is short of breath since he is dying, will waste his breath on Richard, is inspired (literally 'breathing in') but about to expire – breathe out for the last time

33 riot: debauchery, extravagance and wasteful living

36 He tires betimes ... betimes: he soon tires who rides too fast too early in the day – betimes means both soon and early

38 Light: trivial; valueless
   insatiate cormorant: insatiable greed. The cormorant was an emblem of gluttony

40 sceptred: a sceptre is wand carried by the monarch

41 seat of Mars: home for the god of war

42 This other Eden: see Act 3 scene 4 for the development of this image
   demi-paradise: like heaven; a partial image of perfection

45 breed: breeder: the place, *not* the population, is described as happy (fortunate), though this distinction is usually ignored when the phrase is quoted
   this little world: this microcosm; the island of Britain as representative of the whole of creation

46 set: see Act 1 scene 3 line 266 above, and note

51 teeming: productive; fertile. Compare Bolingbroke's prophetic words at Act 1 scene 3 line 307

52 Feared by their breed: inspiring fear in others because of their breeding (see line 45, above)

55–56 As is the ... Mary's son: English monarchs are renowned far away – like Christ's tomb in Jerusalem – and as far as Jerusalem. Gaunt is perhaps reminding his audience that Richard I (the second Plantagenet king) fought in the Crusades. The Bible depicts Christ, the son of Mary, as ransoming humanity through his death (Matthew chapter 20 verse 28). Jewry, the land of the Jews, is stubborn since it does not recognise Christ as the Messiah

57 dear souls: costly, since bought at the price of Christ's death – with a quibble on the word meaning 'beloved' in the next phrase

60 tenement or pelting farm: piece of land held by a tenant or a paltry, worthless, farm; small-holding

63 Neptune: Roman god of the sea

Then all too late comes counsel to be heard,
Where will doth mutiny with wit's regard.
Direct not him whose way himself will choose
'Tis breath thou lackest, and that breath wilt thou
    lose.   30

JOHN OF GAUNT Methinks I am a prophet new-inspired,
And thus expiring do foretell of him,
His rash fierce blaze of riot cannot last,
For violent fires soon burn out themselves.
Small showers last long, but sudden storms are short.
He tires betimes that spurs too fast betimes.
With eager feeding food doth choke the feeder.
Light vanity, insatiate cormorant,
Consuming means, soon preys upon itself.
This royal throne of kings, this sceptred isle,   40
This earth of majesty, this seat of Mars,
This other Eden, demi-paradise,
This fortress built by nature for herself
Against infection and the hand of war,
This happy breed of men, this little world,
This precious stone set in the silver sea,
Which serves it in the office of a wall,
Or as a moat defensive to a house,
Against the envy of less happier lands;
This blessed plot, this earth, this realm, this England,   50
This nurse, this teeming womb of royal kings,
Feared by their breed, and famous by their birth,
Renowned for their deeds as far from home,
For Christian service and true chivalry,
As is the sepulchre in stubborn Jewry
Of the world's ransom, blessed Mary's son.
This land of such dear souls, this dear dear land,
Dear for her reputation through the world,
Is now leased out – I die pronouncing it –
Like to a tenement or pelting farm.   60
England, bound in with the triumphant sea,
Whose rocky shore beats back the envious siege
Of watery Neptune, is now bound in with shame,

The King, the Queen, Aumerle and the King's favourites arrive. Gaunt plays upon his name and blames Richard for making him gaunt through the exile of Bolingbroke. Gaunt tells Richard that they are as sick as each other: England has become Richard's deathbed.

64 With inky blots ... bonds: the documents required to lease out the land. See *to farm our royal realm* (Act 1 scene 4 line 45)

72–85 Gaunt: Richard quibbles on *gaunt*, meaning haggard or lean from fasting. The Duke recognises the cruel pun and develops it, to Richard's discomfort, in the following lines

73 composition: physical and mental state

77 watched: kept vigil

79–80 The pleasure ... looks: the pleasure of seeing his children, which a father feeds upon, I have been denied – I have fasted through lack of my exiled son

84 nicely: subtly; cleverly

85 misery makes sport to mock itself: misery's pleasure is to make fun of itself

86 Since thou dost ... me: since, by banishing my son, you have ensured that my family's name will die with me. 'Name' means both title and reputation

87–94 I mock ... seeing ill: an example of stichomythia, a rhetorical device popular at the time (see Glossary p. 246). The characters joust verbally, often in rhyming couplets and with many quibbles

94 Ill: Gaunt puns on his own illness which affects his sight and the sickness, both political and moral, which he sees in Richard

With inky blots and rotten parchment bonds.
That England that was wont to conquer others,
Hath made a shameful conquest of itself.
Ah would the scandal vanish with my life,
How happy then were my ensuing death!

Enter KING, QUEEN, AUMERLE, BUSHY, GREEN,
BAGOT, ROSS, *and* WILLOUGHBY

YORK   The King is come; deal mildly with his youth,
                For young hot colts being raged do rage the more.   70

QUEEN ISABEL   How fares our noble uncle Lancaster?

KING RICHARD   What comfort, man? How is't with aged Gaunt?

JOHN OF GAUNT   O how that name befits my composition!
                Old Gaunt indeed, and gaunt in being old.
                Within me grief hath kept a tedious fast,
                And who abstains from meat that is not gaunt?
                For sleeping England long time have I watched,
                Watching breeds leanness, leanness is all gaunt.
                The pleasure that some fathers feed upon
                Is my strict fast – I mean my children's looks,   80
                And therein fasting hast thou made me gaunt.
                Gaunt am I for the grave, gaunt as a grave,
                Whose hollow womb inherits naught but bones.

KING RICHARD   Can sick men play so nicely with their names?

JOHN OF GAUNT   No, misery makes sport to mock itself.
                Since thou dost seek to kill my name in me,
                I mock my name, great King, to flatter thee.

KING RICHARD   Should dying men flatter with those that live?

JOHN OF GAUNT   No, no, men living flatter those that die.

KING RICHARD   Thou now a-dying sayst thou flatterest me.   90

JOHN OF GAUNT   O no, thou diest, though I the sicker be.

KING RICHARD   I am in health, I breathe, and see thee ill.

JOHN OF GAUNT   Now he that made me knows I see thee ill,
                Ill in myself to see, and in thee, seeing ill.
                Thy death-bed is no lesser than thy land,

Gaunt tells Richard that he has betrayed his royal inheritance and is merely landlord of England, not King. Richard is furious, telling Gaunt that he would kill him were he not his uncle. Gaunt accuses him of having killed his other uncle, Gloucester. He taunts Richard.

98 **anointed body:** a sick patient might be anointed with medicine but Richard has been anointed with holy oil at his coronation to signify God's blessing and that the king is God's deputy. Gaunt may also be alluding to the last rites, extreme unction, when a priest anoints a dying person

101 **compass:** circumference

102 **verge:** limit; also, the area within a twelve-mile radius of the king

103 **waste:** damage done to a property by a tenant

104 **grandsire:** Edward III, his predecessor as king

106 **forth:** out of
thy shame: i.e. the monarchy

107–108 **possessed ... possessed:** possessed of the crown and possessed by the devil

109 **regent:** ruler, especially someone who rules during the childhood of a king. Gaunt had been regent to Richard and is reminding him of his authority to speak in this way

109–112 **wert thou regent ... so?:** were you ruler of the whole world it would shame you to lease out England, but since this land is your only possession does it not more than shame you to shame the land in this way?

114 **bondslave to the law:** instead of being its master

115 **A lunatic lean-witted fool:** Richard's attempt to turn Gaunt's words against him is ironic since he may appear to be describing himself as mad

116 **ague:** fever – which generates a quibble on *frozen*

119 **native residence:** natural home; his face

121 **great Edward's son:** Edward, the Black Prince

122 **roundly:** outspokenly, severely, fluently

126 **pelican:** the pelican was thought to be so devoted to its young that it revived them by opening its breast so that they could drink its blood. Gaunt turns the image in order to praise Edward III while commenting on Richard's squandering of his inheritance and his debauched lifestyle

127 **tapped out ... caroused:** helped yourself from the barrel and drukenly consumed

129 **fair befall:** may have good fortune

130 **precedent:** example; previous incidence

Wherein thou liest in reputation sick;
And thou, too careless patient as thou art,
Committest thy anointed body to the cure
Of those physicians that first wounded thee.
A thousand flatterers sit within thy crown,   100
Whose compass is no bigger than thy head,
And yet, encaged in so small a verge,
The waste is no whit lesser than thy land.
O had thy grandsire with a prophet's eye
Seen how his son's son should destroy his sons,
From forth thy reach he would have laid thy shame,
Deposing thee before thou wert possessed,
Which art possessed now to depose thyself.
Why cousin, wert thou regent of the world,
It were a shame to let this land by lease.   110
But for thy world enjoying but this land,
Is it not more than shame to shame it so?
Landlord of England art thou now, not king;
Thy state of law is bondslave to the law,
And thou –

KING RICHARD   – A lunatic lean-witted fool,
Presuming on an ague's privilege,
Darest with thy frozen admonition
Make pale our cheek, chasing the royal blood
With fury from his native residence.
Now by my seat's right royal majesty,   120
Wert thou not brother to great Edward's Son,
This tongue that runs so roundly in thy head
Should run thy head from thy unreverent shoulders.

JOHN OF GAUNT O, spare me not, my brother Edward's son,
For that I was his father Edward's son.
That blood already, like the pelican,
Hast thou tapped out and drunkenly caroused.
My brother Gloucester, plain well-meaning soul,
Whom fair befall in heaven 'mongst happy souls,
May be a precedent and witness good   130
That thou respectest not spilling Edward's blood.
Join with the present sickness that I have,

Gaunt exits and York attempts to appease Richard. The King comments that Gaunt and Bolingbroke hate Richard as much as he hates them. Northumberland brings news that Gaunt has died. York foresees his own death. Richard turns his attention to seizing Gaunt's possessions in order to finance his Irish war.

133 **unkindness:** unnatural behaviour. 'Kind' described the nature, qualities or inherited characteristics of a living thing and was a much stronger word than now

138 **Love they ... have:** Only those who have love and honour enjoy life

139 **sullens:** sulks

140 **become:** are fit for; suit

149 **His tongue ... instrument:** compare Mowbray's words: Act 1 scene 3 lines 161–162

151 **bankrupt:** suggested by *spent* in the previous line and leading to *poor* in the next.

152 **death:** the condition of being dead
    mortal: both 'earthly' and 'the process of dying'

153 **The ripest fruit first falls:** a proverb

154 **our pilgrimage must be:** our journey through life is still to come

155 **Irish wars:** England had nominally ruled Ireland for more than two centuries but had neglected and lost control of most of the country. The English Governor, the Earl of March, had recently been killed

156 **rug-headed:** shaggy-haired
    kerns: lightly-armed Irish foot-soldiers

157 **venom:** snakes – an example of synecdoche, a figure of speech in which a part is used to represent the whole. The reference here is to the legend that St Patrick banished all the snakes from Ireland

159 **And for these ... charge:** and because these matters of state will be costly

161 **The plate ... moveables:** The gold and silver plate, money, income from rents and furniture, clothing and jewellery

---

- *How would you describe Richard's mood and behaviour when he comments here on Gaunt and Bolingbroke?*

And thy unkindness be like crooked age,
To crop at once a too long withered flower.
Live in thy shame, but die not shame with thee.
These words hereafter thy tormentors be.
Convey me to my bed, then to my grave.
Love they to live that love and honour have.

[*Exit with attendants*

KING RICHARD And let them die that age and sullens have,
For both hast thou, and both become the grave.   140

YORK I do beseech your majesty, impute his words
To wayward sickliness and age in him.
He loves you, on my life, and holds you dear
As Harry Duke of Herford, were he here.

KING RICHARD Right, you say true; as Herford's love, so his;
As theirs, so mine; and all be as it is.

Enter NORTHUMBERLAND

NORTHUMBERLAND My liege, old Gaunt commends him to your
majesty.

KING RICHARD What says he?

NORTHUMBERLAND   Nay nothing, all is said.
His tongue is now a stringless instrument,
Words, life, and all, old Lancaster hath spent.   150

YORK Be York the next that must be bankrupt so.
Though death be poor, it ends a mortal woe.

KING RICHARD The ripest fruit first falls, and so doth he;
His time is spent, our pilgrimage must be.
So much for that. Now for our Irish wars.
We must supplant those rough rug-headed kerns
Which live like venom where no venom else
But only they have privilege to live.
And for these great affairs do ask some charge,
Towards our assistance we do seize to us   160
The plate, coin, revenues, and moveables
Whereof our uncle Gaunt did stand possessed.

YORK How long shall I be patient? Ah, how long
Shall tender duty make me suffer wrong?

York loses his temper: after the death of Gloucester, Bolingbroke's exile and other deeds against the family this confiscation of Gaunt's wealth is the last straw. He contrasts Richard unfavourably with his noble father Edward, the Black Prince. York argues that if Bolingbroke is deprived of his inheritance it will undermine the same principle by which Richard inherited his throne.

167–168 the prevention … marriage: This event is not mentioned elsewhere in the play. According to Shakespeare's sources Bolingbroke had hoped to marry a cousin of the French King but Richard had intervened

168 his own disgrace: one of Shakespeare's possible sources, the anonymous play *Woodstock*, suggests that Richard banished York and Gloucester from Court and 'Disgraced our names'

169 sour my patient cheek: scowl; give a sour look

170 bend one wrinkle … face: frowned at the King

177 Accomplished … hours: at your age

180 win: earn through some effort

185–186 between … matter?: York breaks off, unable to complete the phrase through grief or a realisation of what he will say about Richard. It is likely that he is about to draw a comparison with the story of Cain and Abel – a motif which runs throughout the play

189 gripe: clutch

190 royalties: a right belonging to the king which he grants to a subject

195–196 Take Herford's … rights: If you take Herford's rights away you disrupt the process by which titles and rights descend through the generations

197 ensue: follow

198 Be not thyself: you will not be King. Not only will Richard not have behaved as a king should but he will have denied the principle of succession by which he became king

- *Is Richard's question at line 186 sarcastic, concerned or mildly puzzled?*
- *What is the basis of York's criticism of Richard's action?*

Not Gloucester's death, nor Herford's banishment,
Nor Gaunt's rebukes, nor England's private wrongs,
Nor the prevention of poor Bolingbroke
About his marriage, nor his own disgrace,
Have ever made me sour my patient cheek,
Or bend one wrinkle on my sovereign's face.   170
I am the last of noble Edward's sons,
Of whom thy father, Prince of Wales, was first.
In war was never lion raged more fierce,
In peace was never gentle lamb more mild,
Than was that young and princely gentleman.
His face thou hast, for even so looked he
Accomplished with the number of thy hours;
But when he frowned it was against the French,
And not against his friends. His noble hand
Did win what he did spend, and spent not that   180
Which his triumphant father's hand had won.
His hands were guilty of no kindred blood,
But bloody with the enemies of his kin.
O Richard! York is too far gone with grief,
Or else he never would compare between –

KING RICHARD   Why uncle, what's the matter?

YORK   O my liege,
Pardon me if you please; if not, I pleased
Not to be pardoned, am content withal.
Seek you to seize and gripe into your hands
The royalties and rights of banished Herford?   190
Is not Gaunt dead? And doth not Herford live?
Was not Gaunt just? And is not Harry true?
Did not the one deserve to have an heir?
Is not his heir a well-deserving son?
Take Herford's rights away, and take from time
His charters and his customary rights;
Let not tomorrow then ensue today.
Be not thyself; for how art thou a king
But by fair sequence and succession?
Now afore God – God forbid I say true –   200
If you do wrongfully seize Herford's rights,

If Bolingbroke is deprived of his inheritance this will make Richard vulnerable to revolt and lose him the affection of many. Richard will not change his mind and York leaves. Richard appoints York Governor of England while he is absent in Ireland.

202–204 Call in the letters ... homage: If you demand the return of the letters you sent permitting his lawyers to apply for his inheritance and to make homage to you on his behalf (so that he could inherit the Dukedom of Lancaster)

205–208 You pluck a ... think: York indicates that he would consider the unthinkable – rebellion – and that there would be many who would revolt against Richard

211 I'll not be by the while: I'll not stay to witness it

213–214 But by bad ... understood: from bad actions it should be understood that good never results. York seems to struggle to find a couplet on which to exit and which matches Richard

215 Earl of Wiltshire: Wiltshire does not appear during the play but Holinshed records that he was Lord Treasurer and one of the chief beneficiaries of Richard's farming of the realm. His death, with other of the King's favourites, is reported in Act 3 scene 1

216 repair: make his way

218 trow: believe

226 Barely: merely; only

228–229 My heart is great ... tongue: my heart is pregnant with emotion but it must break silently before I unburden it by speaking too freely

231 That speaks words again: whoever repeats your words

- *What do we learn about Richard from his reaction to York's speech?*
- *What reasons might Richard have for making York*

Call in the letters patents that he hath
By his attorneys-general to sue
His livery, and deny his offered homage,
You pluck a thousand dangers on your head,
You lose a thousand well-disposed hearts,
And prick my tender patience to those thoughts
Which honour and allegiance cannot think.

KING RICHARD Think what you will, we seize into our hands
His plate, his goods, his money, and his lands.   210

YORK I'll not be by the while. My liege farewell.
What will ensue hereof there's none can tell;
But by bad courses may be understood
That their events can never fall out good.

[*Exit*

KING RICHARD Go Bushy to the Earl of Wiltshire straight,
Bid him repair to us to Ely House
To see this business. Tomorrow next
We will for Ireland, and 'tis time I trow.
And we create in absence of ourself
Our uncle York Lord Governor of England;   220
For he is just and always loved us well.
Come on, our Queen, tomorrow must we part.
Be merry, for our time of stay is short.

[*Flourish. Exeunt* KING *and* QUEEN, BUSHY,
BAGOT, GREEN. NORTHUMBERLAND,
WILLOUGHBY, *and* ROSS *remain*

NORTHUMBERLAND Well lords, the Duke of Lancaster is dead.

ROSS And living too, for now his son is duke.

WILLOUGHBY Barely in title, not in revenues.

NORTHUMBERLAND Richly in both, if justice had her right.

ROSS My heart is great, but it must break with silence,
Ere't be disburdened with a liberal tongue.

NORTHUMBERLAND Nay speak thy mind, and let him ne'er speak
more   230
That speaks thy words again to do thee harm.

After Richard leaves, Northumberland, Ross and Willoughby speak of their sympathy for the exiled Bolingbroke. Northumberland suggests that Richard's treatment of Bolingbroke and the influence which flatterers have over him threatens them all. They agree that the King is wasting his resources.

232 **Tends that thou wouldst speak:** are you disposed to speak?

237 **Bereft ... patrimony:** bereaved, and with the inheritance from his father cut off

239 **me:** more

243 **Merely in hate:** solely motivated by hatred

246 **pilled:** pillaged; plundered

249 **exactions:** exorbitant demands

250 **blanks:** blank charters – see Act 1 scene 4 line 48 and note
benevolences: forced loans

251 **a:** in

253 **basely yielded upon compromise:** dishonourably gave away, after arbitration. This probably refers to Richard's cessation of Brest to the Duke of Brittany in 1596

256 **hath the realm in farm:** has purchased the right to collect taxes. See Act 1 scene 4 line 45

257 **bankrupt:** see line 151, above
broken: financially ruined

258 **dissolution:** immorality; extravagance; ruin

260 **His burthenous ... not withstanding:** despite the excessive tax burden

- *When Richard exits the three remaining lords establish a very different atmosphere. How should they seem to be behaving?*
- *For what reasons, do you think, do the lords list Richard's behaviour in the way that they do?*

WILLOUGHBY	Tends that thou wouldst speak to the Duke of Herford?
	If it be so, out with it boldly, man.
	Quick is mine ear to hear of good towards him.
ROSS	No good at all that I can do for him,
	Unless you call it good to pity him,
	Bereft, and gelded of his patrimony.
NORTHUMBERLAND	Now afore God 'tis shame such wrongs are borne
	In him, a royal prince, and many moe
	Of noble blood in this declining land.
	The King is not himself, but basely led
	By flatterers; and what they will inform,
	Merely in hate, 'gainst any of us all,
	That will the King severely prosecute
	'Gainst us, our lives, our children, and our heirs.
ROSS	The commons hath he pilled with grievous taxes,
	And quite lost their hearts. The nobles hath he fined
	For ancient quarrels, and quite lost their hearts.
WILLOUGHBY	And daily new exactions are devised,
	As blanks, benevolences, and I wot not what.
	But what a God's name doth become of this?
NORTHUMBERLAND	Wars hath not wasted it, for warred he hath not,
	But basely yielded upon compromise
	That which his noble ancestors achieved with blows.
	More hath he spent in peace than they in wars.
ROSS	The Earl of Wiltshire hath the realm in farm.
WILLOUGHBY	The King's grown bankrupt like a broken man.
NORTHUMBERLAND	Reproach and dissolution hangeth over him.
ROSS	He hath not money for these Irish wars,
	His burdenous taxations notwithstanding,
	But by the robbing of the banished Duke.

240

250

260

Northumberland says that it is time they acted to prevent
further disasters. He reveals that Bolingbroke is planning to
invade England as soon as Richard has departed for Ireland. He
may already be on his way.

263–266 we hear this ... perish: Northumberland pictures the
    lords as being like sailors caught in a storm who hear the wind
    in the rigging but do not look for a safe harbour or reduce
    ('strike') sail and so are drowned through over-confidence

267 the very wrack: the true danger of shipwreck

268 unavoided: unavoidable

269 suffering so: putting up with

270 the hollow eyes of death: the eye-sockets of the skull (of an
    imagined drowned sailor)

272 tidings: news; intelligence – with a pun on 'the ebb and flow
    of the tide', suggested by the nautical imagery in the previous
    lines

278 Brittaine: Brittany

280 The son of Richard Earl of Arundel: this line, which is not
    in the Folio or Quarto, is usually now added because it was not
    Cobham that 'broke from the Duke of Exeter' but Arundel's
    son, who was also the nephew of the recently banished
    Archbishop of Canterbury. The Duke of Exeter, according to
    Holinshed, accompanied Richard in Ireland and on his return
    to Wales

286 tall: fine

287 expedience: speed

289–290 Perhaps they had ... Ireland: perhaps they already have,
    though they may first wait for the King to depart for Ireland

292 Imp out: graft extra feathers to. The term is taken from
    falconry where imping was used to improve or repair a bird's
    flight

293 Redeem from broking pawn: recover [the realm] from the
    money lenders. The image refers back to lines 256–257,
    comparing the King to a ruined man who has pawned his
    possessions

294 gilt: a play on 'guilt'

296 Ravenspurgh: a port on the Humber – the 'northern shore'
    of line 288, above

> • *Why does Northumberland list those who are with
> Bolingbroke?*

NORTHUMBERLAND   His noble kinsman – most degenerate King.
But lords, we hear this fearful tempest sing,
Yet seek no shelter to avoid the storm.
We see the wind sit sore upon our sails,
And yet we strike not, but securely perish.

ROSS   We see the very wrack that we must suffer,
And unavoided is the danger now,
For suffering so the causes of our wrack.

NORTHUMBERLAND   Not so; even through the hollow eyes of death   270
I spy life peering; but I dare not say
How near the tidings of our comfort is.

WILLOUGHBY   Nay let us share thy thoughts as thou dost ours.

ROSS   Be confident to speak Northumberland.
We three are but thyself, and speaking so
Thy words are but as thoughts; therefore be bold.

NORTHUMBERLAND   Then thus: I have from Le Port Blanc,
A bay in Brittaine, received intelligence
That Harry Duke of Herford, Rainold Lord
   Cobham,
The son of Richard Earl of Arundel   280
That late broke from the Duke of Exeter,
His brother, Archbishop late of Canterbury,
Sir Thomas Erpingham, Sir John Ramston,
Sir John Norbery, Sir Robert Waterton, and
   Francis Coint;
All these well-furnished by the Duke of Brittaine
With eight tall ships, three thousand men of war,
Are making hither with all due expedience,
And shortly mean to touch our northern shore.
Perhaps they had ere this, but that they stay
The first departing of the King for Ireland.   290
If then we shall shake off our slavish yoke,
Imp out our drooping country's broken wing,
Redeem from broking pawn the blemished crown
Wipe off the dust that hides our sceptre's gilt,
And make high majesty look like itself,
Away with me in post to Ravenspurgh.

Ross and Willoughby enthusiastically agree to accompany Northumberland to meet Bolingbroke when he lands in England.

297 **faint:** lack courage; are half-hearted
299 **urge doubts ... fear:** only encourage those who are afraid to be frightened
300 **Hold out my horse, and:** so long as my horse lasts out

The Queen enters with Bushy and Bagot, two of Richard's favourites. Richard has departed for Ireland, but the Queen is more grief-stricken than she can explain solely by their parting. Bushy tells her that grief tends to grow by feeding upon itself.

  3 **heaviness:** grief
 11 **inward:** innermost
 14 **Each substance ... shadows:** for each real cause of grief we experience the emotion twenty times
 15 **Which shows ... is:** this singular phrase refers to the plural subject, *twenty shadows*
17–20 **Divides one thing ... form:** divides the whole into many parts, like an optical illusion which confuses when viewed normally but becomes clear when seen from a particular angle. The use of perspective to create such illusions was popular in late Renaissance painting
 21 **Looking awry:** viewed wrongly – opposed to *eyed awry*, 'view from a particular angle', in line 19
21–27 **Looking awry ... imaginary:** Bushy's argument is that Isabel sees things wrongly, creating griefs which do not exist, because she is seeing the world through her tears. Her real sorrow for Richard creates *false sorrows* because *blinding tears* create *shadows Of what is not*

> • *What view of Richard is offered at the beginning of scene 2? How does it contrast with previous perceptions of him in the play?*

But if you faint, as fearing to do so,
Stay, and be secret, and myself will go.

ROSS   To horse, to horse, urge doubts to them that fear.

WILLOUGHBY   Hold out my horse, and I will first be there.   300

[Exeunt

Scene 2

Enter the QUEEN, BUSHY, *and* BAGOT

BUSHY   Madam, your majesty is too much sad.
You promised, when you parted with the King,
To lay aside life-harming heaviness,
And entertain a cheerful disposition.

QUEEN ISABEL To please the King I did; to please myself
I cannot do it. Yet I know no cause
Why I should welcome such a guest as grief,
Save bidding farewell to so sweet a guest
As my sweet Richard. Yet again methinks
Some unborn sorrow ripe in fortune's womb   10
Is coming towards me, and my inward soul
With nothing trembles. At something it grieves
More than with parting from my lord the King.

BUSHY   Each substance of a grief hath twenty shadows,
Which shows like grief itself, but is not so.
For sorrow's eye, glazed with blinding tears,
Divides one thing entire to many objects,
Like perspectives which, rightly gazed upon,
Show nothing but confusion; eyed awry,
Distinguish form. So your sweet majesty,   20
Looking awry upon your lord's departure,
Find shapes of grief more than himself to wail,
Which looked on as it is, is naught but shadows
Of what it is not. Then, thrice-gracious Queen,

The Queen is not convinced by Bushy's consoling words.
There is a 'nameless woe' which haunts her. Greene enters
with news that Bolingbroke has landed in England. He hopes
that the king has not yet left for Ireland. Many of the
nobility have joined in support of Bolingbroke.

31 though on thinking … think: even though I try to think
   of nothing
33 conceit: imagination
34–40 'Tis nothing less … I wot: it is anything but
   imagination: such imaginary grief is always created by some
   real grief; my grief is not like that since nothing has created
   the grief I feel. Perhaps, my grief really arises from
   something else and has become mine by default. Since I
   don't know what my grief is I cannot name it: I suppose it's
   a nameless woe
44 his designs crave … hope: his plans require speed, his
   speed depends upon an expectation of success
46 That he … power: that he, our source of rescue, might
   have withdrawn his army [from an attack on Ireland]
49 repeals himself: recalls himself from exile
50 with uplifted arms: having raised an army; carrying
   weapons

> • *Grief will become an increasingly important theme in the
> play. Here Isabel recognises that sadness may sometimes be
> a premonition of worse to come.*

More than your lord's departure weep not, more
   is not seen;
Or if it be, 'tis with false sorrow's eye,
Which for things true weeps things imaginary.

QUEEN ISABEL It may be so; but yet my inward soul
Persuades me it is otherwise. Howe'er it be,
I cannot but be sad; so heavy-sad   30
As, though on thinking on no thought I think,
Makes me with heavy nothing faint and shrink.

BUSHY 'Tis nothing but conceit, my gracious lady.

QUEEN ISABEL 'Tis nothing less. Conceit is still derived
From some forefather grief. Mine is not so,
For nothing hath begot my something grief,
Or something hath the nothing that I grieve –
'Tis in reversion that I do possess –
But what it is that is not yet known what,
I cannot name; 'tis nameless woe, I wot.   40

Enter GREEN

GREEN God save your majesty, and well met, gentlemen.
I hope the King is not yet shipped for Ireland.

QUEEN ISABEL Why hopest thou so? 'tis better hope he is,
For his designs crave haste, his haste good hope.
Then wherefore dost thou hope he is not shipped?

GREEN That he, our hope, might have retired his power,
And driven into despair an enemy's hope,
Who strongly hath set footing in this land.
The banished Bolingbroke repeals himself,
And with uplifted arms is safe arrived   50
At Ravenspurgh.

QUEEN ISABEL Now God in heaven forbid.

GREEN Ah madam, 'tis too true; and, that is worse,
The Lord Northumberland, his son young Henry
   Percy,
The Lords of Ross, Beaumont, and Willoughby,
With all their powerful friends are fled to him.

The Queen now understands why she had a sense of foreboding and is in despair. York enters, dressed for battle but despondent: Richard is in Ireland and his flattering friends are not to be relied upon.

57 **all the rest ... faction:** the others in his conspiracy
59 **hath broken his staff:** has destroyed the symbol of his royal office; resigned
62–65 **thou art the midwife ... mother:** the image continues Isabel's conceit in lines 10 and 34–35, above
64 **prodigy:** something extraordinary or monstrous; an omen
69 **cozening:** cheating
71 **Who:** i.e. Death
72 **lingers in extremity:** prolongs to the utmost, when things are at their worst
74 **signs of war ... neck:** armour, especially the gorget which protected the throat
75 **careful business:** anxious preoccupation
76 **comfortable:** comforting
80 **to save far off:** protect something remote
82 **underprop:** support; protect
84 **Now comes ... surfeit made:** The time has now come when we shall experience the illness which is the consequence of his excess
85 **try:** test; find the true worth of
86 **your son ... came:** i.e. Aumerle had gone to join the King in Ireland before I could intercept him
87 **Go all ... will:** what will be will be

- *What significant information is revealed to the audience by Greene?*
- *What familiar aspects of York's character are emphasised here?*

BUSHY	Why have you not proclaimed Northumberland
	And all the rest revolted faction traitors?
GREEN	We have; whereupon the Earl of Worcester
	Hath broken his staff, resigned his stewardship,
	And all the household servants fled with him 60
	To Bolingbroke.
QUEEN ISABEL	So Green, thou art the midwife to my woe,
	And Bolingbroke my sorrow's dismal heir.
	Now hath my soul brought forth her prodigy,
	And I, a gasping new-delivered mother,
	Have woe to woe, sorrow to sorrow joined.
BUSHY	Despair not madam.
QUEEN ISABEL	Who shall hinder me?
	I will despair, and be at enmity
	With cozening hope. He is a flatterer,
	A parasite, a keeper-back of death, 70
	Who gently would dissolve the bands of life,
	Which false hope lingers in extremity.

Enter YORK

GREEN	Here comes the Duke of York.
QUEEN ISABEL	With signs of war about his aged neck.
	O full of careful business are his looks.
	Uncle, for God's sake speak comfortable words.
YORK	Should I do so I should belie my thoughts.
	Comfort's in heaven, and we are on the earth,
	Where nothing lives but crosses, cares, and grief.
	Your husband, he is gone to save far off, 80
	Whilst others come to make him lose at home.
	Here am I left to underprop his land,
	Who weak with age cannot support myself.
	Now comes the sick hour that his surfeit made,
	Now shall he try his friends that flattered him.

Enter a SERVANT

| SERVANT | My lord, your son was gone before I came. |
| YORK | He was? Why, so. Go all which way it will. |

A servant reports that the Duchess of Gloucester has died. For a brief moment York takes command and gives orders in preparation for war. However, he feels his loyalty is divided between his two nephews: Richard his King and the wronged Bolingbroke.

90 **Sirrah:** a mode of address used towards servants or other social inferiors
Pleshey: the Essex home of the Duchess of Gloucester (see Act 1 scene 2 line 66)
Sister: sister-in-law
91 **presently:** immediately
92 **take my ring:** his seal ring, bearing his crest, to authenticate the request
96 **knave:** boy; servant
98–121 **God for his ... seven:** This speech is metrically uneven: the text might be corrupt and editors have made various attempts to determine Shakespeare's intention. The poetic inadequacies are best viewed as representing the disordered state of York's thought and emotion
101 **So my untruth:** so long as my disloyalty
105 **sister:** the distressed York is still thinking of the Duchess of Gloucester
108 **muster men:** raise a fighting force from amongst their retainers and tenants
111 **Both:** i.e. Richard and Bolingbroke
117 **dispose of you:** give you your orders. In this and the next line York shows a fleeting decisiveness
118 **presently:** immediately
Berkeley: a castle in Gloucestershire. The Elizabethan audience would have recognised that Berkeley was the scene of the murder of another Plantagenet king, Edward II, in Marlowe's play of 1593
121 **at six and seven:** in chaos; at extreme hazard. The phrase is originally from gambling with dice

> • *'What a tide of woes ...'* What are the problems with which Richard is now faced? How likely is it that York will be able to find a solution?

	The nobles they are fled, the commons they are
	cold,
	And will, I fear, revolt on Herford's side.
	Sirrah, get thee to Pleshey to my sister Gloucester, 90
	Bid her send me presently a thousand pound –
	Hold, take my ring.
SERVANT	My lord, I had forgot to tell your lordship.
	Today as I came by I called there –
	But I shall grieve you to report the rest.
YORK	What is't, knave?
SERVANT	An hour before I came the Duchess died.
YORK	God for his mercy, what a tide of woes
	Comes rushing on this woeful land at once!
	I know not what to do. I would to God, 100
	So my untruth had not provoked him to it,
	The King had cut off my head with my brother's.
	What, are there no posts dispatched for Ireland?
	How shall we do for money for these wars?
	Come, sister – cousin, I would say – pray pardon
	me.
	Go fellow, get thee home, provide some carts,
	And bring away the armour that is there.
	Gentlemen, will you go muster men?
	If I know how or which way to order these affairs
	Thus disorderly thrust into my hands, 110
	Never believe me. Both are my kinsmen.
	Th one is my sovereign, whom both my oath
	And duty bids defend. Th other again
	Is my kinsman, whom the King hath wronged,
	Whom conscience and my kindred bids to right.
	Well, somewhat we must do. Come, cousin,
	I'll dispose of you. Gentlemen, go muster up your
	men,
	And meet me presently at Berkeley.
	I should to Pleshey, too,
	But time will not permit. All is uneven, 120
	And everything is left at six and seven.

York departs for Gloucestershire where he will assemble his forces. Bushy, Greene and Bagot fear defeat and know that their closeness to the King will be their own downfall. Greene and Bushy decide to go to Bristol while Bagot intends to find the King in Ireland. The favourites have little faith in York's capacity to defeat Bolingbroke. They depart, fearing they will never meet again.

122–123 The wind sits ... returns: the wind is in the right direction for messages to go to Ireland but neither news nor people return

124 Proportionable to: of equivalent power and strength to

126–127 our nearness ... king: our close relationship with the king causes his enemies to hate us

132 If judgment ... we: if it is the common people who are to judge, then we shall be condemned too

136 office: service

138 curs: ill-bred, cowardly dogs

141 heart's presages: foreboding; intuition

145 numbering: counting. Both comparisons in this line are proverbial expressions for attempting the impossible

- *The three favourites, Bushy, Green and Bagot, have been shadowy figures so far in the play. How do you feel about their behaviour here?*

[*Exeunt* YORK *and the* QUEEN

BUSHY
The wind sits fair for news to go for Ireland,
But none returns. For us to levy power
Proportionable to the enemy
Is all unpossible.

GREEN
Besides, our nearness to the King in love
Is near the hate of those love not the King.

BAGOT
And that's the wavering commons, for their love
Lies in their purses, and whoso empties them
By so much fills their hearts with deadly hate.   130

BUSHY
Wherein the King stands generally condemned.

BAGOT
If judgment lie in them, then so do we,
Because we ever have been near the King.

GREEN
Well I will for refuge straight to Bristol Castle.
The Earl of Wiltshire is already there.

BUSHY
Thither will I with you; for little office
Will the hateful commons perform for us,
Except like curs to tear us all to pieces.
Will you go along with us?

BAGOT
No, I will to Ireland to his majesty.   140
Farewell. If heart's presages be not vain,
We three here part that ne'er shall meet again.

BUSHY
That's as York thrives to beat back Bolingbroke.

GREEN
Alas poor Duke, the task he undertakes
Is numbering sands, and drinking oceans dry.
Where one on his side fights, thousands will fly.

BAGOT
Farewell at once, for once, for all, and ever.

BUSHY
Well, we may meet again.

BAGOT
I fear me never.   [*Exeunt*

Bolingbroke, having met Northumberland on his arrival at Ravenspurgh, has made rapid progress to Gloucestershire in order to meet with other supporters and intercept York at Berkeley Castle. Northumberland flatters Bolingbroke. They are met by Northumberland's son, Henry Percy (known as Harry or Hotspur).

7 **delectable:** the stress is on the first and third syllables
9 **Cotswold:** spelt Cotshall in the Quarto
10 **In:** by
   wanting: lacking
11 **beguiled:** pleasantly diverted my attention from
15–16 **hope to joy ... enjoyed:** hope of happiness is only a little less enjoyable than the enjoyment of that which was hoped for
16 **this:** i.e. the hope of Bolingbroke's company
22 **whencesoever:** from somewhere or other
26–28 **he hath forsook ... King:** see Act 2 scene 2 lines 58–61

- *Why, do you think, does Northumberland flatter Bolingbroke in the way that he does?*
- *What is the significance of the juxtaposition of the beginning of scene 3 with the end of scene 2?*

Scene 3

Enter BOLINGBROKE *and* NORTHUMBERLAND

BOLINGBROKE   How far is it, my lord, to Berkeley now?

NORTHUMBERLAND   Believe me noble lord,
I am a stranger here in Gloucestershire.
These high wild hills and rough uneven ways
Draws out our miles, and makes them wearisome.
And yet your fair discourse hath been as sugar,
Making the hard way sweet and delectable.
But I bethink me what a weary way
From Ravenspurgh to Cotswold will be found
In Ross and Willoughby, wanting your company,   10
Which I protest hath very much beguiled
The tediousness and process of my travel.
But theirs is sweetened with the hope to have
The present benefit which I possess;
And hope to joy is little less in joy
Than hope enjoyed. By this the weary lords
Shall make their way seem short as mine hath done
By sight of what I have, your noble company.

BOLINGBROKE   Of much less value is my company
Than your good words. But who comes here?   20

Enter HARRY PERCY

NORTHUMBERLAND   It is my son young Harry Percy,
Sent from my brother Worcester whencesoever.
Harry, how fares your uncle?

PERCY   I had thought my lord to have learned his health of
you.

NORTHUMBERLAND   Why, is he not with the Queen?

PERCY   No my good lord, he hath forsook the court,
Broken his staff of office, and dispersed
The household of the King.

NORTHUMBERLAND   What was his reason?
He was not so resolved when last we spake together.

Harry Percy has been discovering the extent of York's support at Berkeley. He does not recognise Bolingbroke, whom he has not previously met. Percy pledges his support to Bolingbroke, who welcomes him with promises of future good fortune. Percy reports that York has only a small force at Berkeley. Ross and Willoughby arrive to join Bolingbroke.

34 What power ... levied there: What army the Duke of York has raised and collected there

43 elder days: in my maturity

44 desert: deserving (of honour)

45–50 and be sure ... seals it: be assured that I am most happy to know that I have a heart which remembers my good friends, and as my fortune grows through your love it will be used to repay your love. This promise I make with my heart and seal it with my hand. In a later play, *Henry IV Part 1* Act 1 scene 3, Shakespeare has Percy (Hotspur) stingingly recall this *candy deal of courtesy* from *the vile politician Bolingbroke*

51 stir: agitation; disorder

61 unfelt: intangible

more enriched: once (my treasury) is richer

- *This is our introduction to Harry Percy. What characteristics are revealed so far?*
- *How does Bolingbroke attempt to win people to his cause? Compare his behaviour with Richard's comments on him in Act 1 scene 4 lines 23–36.*

PERCY   Because your lordship was proclaimed traitor.   30
But he my lord is gone to Ravenspurgh
To offer service to the Duke of Herford,
And sent me over by Berkeley to discover
What power the Duke of York had levied there
Then with directions to repair to Ravenspurgh.

NORTHUMBERLAND   Have you forgot the Duke of Herford, boy?

PERCY   No my good lord, for that is not forgot
Which ne'er I did remember. To my knowledge
I never in my life did look on him.

NORTHUMBERLAND   Then learn to know him now. This is the Duke.   40

PERCY   My gracious lord, I tender you my service,
Such as it is, being tender, raw, and young,
Which elder days shall ripen and confirm
To more approved service and desert.

BOLINGBROKE   I thank thee gentle Percy, and be sure
I count myself in nothing else so happy
As in a soul remembering my good friends;
And as my fortune ripens with thy love,
It shall be still thy true love's recompense.
My heart this covenant makes, my hand thus seals
    it.   50

NORTHUMBERLAND   How far is it to Berkeley, and what stir
Keeps good old York there with his men of war?

PERCY   There stands the castle by yon tuft of trees,
Manned with three hundred men, as I have heard,
And in it are the Lords of York, Berkeley, and
    Seymour,
None else of name and noble estimate.

Enter ROSS *and* WILLOUGHBY

NORTHUMBERLAND   Here comes the Lords of Ross and Willoughby,
Bloody with spurring, fiery red with haste.

BOLINGBROKE   Welcome my lords. I wot your love pursues
A banished traitor. All my treasury   60
Is yet but unfelt thanks, which more enriched

Bolingbroke promises future rewards to Willoughby and
Ross. Lord Berkeley arrives with a message from York. He
initially fails to address Bolingbroke with the title of Duke of
Lancaster, which Bolingbroke claims following his father's
death. York enters and Bolingbroke kneels before him. York
berates Bolingbroke for his armed invasion of England and
for defying the order of banishment.

64 **far surmounts ... attain it:** [your presence] is of much
   greater value than the cost to us of meeting you here
65 **Evermore thank's ... poor:** gratitude is always (or always
   will be) the only wealth of the poor
66 **comes to years:** grows up; comes of age
67 **Stands for my bounty:** represents my gifts
70 **my answer is to 'Lancaster':** I only answer to the title
   Duke of Lancaster
75 **raze one title:** pun on 'tittle', meaning 'a very small part'.
   See also Act 3 scene 1 line 25
78 **what pricks you on:** what provokes you; what spurs you
   on
79 **the absent time:** the time during which the king is absent
80 **self-borne arms:** arms created and carried by you and for
   your own selfish purposes – a quibble on 'born'
84 **Whose duty is deceivable:** whose act of kneeling is
   deceptive
87 **grace:** is both the title given to a Duke and describes God's
   favour, hence its opposition to 'profane', ungodly, in the
   next line
90 **a dust:** a grain of dust

> • *Berkeley brings a message from York who immediately*
>   *appears in person. In what ways is this consistent with*
>   *York's behaviour throughout the play?*

	Shall be your love and labour's recompense.
ROSS	Your presence makes us rich, most noble lord.
WILLOUGHBY	And far surmounts our labour to attain it.
BOLINGBROKE	Evermore thank's the exchequer of the poor,
	Which till my infant fortune comes to years
	Stands for my bounty. But who comes here?

Enter BERKELEY

NORTHUMBERLAND	It is my Lord of Berkeley, as I guess.
BERKELEY	My Lord of Herford, my message is to you.
BOLINGBROKE	My lord, my answer is to 'Lancaster'. 70
	And I am come to seek that name in England,
	And I must find that title in your tongue
	Before I make reply to aught you say.
BERKELEY	Mistake me not my lord. 'Tis not my meaning
	To raze one title of your honour out.
	To you my lord I come, what lord you will,
	From the most gracious regent of this land,
	The Duke of York, to know what pricks you on
	To take advantage of the absent time,
	And fright our native peace with self-borne arms. 80

Enter YORK

BOLINGBROKE	I shall not need transport my words by you,
	Here comes his grace in person. My noble uncle.

[Kneels

YORK	Show me thy humble heart, and not thy knee,
	Whose duty is deceivable and false.
BOLINGBROKE	My gracious uncle –
YORK	Tut, tut, grace me no grace, nor uncle me no uncle.
	I am no traitor's uncle, and that word 'grace'
	In an ungracious mouth is but profane.
	Why have those banished and forbidden legs
	Dared once to touch a dust of England's ground? 90
	But then more 'why' – why have they dared to march
	So many miles upon her peaceful bosom,

Bolingbroke claims that the death of his father has changed the situation and he comes to claim his rightful title. He claims that Richard's actions in depriving him of his material inheritance and the Dukedom of Lancaster give him the right to return to England and seek justice.

94 ostentation of despised arms: exhibiting despicable weapons

99–101 As when ... French: It is not known to what, if any, historical incident these lines refer

100 Mars: Roman god of war

103 palsy: paralysis; disorder of the nervous and muscular system
chastise: accent on first syllable

104 minister correction ... fault: administer punishment

106 condition: personal quality or act of mine

107 Even in ... degree: it is behaviour of the worst kind

111 braving: defiant; showy; daring

115 indifferent: impartial; just and fair

119 royalties: rights belonging to the king which he grants to a subject (see Act 2 scene 1 line 190, above)

120 perforce: compulsorily; by force

121 unthrifts: spendthrifts; wastrels
Wherefore was I born?: for what reason was I born into the Royal family? This begins a line of argument which mirrors York's own appeal to Richard in Act 2 scene 1 lines 191–208

127 To rouse his ... bay: to startle his wrongdoers from their place of hiding and pursue them to their last stand. The metaphor is taken from stag hunting

128–129 I am denied ... leave: I am refused my right to claim my inheritance despite legal permission to do so. (See Act 2 scene 1 lines 202–204 and note.)

130 distrained: seized by the crown

> • *How does Bolingbroke use York's emotional involvement in the situation to persuade him of the rightness of his cause?*

Frighting her pale-faced villages with war,
And ostentation of despised arms?
Comest thou because the anointed King is hence?
Why, foolish boy, the King is left behind,
And in my loyal bosom lies his power.
Were I but now lord of such hot youth
As when brave Gaunt, thy father, and myself
Rescued the Black Prince, that young Mars of men,   100
From forth the ranks of many thousand French,
O then how quickly should this arm of mine,
Now prisoner to the palsy, chastise thee,
And minister correction to thy fault.

BOLINGBROKE   My gracious uncle, let me know my fault.
On what condition stands it and wherein?

YORK   Even in condition of the worst degree,
In gross rebellion and detested treason.
Thou art a banished man, and here art come
Before the expiration of thy time   110
In braving arms against thy sovereign.

BOLINGBROKE   As I was banished, I was banished Herford;
But as I come, I come for Lancaster.
And noble uncle I beseech your grace
Look on my wrongs with an indifferent eye.
You are my father, for methinks in you
I see old Gaunt alive. O then my father,
Will you permit that I shall stand condemned
A wandering vagabond, my rights and royalties
Plucked from my arms perforce, and given away   120
To upstart unthrifts? Wherefore was I born?
If that my cousin King be King in England,
It must be granted I am Duke of Lancaster.
You have a son, Aumerle, my noble cousin.
Had you first died, and he been thus trod down,
He should have found his uncle Gaunt a father
To rouse his wrongs and chase them to the bay.
I am denied to sue my livery here,
And yet my letters patents give me leave.
My father's goods are all distrained and sold,   130

Northumberland, Ross and Willoughby support Bolingbroke.
York agrees that Bolingbroke has been wronged but tells them
that their open rebellion is unjustifiable. Northumberland
insists on Bolingbroke's right to claim his inheritance. York is
helpless to defeat the rebellion so tells them that he will
remain impartial and offers them the hospitality of Berkeley
Castle. Bolingbroke accepts but expresses his intention to go
to Bristol to destroy Bushy and Bagot.

131 **and all ... employed:** and everything else are misused
133 **challenge law:** demand my right to proper legal process
      Attorneys ... me: My lawyers are denied audience with the
      king
134 **personally:** in person
135 **inheritance of free descent:** direct, undisputed inheritance
137 **It stands ... upon:** it is your grace's duty
138 **Base men ... great:** Ignoble men are made great by
      property which is rightfully his
142 **in this kind:** in this manner
143 **Be his own carver:** help himself
144 **find our right with wrong:** achieve his rights through
      doing wrong
147–148 **his coming ... own:** he has come only to claim back
      what is rightfully his, not to gain anything more
151 **I see ... arms:** I perceive what will come of this armed
      presence
153 **my power ... left:** my army is weak and poorly prepared
155 **attach:** arrest
158 **as neuter:** neutral; helpless; impotent
165 **caterpillars:** destroyers; rapacious extortioners
166 **weed:** see Act 3 scene 4, the 'garden' scene, below

> • *'It stands your grace upon to do him right.' How could
>   York now resolve the crisis?*
> • *In what way does Northumberland take a different
>   approach to that of Bolingbroke?*

And these, and all, are all amiss employed.
What would you have me do? I am a subject,
And I challenge law. Attorneys are denied me,
And therefore personally I lay my claim
To my inheritance of free descent.

NORTHUMBERLAND   The noble Duke hath been too much abused.

ROSS   It stands your grace upon to do him right.

WILLOUGHBY   Base men by his endowments are made great.

YORK   My lords of England, let me tell you this:
I have had feeling of my cousin's wrongs,   140
And laboured all I could to do him right.
But in this kind to come, in braving arms,
Be his own carver, and cut out his way,
To find our right with wrong – it may not be.
And you that do abet him in this kind
Cherish rebellion, and are rebels all.

NORTHUMBERLAND   The noble Duke hath sworn his coming is
But for his own, and for the right of that
We all have strongly sworn to give him aid.
And let him never see joy that breaks that oath.   150

YORK   Well well, I see the issue of these arms.
I cannot mend it, I must needs confess,
Because my power is weak and all ill-left.
But if I could, by Him that gave me life,
I would attach you all, and make you stoop
Unto the sovereign mercy of the King.
But since I cannot, be it known unto you
I do remain as neuter. So fare you well,
Unless you please to enter in the castle,
And there repose you for this night.   160

BOLINGBROKE   An offer, uncle, that we will accept;
But we must win your grace to go with us
To Bristol Castle, which they say is held
By Bushy, Bagot, and their complices,
The caterpillars of the commonwealth,
Which I have sworn to weed and pluck away.

169 **Nor friends ... are:** neither as friends nor as foes can I
make you welcome

170 **Things past ... care:** what I can't cure is past caring about
(a proverbial expression)

Somewhere in Wales the Earl of Salisbury, a supporter of
Richard, is waiting for the King's return from Ireland. A
Welsh Captain says that he cannot persuade his men to wait
any longer. They have heard rumours that the King is dead
and there have been portents and prophecies of disaster.
Salisbury foresees the defeat of Richard.

SD **a Welsh Captain:** One of Shakespeare's sources,
Holinshed, identifies him as Owen Glendower. He is an
important character in *1 Henry IV,* where Hotspur scorns
his superstitious nature. He is mentioned again in Act 3
scene 1 line 43, below

2 **hardly:** with difficulty

8 **bay trees:** laurel: an evergreen tree whose leaves were
woven into a wreath to reward a conqueror or poet. The
withering of the laurel is therefore seen by the Captain as
an evil omen; more follow

9 **the fixed stars:** In the Ptolemaic description of the
universe which was widely believed until the seventeenth
century, the stars were fixed in a crystalline sphere beyond
the sun, moon and planets. They symbolised stability; the
meteor was a sign of disorder. See lines 19–20 below

10 **looks:** both appears bloody and prophesies blood on earth

11 **lean-looked:** lean-looking
prophets: soothsayers

14 **to enjoy:** in the hope of enjoying riches
rage: madness; violence

17 **As well assured:** already convinced

20 **the firmament:** the heavens; the fixed sphere of stars which
surround the earth

23 **to wait upon:** to serve

24 **crossly to thy good:** against your good fortune

> • *The previous scene has presented the crisis as a family
> affair. How does this brief interlude ask us to view events
> in a very different way?*

YORK It may be I will go with you; but yet I'll pause,
      For I am loath to break our country's laws.
      Nor friends, nor foes, to me welcome you are.
      Things past redress are now with me past care.   170
                                    [*Exeunt*

Scene 4

Enter EARL OF SALISBURY *and a* WELSH CAPTAIN

CAPTAIN My Lord of Salisbury, we have stayed ten days
         And hardly kept our countrymen together,
         And yet we hear no tidings from the King
         Therefore we will disperse ourselves. Farewell.

SALISBURY Stay yet another day, thou trusty Welshman.
           The King reposeth all his confidence in thee.

CAPTAIN 'Tis thought the King is dead. We will not stay.
         The bay trees in our country are all withered,
         And meteors fright the fixed stars of heaven.
         The pale-faced moon looks bloody on the earth,   10
         And lean-looked prophets whisper fearful change;
         Rich men look sad, and ruffians dance and leap,
         The one in fear to lose what they enjoy,
         The other to enjoy by rage and war.
         These signs forerun the death or fall of kings.
         Farewell. Our countrymen are gone and fled,
         As well assured Richard their king is dead.
                                    [*Exit*

SALISBURY Ah Richard! With the eyes of heavy mind
           I see thy glory like a shooting star
           Fall to the base earth from the firmament.   20
           Thy sun sets weeping in the lowly west,
           Witnessing storms to come, woe, and unrest.
           Thy friends are fled to wait upon thy foes,
           And crossly to thy good all fortune goes.
                                    [*Exit*

ACTIVITIES

Keeping track

Scene 1

1 Why does Gaunt wish Richard to visit him?
2 List three criticisms which Gaunt makes of Richard's conduct.
3 What is Richard's response to Gaunt's words?
4 How does Richard react to Gaunt's death?
5 York lists six reasons for his anger at Richard's behaviour. What are they?
6 Why does York accuse Richard of making a serious mistake when he confiscates Bolingbroke's inheritance?
7 What reason does Ross give for fearing and objecting to the king's actions?

Scene 2

1 What feelings for Richard does the queen reveal?
2 Why does Green hope to have arrived at Court before Richard has departed for Ireland?
3 How is York attired on his entrance? Why?
4 Whose death upsets York?
5 York leaves for Berkeley. Where do Bushy, Green and Bagot plan to go?

Scene 3

1 What characterises the behaviour of Bolingbroke and the rebellious lords towards each other?
2 What reasons does York give for his displeasure at Bolingbroke's behaviour?
3 Why is York unable to do anything about Bolingbroke's rebellion?

Scene 4

1 Why do the Welshmen desert Richard?
2 What does Salisbury now expect?

Characters

King Richard

- In this Act we see Richard very much through the words and actions of others. Much of their judgement on him is negative, though Isabel presents a contrasting view. Sum up the arguments for and against Richard's character and behaviour. (You could do this as a chart or diagram.)

Bolingbroke

- Almost as soon as Richard has left the stage Bolingbroke returns.
1 How does his behaviour contrast with that of the king?
2 Why, do you think, are people attracted to Bolingbroke and his cause?

John of Gaunt

- Do the Close Study, below, to investigate Gaunt's famous speech in detail. Then make notes summing up Gaunt's dramatic function in the play. How are his age and character used to contrast with those of Richard?

Duke of York

- Richard says that York 'is just and always loved us well'.
1 What is the evidence in this Act which would support Richard's judgement?
2 Look at all the statements made by York in this Act. Do you think he is indecisive or simply a good man in an impossible situation?

Northumberland

- Northumberland emerges from the shadows during this Act. His first action is to bring the news of Gaunt's death, and soon afterwards he is introducing Ross and Willoughby to the possibility of a conspiracy against Richard.
1 What is the evidence that Northumberland's behaviour is largely motivated by a desire to manipulate others?

Queen Isabel

- The character of Queen Isabel is not based upon any historical reality. Shakespeare develops her role with a particular dramatic intention.
1 How does she present an alternative view of events and characters in the play?
2 How is she used to create atmosphere and expectations in scene 2?

Themes

1 **Flattery or good counsel** The perennial problem for a king, or any leader, is to decide whom he should trust. This is a particular difficulty for one who is not accountable to a representative body such as a parliament. Shakespeare dramatises the issue for us by refusing to paint any of the people who surround Richard in simple black or white. What difficulties does the King face in trying to make an assessment of the advice he receives from York, Gaunt and the 'favourites', Bushy, Green and Bagot? How far, on the basis of the evidence in the play, can any one of them be trusted?

2 **Revolt** Another concern for the subjects of an absolute monarch is how far it is possible to dissent, especially when the ruler is seen to be unjust or incompetent. Shakespeare explores this theme constantly in his history plays, including in the second half of Act 2 scene 3 of *Richard II*. Give an account of York's changing thoughts and feelings between lines 83 and 170. Is his behaviour at the end of the scene simply a sign of weakness or is there any political or moral justification you could offer?

Drama

1 **Act 2 scene 1**
   • Work in groups of four.
   • Members of the group should take the roles of Richard, Northumberland, York and Gaunt.
   • Read lines 69–223.
   • Now imagine you are in the position of a modern cabinet and your agenda includes (1) the situation in Ireland, (2) taxation policy and (3) the behaviour of the exiled Bolingbroke.
   • Working in role, with attitudes appropriate to those taken by the characters in the play, decide what to do about each of the issues.
   • Compare the conclusions you have reached with those in the play. Is the outcome of your discussion very different from that in the play? If it is, why did you reach different conclusions?

2 **Freeze Frame: Act 2 scene 3 line 86**
   • Cast the characters of Bolingbroke, Northumberland, Harry Percy, Ross, Willoughby, Berkeley and York.
   • Read the scene from the beginning to line 86.

- Create the tableau which might exist on the stage at line 86. Note that this is a potentially very dangerous situation for all concerned. The characters must be asking themselves questions such as 'Will there be violence?', 'Who has the greatest power?', 'What is the consequence of this situation?' The positioning and body language of the characters must reflect these concerns.
- Once you have frozen the scene, ask each of the characters how they feel about their own predicament and about their attitude and behaviour towards the other people around them.

(For further advice see notes about Stopping the action on page 234–35.)

Close Study

Act 2 scene 1 lines 31–68: John of Gaunt's speech

1 Lines 31–33. These lines link this speech with that of the Captain in the last scene of the Act (Act 2 scene 4 line 11). It is one of a number of prophetic statements in the play. In each case the prophecy is the last words of a person before they depart the scene. The message seems to be: 'I can no longer change events; all that remains is to foretell disaster.'
   - If the image in line 33 is taken literally, why cannot the '*blaze of riot*' last?

2 Lines 34–39. How do these lines develop the idea contained in line 33? What do these lines prophesy about Richard?

3 Lines 40–60. These twenty-one lines are a single, periodic, sentence. That is, the sentence does not reveal its meaning until the end. It has one short and simple main clause, and many dependent clauses. The main verb does not appear until the penultimate line: '*This … England … is now leased out.*'
   - List the things with which England is compared.
   - How do these comparisons give weight to the main verb '*leased*'?
   - What is the rhythmical impact of the repetition of the word '*this*'? How does the repetition help the audience's understanding of the extended metaphor?
   - How does the final simile emphasise the scorn and despair felt by Gaunt?

4 Lines 61–68. This concluding section repeats in miniature the form of the previous twenty-one lines: praise of England followed by a sad simile. What does Gaunt mean by the antithesis in his final couplet?

5 Read the speech aloud. Note examples of the way in which the rhythm and meaning are emphasised, for example in lines 35 and 37, by alliteration and assonance (see glossary).

6 Some of Gaunt's images are strongly religious. Why, do you think, does he make these comparisons?

7 The speech is artificial and in a high, rhetorical style, yet Shakespeare delays the entry of its chief target, Richard, until Gaunt has finished. Why do you think he does this? How would the dramatic nature of the ensuing scene be changed if Richard (and other characters) had heard the speech?

Key scene

Scene 3 lines 81– end
Keying it in

1 Bolingbroke has been absent from the stage since the end of Act 1 scene 3. The audience's sympathy for him has been engaged by his friends, by his predicament following the death of his father, and even by Richard's account of his leaving England. Now, however, he must speak for himself.

- How does he behave towards the nobles who have joined him in the earlier part of this scene?

The scene itself

2 **Lines 81–105**
- How does Bolingbroke behave towards his uncle, York? How is this consistent with his behaviour earlier in the play and in this scene?
- How does York respond to Bolingbroke's greeting? In what ways does his language seek to undermine the impression of Bolingbroke given earlier in the scene?

3 **Lines 105–138**
- York charges Bolingbroke with treason. What are his reasons for viewing Bolingbroke's behaviour in this way?
- Summarise Bolingbroke's rebuttal of the charge of treason.
- Neither York nor Bolingbroke mentions the cause of Bolingbroke's banishment in Act 1. Why would it not help either's argument to allude to this?
- Bolingbroke's speech is highly rhetorical; that is, it is written in artificial and impressive language in order to be persuasive. Read it aloud to get a sense of its rhythm and power. Note at least one example of each of the following: rhetorical questions, alliteration, assonance.
- How does Shakespeare show that we are meant to find Bolingbroke persuasive? Considering both the technique of his speech and the logic of his argument, do you find him so?

4 **Lines 136–170**
   - Northumberland is much less subtle than Bolingbroke. What is the evidence for this?
   - How do you think an actor should play lines 157–160? York could appear sympathetic or merely foolish, comic or politically astute: what would you think most appropriate?
   - Why does Bolingbroke mention Bushy and Bagot? In what way does his final speech in this scene demonstrate his political skill?

Overview
5 The scene illustrates the characters of Bolingbroke, York and Northumberland.
   - What emotional stages does York go through in these lines? How does he modify his view as the scene develops?
   - What diplomatic and leadership skills does Bolingbroke exhibit here?

Writing

1 Imagine that Northumberland is discussing the events of Act 2 with his son, Harry Percy. He:
   - makes it clear why he thinks their family interest will be served by supporting Bolingbroke
   - comments on the character and behaviour of the King and his uncles
   - forecasts what will happen once they have destroyed Bushy and Bagot and considers the consequences of the Welsh defection.
   Write the conversation as a script.
2 You have been retained by Bolingbroke as one of his attorneys to plead his case for inheriting his estates and titles. Prepare the argument, being sure to consider any possible counter arguments which may be made by the opposition.
3 Suppose that Bolingbroke and his supporters publish a manifesto in order to gain popular support and rally the nobility to his side. Write it.
4 Imagine that you are the art director on a forthcoming film of *Richard II*.
   - Through a combination of illustrations and notes, describe the locations you would use for this act. Consider how you could use the settings to provide dramatic contrasts and to intensify emotion.
   - What is gained and what is lost by transferring the action of the play from a bare Elizabethan stage to the complex possibilities of modern cinema?

Bolingbroke has captured Bushy and Green and sentenced them to death. He explains that their crime has been to provide Richard with bad advice and to divide him from his queen. Bolingbroke suggests that they poisoned Richard's opinion of him and have profited from his exile. He charges them with despoiling his lands and buildings.

2 **vex:** trouble; afflict

3 **presently:** immediately

4 **too much urging ... lives:** stressing too strongly the evil and destructive nature of your lives

5–6 **to wash your blood ... men:** Bolingbroke compares himself, perhaps unconsciously, to Pilate washing his hands before condemning Christ to death. See below, Act 4 scene 1 line 239 and note.

7 **causes of:** reasons for

9 **happy:** fortunate
   blood and lineaments: birth and appearance

10 **By your unhappied ... clean:** you have, in fortune and appearance, ruined him entirely

11 **in manner:** so to speak; as it were

12 **Made a divorce betwixt:** separated

13–15 **Broke the possession ... wrongs:** Bolingbroke is vague but implies that Richard has been led into sexual unfaithfulness. Some productions of the play suggest an analogy with Marlowe's *Edward II* (1593) in which the King's homosexual relationship with his favorite, Gaveston, is a principal reason for his overthrow. Bolingbroke's charge needs to be placed in the context of the scenes between Richard and the Queen and her grief for him

20 **in foreign clouds:** The same image is used in *Romeo and Juliet* (Act 1 scene 1 line 131) which Shakespeare wrote at about this time
   in: into; amongst

22 **signories:** estates; the lands over which he has lordship

23 **Disparked my parks:** a park was originally land enclosed for hunting, so the implication is that fences have been untended, noble pursuits have declined and the land put to other uses

24 **torn my household coat:** destroyed the stained-glass coats-of-arms

25 **Razed out my imprese:** utterly destroyed my heraldic devices

---

• *Bolingbroke is confident of the charges he brings against Bushy and Green but how much evidence have we had in the play to substantiate his assertions?*

Act three

Scene

Enter BOLINGBROKE, YORK, NORTHUMBERLAND,
PERCY, ROSS, WILLOUGHBY, *with* BUSHY *and* GREEN,
prisoners

BOLINGBROKE   Bring forth these men.
Bushy and Green, I will not vex your souls,
Since presently your souls must part your bodies,
With too much urging your pernicious lives,
For 'twere no charity; yet to wash your blood
From off my hands, here in the view of men
I will unfold some causes of your deaths.
You have misled a prince, a royal king,
A happy gentleman in blood and lineaments,
By you unhappied and disfigured clean.   10
You have in manner with your sinful hours
Made a divorce betwixt his Queen and him,
Broke the possession of a royal bed,
And stained the beauty of a fair queen's cheeks
With tears, drawn from her eyes by your foul
   wrongs.
Myself a prince by fortune of my birth,
Near to the King in blood, and near in love
Till you did make him misinterpret me,
Have stooped my neck under your injuries,
And sighed my English breath in foreign clouds,   20
Eating the bitter bread of banishment
Whilst you have fed upon my signories,
Disparked my parks, and felled my forest woods,
From my own windows torn my household coat,
Razed out my imprese, leaving me no sign
Save men's opinions and my living blood
To show the world I am a gentleman.

Bushy and Green go courageously to their deaths.
Bolingbroke sends greetings to the Queen, who is in the
custody of Northumberland, and then departs in search of
Richard's Welsh supporters.

34 **plague injustice ... hell:** punish in hell those who judge us
35 **dispatched:** executed; sent to the next world
37 **intreated:** treated
41 **at large:** in full
43 **complices:** allies, accomplices

> • *What role has Bolingbroke assumed and how effective does*
> *he seem to be? How far do you sympathise with*
> *Bolingbroke now?*

Richard has arrived in North Wales accompanied by Aumerle
and the Bishop of Carlisle. He weeps for joy on returning to
his kingdom.

SD *flourish and colours:* fanfare and flags
  1 **Barkloughly:** The name is used by Holinshed apparently in
    error for Harlech in north-west Wales
    at hand: close by
  2 **How brooks:** how do you like
  4 **Needs must ... well:** Necessity makes me be satisfied by it
  6 **salute:** greet. Richard apparently stoops to touch the
    ground.
  9 **Plays fondly with:** alternates fondly between
    Both *play* and *fond* are used affectionately

This and much more, much more than twice all this,
Condemns you to the death. See them delivered over
To execution and the hand of death.   30

BUSHY

More welcome is the stroke of death to me
Than Bolingbroke to England. Lords farewell.

GREEN

My comfort is that heaven will take our souls,
And plague injustice with the pains of hell.

BOLINGBROKE

My Lord Northumberland, see them dispatched.

[*Exit* NORTHUMBERLAND *with* BUSHY *and* GREEN

Uncle, you say the Queen is at your house.
For God's sake fairly let her be intreated.
Tell her I send to her my kind commends.
Take special care my greetings be delivered.

YORK

A gentleman of mine I have dispatched   40
With letters of your love to her at large.

BOLINGBROKE

Thanks, gentle uncle. Come lords, away,
To fight with Glendower and his complices.
A while to work, and after holiday.   [*Exeunt*

Scene ❷

Drums; flourish and colours. Enter KING RICHARD,
AUMERLE, *the* BISHOP OF CARLISLE, *and* SOLDIERS

KING RICHARD

Barkloughly Castle call they this at hand?

AUMERLE

Yea my lord. How brooks your grace the air
After your late tossing on the breaking seas?

KING RICHARD

Needs must I like it well. I weep for joy
To stand upon my kingdom once again.
Dear earth I do salute thee with my hand,
Though rebels wound thee with their horses' hoofs.
As a long-parted mother with her child
Plays fondly with her tears and smiles in meeting,

Richard invokes the earth to defeat his enemies. The Bishop
reassures him that God will help him, providing he helps
himself. Aumerele believes that Richard has been careless in the
face of Bolingbroke's threat.

11 **do thee favours:** treat you kindly. Richard makes the contrast
with the wounds delivered by the rebels' horses (above)
13 **with thy sweets ... sense:** feed his greedy appetite with your
produce; give yourself to him
14,15 **spiders, toads:** both considered to be poisonous. It was
thought that spiders sucked their poison from the earth
15 **heavy-gaited:** clumsily walking
18 **Yield:** give in return
21 **double tongue:** forked tongue
mortal: deadly
23 **senseless:** because he is addressing the inanimate, unfeeling,
earth. The word immediately suggests to him, however, that
the idea is not entirely 'senseless' since the earth must
recognise his God-given sovereignty and rise up on his behalf
(lines 24–26)
conjuration: solemn and sacred appeal
24–25 **these stones ... soldiers:** an illusion both to the Greek
myths of Deucalion, who casts stones to recreate men after the
Deluge, and Cadmus, who sowed dragon's teeth to create an
army, as well as to the Bible (see Luke chapter 3 verse 8 and
chapter 19 verse 40)
27 **that power:** i.e God
29–32 **The means ... redress:** these lines are not in the First
Folio, presumably because the compositor's eye skipped from
'The means ... ' to 'He means'
29 **yield:** give
30–31 **else heaven ... not:** otherwise heaven would help us when
we will not assist ourselves
31–32 **heaven's offer ... redress:** we are in danger of refusing the
means by which God has chosen to help and restore us
34 **security:** over-confidence
36 **Discomfortable:** disheartening; unsettling
37 **the searching eye of heaven:** the sun. As the speech develops
we see Richard's conceit to be a development of Salisbury's in
Act 2 scene 4 lines 19–22
38 **and lights the lower world:** shines in the Antipodes, the
other side of the world. (The First Folio and Quarto read 'that'
for 'and')
41 **this terrestrial ball:** the earth

So weeping, smiling, greet I thee my earth,   10
And do thee favours with my royal hands.
Feed not thy sovereign's foe, my gentle earth,
Nor with thy sweets comfort his ravenous sense,
But let thy spiders that suck up thy venom,
And heavy-gaited toads lie in their way,
Doing annoyance to the treacherous feet,
Which with usurping steps do trample thee.
Yield stinging nettles to mine enemies;
And when they from thy bosom pluck a flower,
Guard it, I pray thee, with a lurking adder,   20
Whose double tongue may with a mortal touch
Throw death upon thy sovereign's enemies.
Mock not my senseless conjuration lords.
This earth shall have a feeling, and these stones
Prove armed soldiers ere her native king
Shall falter under foul rebellion's arms.

BISHOP OF CARLISLE   Fear not my lord, that power that made you
    king
Hath power to keep you king in spite of all.
The means that heavens yield must be embraced
And not neglected; else heaven would,   30
And we will not – heaven's offer we refuse,
The proffered means of succour and redress.

AUMERLE   He means my lord that we are too remiss,
Whilst Bolingbroke through our security
Grows strong and great in substance and in power.

KING RICHARD   Discomfortable cousin knowest thou not
That when the searching eye of heaven is hid
Behind the globe, and lights the lower world,
Then thieves and robbers range abroad unseen
In murders and in outrage boldly here;   40
But when from under this terrestrial ball
He fires the proud tops of the eastern pines,
And darts his light through every guilty hole,

Richard says that, though Bolingbroke has prospered in his absence, now that he has returned the traitor will quickly fade away. He is sure that none can defeat God's anointed King. However, Salisbury enters with the news that all Richard's Welsh supporters have fled or joined Bolingbroke.

49 **we were … Antipodes:** a comparison with Richard's journey to Ireland
53 **self-affrighted:** frightened by what he has done
54 **rude:** turbulent; violent
55 **balm:** the oil of consecration used at the monarch's coronation (see *Background* page xii)
56 **breath:** words; life
   worldly: mortal
58 **pressed:** forced to fight; conscripted
59 **shrewd:** dangerous
60 **pay:** this suggestion of mercenary angels is created in Richard's mind because he plays on *crown* and *angel*, which were silver and gold coins
62 **still:** always
SD *Enter* **SALISBURY:** Salisbury's news, following Richard's rhetoric, is ironic but his entrance follows appropriately from the events of Act 2 scene 4
63 **power:** army; strength
64 **Nor near:** neither nearer
65 **discomfort:** bad news
68 **clouded:** a further allusion to the 'sun' metaphor
76–81 **But now … pride:** These lines have the rhythm and rhyme of a sestet – lines 9–14 of a Shakespearean sonnet (see Glossary page 245). The sonnet craze of the early 1590s suggested the form as appropriate for the expression of high emotion (compare John of Gaunt, Act 2 scene 1 lines 9–14 as well as *Romeo and Juliet* Act 1 scene 5 lines 92–105)
76 **But now:** until this moment

- *On what is Richard relying to safeguard his throne?*
- *Compare Salisbury's couplets with the way in which Richard speaks. What dramatic contrasts does Shakespeare create?*

Then murders, treasons, and detested sins,
The cloak of night being plucked from off their
    backs,
Stand bare and naked, trembling at themselves?
So when this thief, this traitor Bolingbroke,
Who all this while hath revelled in the night,
Whilst we were wandering with the Antipodes,
Shall see us rising in our throne the east,   50
His treasons will sit blushing in his face,
Not able to endure the sight of day,
But self-affrighted, tremble at his sin.
Not all the water in the rough rude sea
Can wash the balm off from an anointed king.
The breath of worldly men cannot depose
The deputy elected by the Lord.
For every man that Bolingbroke hath pressed
To lift shrewd steel against our golden crown,
God for his Richard hath in heavenly pay   60
A glorious angel. Then if angels fight,
Weak men must fall for heaven still guards the right.

Enter SALISBURY

KING RICHARD   Welcome my lord. How far off lies your power?

SALISBURY   Nor near nor farther off, my gracious lord,
Than this weak arm. Discomfort guides my tongue
And bids me speak of nothing but despair.
One day too late, I fear me, noble lord,
Hath clouded all thy happy days on earth.
O call back yesterday, bid time return,
And thou shalt have twelve thousand fighting men.   70
Today, today, unhappy day too late,
O'erthrows thy joys, friends, fortune, and thy state;
For all the Welshmen, hearing thou wert dead,
Are gone to Bolingbroke, dispersed and fled.

AUMERLE   Comfort my liege, why looks your grace so pale?

KING RICHARD   But now the blood of twenty thousand men
Did triumph in my face, and they are fled.
And till so much blood thither come again,

Richard is taken aback, but with Aumerle's encouragement, he remembers that he is the King and that his uncle, the Duke of York, should have a sufficient army. Sir Stephen Scroop arrives, saying that he brings bad news. The King claims that no disaster has the power to hurt him.

81 **set a blot ... pride:** stained my greatness; marked my arrogance

SD *Enter* **SCROOP:** Sir Stephen Scroop was a courageous soldier, loyal to Richard. Holinshed describes him carrying the sword of state ceremoniously before the King

92 **care-tuned:** tuned to the key which best expresses sorrow
deliver: provide; communicate

94 **The worst ... unfold:** the worst you can tell me is that I have lost earthly (as opposed to spiritual) things

95 **care:** trouble; responsibility

98–99 **Greater he shall ... so:** he cannot be greater than I am because the greatest status that a man can aspire to is to serve God, so I shall serve Him too and be Bolingbroke's equal partner in doing so

101 **They break ... us:** by revolting against the king they break their duty to God (because I am God's deputy)

109 **limits:** banks; ordained position

> • *How is Shakespeare creating dramatic irony in the scene, and what is its impact upon the audience?*

	Have I not reason to look pale and dead?	
	All souls that will be safe fly from my side,	80
	For time hath set a blot upon my pride.	
AUMERLE	Comfort my liege, remember who you are.	
KING RICHARD	I had forgot myself, am I not King?	

KING RICHARD   I had forgot myself, am I not King?
                 Awake thou coward majesty; thou sleepest.
                 Is not the King's name twenty thousand names?
                 Arm, arm, my name, a puny subject strikes
                 At thy great glory. Look not to the ground,
                 Ye favourites of a King, are we not high?
                 High be our thoughts. I know my uncle York
                 Hath power enough to serve our turn. But who
                    comes here?   90

                 Enter SCROOP

SCROOP   More health and happiness betide my liege
                 Than can my care-tuned tongue deliver him.

KING RICHARD   Mine ear is open and my heart prepared.
                 The worst is worldly loss thou canst unfold.
                 Say, is my kingdom lost? Why, 'twas my care,
                 And what loss is it to be rid of care?
                 Strives Bolingbroke to be as great as we?
                 Greater he shall not be. If he serve God,
                 We'll serve Him too, and be his fellow so.
                 Revolt our subjects? That we cannot mend;   100
                 They break their faith to God as well as us.
                 Cry woe, destruction, ruin, and decay.
                 The worst is death, and death will have his day.

SCROOP   Glad am I that your highness is so armed
                 To bear the tidings of calamity.
                 Like an unseasonable stormy day
                 Which makes the silver rivers drown their shores,
                 As if the world were all dissolved to tears
                 So high above his limits swells the rage
                 Of Bolingbroke, covering your fearful land   110
                 With hard bright steel, and hearts harder than steel.

Scroop tells Richard that the whole population has risen up against him. Richard asks what has become of his favourites and initially thinks that Scroop is telling him that they too have defected to Bolingbroke. Scroop explains that Bushy, Green and the Earl of Wiltshire have been executed.

112 **Whitebeards:** old men

114–15 **clap their ... arms:** encase their soft, unmanly limbs in hard and inflexible armour

116 **beadsmen:** men of prayer, especially those provided with a pension to say prayers for the soul of a benefactor

117 **double-fatal yew:** because the wood is used to make longbows and the berries are poisonous

118 **distaff-women:** the women of the house. A distaff is a short staff on which wool is wound during hand-spinning **rusty bills:** old and long-unused weapons. The bill is a very long staff with a spiked blade or axe head

119 **seat:** throne – and the monarchy symbolised by it

121 **a tale so ill:** such a desperate story

125 **Measure our confines ... steps:** pass through our lands without being attacked

127 **I warrant:** I'm certain

129 **vipers:** venomous snakes

130 **fawn:** grovel; make a show of affection

131 **Snakes ... heart:** a proverbial reference to treachery. A man found a snake dying from cold, warmed it on his chest and was bitten by it

132 **Three Judases:** Judas, the betrayer of Jesus, was a common symbol of treachery and this usage echoes other references to Richard as Christ-like.

133 **Would they:** did they desire to. This line is metrically short, presumably to allow the actor to give more emotional weight to *Terrible hell* which is part exclamation, part imprecation (curse)

134 **spotted:** corrupt; stained – and the epithet was associated with snakes

135 **property:** condition: quality

138 **with hands:** through a signature or hand-shake

140 **lie full low ... ground:** buried. Scroop repeats for emphasis: this is the completion of the 'tidings' he began at line 104

144 **of comfort:** i.e. as represented by the Duke of York's imagined army

Whitebeards have armed their thin and hairless
   scalps
Against thy majesty; boys with women's voices
Strive to speak big and clap their female joints
In stiff unwieldy arms against thy crown;
Thy very beadsmen learn to bend their bows
Of double-fatal yew against thy state;
Yea distaff-women manage rusty bills
Against thy seat; both young and old rebel,
And all goes worse than I have power to tell.   120

KING RICHARD   Too well, too well thou tellest a tale so ill.
Where is the Earl of Wiltshire? Where is Bagot?
What is become of Bushy, where is Green,
That they have let the dangerous enemy
Measure our confines with such peaceful steps?
If we prevail, their heads shall pay for it.
I warrant they have made peace with Bolingbroke.

SCROOP   Peace have they made with him indeed, my lord.

KING RICHARD   O villains, vipers, damned without redemption,
Dogs easily won to fawn on any man,   130
Snakes in my heart-blood warmed, that sting my
   heart;
Three Judases, each one thrice worse than Judas.
Would they make peace? Terrible hell
Make war upon their spotted souls for this.

SCROOP   Sweet love, I see, changing his property,
Turns to the sourest and most deadly hate.
Again uncurse their souls; their peace is made
With heads and not with hands. Those whom you
   curse
Have felt the worst of death's destroying wound,
And lie full low, graved in the hollow ground.   140

AUMERLE   Is Bushy, Green, and the Earl of Wiltshire dead?

SCROOP   Ay, all of them at Bristol lost their heads.

AUMERLE   Where is the Duke my father with his power?

KING RICHARD   No matter where – of comfort no man speak.

Richard despairs, and meditates upon the death of kings. He
realises that monarchs are as subject to death and destruction as
other mortals. The Bishop tells him that such defeatism saps his
strength.

146 dust: the earth – but with overtones of death and impermanence

148 executors: people who execute the will of the dead person

150 deposed: laid in safety; but also 'put down from office'. The
word has three syllables stressed on the second

153–154 that small mode ... bones: both flesh and blood (our
'earth' or 'clay') and tomb, and thus by extension the effigy upon
the tomb of a king. *Paste* means pastry or dough

156 tell sad ... kings: there was a popular genre of such stories, told
with moral purpose. The best known is *The Mirror for
Magistrates* which had been in print since 1559

158 the ghosts: the ghosts of those that

161 rounds the mortal temples: encircles the head which will one
day die. The quibble on 'temples' establishes an image of the
crown like a defensive wall around a castle containing temple,
court and jester. Since the jester is also Death, the *mortal temples*
are a *momento mori*, a reminder of the grinning skull beneath the
skin

162 antic: fool; jester. His role was to scoff at the vanity of the
monarch and court just as Death perpetually ridicules human
achievement

165 monarchize: play the part of monarch

166 self: self-centred (*self* qualifies *conceit*)

168 brass: a symbol of imperishability and of the eternal. Compare
Sonnet 64 and Job Chapter 6 verse 12

humoured thus: [Death] being of this mind; having amused
himself; having been indulged – all three meanings are present

171–172 Cover your heads ... reverence: Richard commands his
companions to replace their headgear which they would always
remove in the presence of royalty. He again seeks to emphasise
his humanity

176 subjected: reduced to the state of subject; submissive

179 presently prevent ... wail: immediately avoid the paths to
suffering and grief

180–182 To fear the foe ... yourself: since fear crushes strength,
fear of your enemy makes you weak and gives him strength, and
thus your weak understanding fights against you

> • *Richard's move to 'sit upon the ground' is a dramatic
> metaphor of his inactivity in this scene. He has heard one
> report after another of events over which he now has no control.*

Let's talk of graves, of worms, and epitaphs,
Make dust our paper, and with rainy eyes
Write sorrow on the bosom of the earth.
Let's choose executors and talk of wills.
And yet not so, for what can we bequeath
Save our deposed bodies to the ground?   150
Our lands, our lives, and all are Bolingbroke's,
And nothing can we call our own but death,
And that small model of the barren earth
Which serves as paste and cover to our bones.
For God's sake let us sit upon the ground
And tell sad stories of the death of kings:
How some have been deposed, some slain in war,
Some haunted by the ghosts they have deposed,
Some poisoned by their wives, some sleeping killed,
All murdered. For within the hollow crown   160
That rounds the mortal temples of a king
Keeps death his court; and there the antic sits,
Scoffing his state and grinning at his pomp,
Allowing him a breath, a little scene,
To monarchize, be feared, and kill with looks,
Infusing him with self and vain conceit,
As if this flesh which walls about our life
Were brass impregnable; and humoured thus,
Comes at the last, and with a little pin
Bores through his castle wall, and farewell king!   170
Cover your heads, and mock not flesh and blood
With solemn reverence; throw away respect,
Tradition, form, and ceremonious duty;
For you have but mistook me all this while.
I live with bread like you, feel want,
Taste grief, need friends. Subjected thus,
How can you say to me, I am a king?

BISHOP OF CARLISLE   My lord, wise men ne'er sit and wail their woes,
But presently prevent the ways to wail.
To fear the foe, since fear oppresseth strength,   180
Gives in your weakness strength unto your foe,
And so your follies fight against yourself.

Aumerle reminds Richard that York has an army. The King asks Scroop what has become of York, only to be told of his defection to Bolingbroke. Richard despairs once more. He decides to dismiss his army and retreat to Flint Castle. Richard will not permit Aumerle to debate his decision.

183–185 **no worse can come ... breath:** nothing worse [than death] can come from a fight: to fight and die is to destroy the power of death by dying, while to fear death is to be a slave to death

186 **power:** army

187 **make ... limb:** make one part do the work of the whole; make one regiment into a whole army

189 **change:** exchange

190 **This ague ... overblown:** this quaking fear has passed

194 **complexion:** appearance

195 **The state and ... day:** the weather and the forecast for the day

198 **by small and small:** little by little

199 **To lengthen out ... spoken:** by prolonging the bad news, which is like stretching the torturer's victim on a rack

202 **gentlemen in arms:** men entitled by their birth to bear arms, perhaps especially gentlemen of the royal bodyguard since Holinshed writes of 'the sudden departing of them whom he most trusted'

203 **Upon his party:** on his side. Richard appears to interrupt this incomplete sentence

204 **Beshrew thee:** Curse you! A mild and usually jocular oath

205 **Of:** out of

209 **Flint Castle:** Flint Castle in North Wales is on the Dee estuary some eighty miles east of Harlech

212 **ear:** cultivate; plough

213 **none:** no hope – of growing prosperity

214 **counsel is but vain:** advice is pointless

215 **double wrong:** in disobeying me and in flattering me. Compare also the snake's *double tongue* in line 21, above

- *In what ways do Richard and the Bishop of Carlisle take, perhaps ironically, opposing views?*
- *How does Shakespeare emphasise the hopelessness of Richard's position?*
- *What is the effect of the sonnet-like rhyme scheme of lines 184–197?*

	Fear, and be slain, no worse can come to fight;
	And fight and die is death destroying death,
	Where fearing dying pays death servile breath.

AUMERLE   My father hath a power; inquire of him,
            And learn to make a body of a limb.

KING RICHARD Thou chidest me well. Proud Bolingbroke, I come
              To change blows with thee for our day of doom.
              This ague fit of fear is overblown;   190
              An easy task it is to win our own.
              Say, Scroop, where lies our uncle with his power?
              Speak sweetly, man, although thy looks be sour.

SCROOP   Men judge by the complexion of the sky
            The state and inclination of the day;
            So may you by my dull and heavy eye,
            My tongue hath but a heavier tale to say.
            I play the torturer, by small and small
            To lengthen out the worst that must be spoken.
            Your uncle York is joined with Bolingbroke,   200
            And all your northern castles yielded up,
            And all your southern gentlemen in arms
            Upon his party.

KING RICHARD   Thou hast said enough.

              [*To* AUMERLE] Beshrew thee cousin, which didst
                lead me forth
              Of that sweet way I was in to despair.
              What say you now? What comfort have we now?
              By heaven I'll hate him everlastingly
              That bids me be of comfort any more.
              Go to Flint Castle, there I'll pine away.
              A king, woe's slave, shall kingly woe obey.   210
              That power I have, discharge, and let them go
              To ear the land that hath some hope to grow,
              For I have none. Let no man speak again
              To alter this, for counsel is but vain.

AUMERLE   My liege, one word.

KING RICHARD   He does me double wrong

217 **Discharge:** release (from their military obligations)
218 **Richard's night ... day:** a further development of the 'sun' image

Bolingbroke is closing in on Richard who, he now knows, has few supporters left. York objects to Northumberland's failure to give Richard the title of King. He warns Bolingbroke not to be over-ambitious. Percy tells Bolingbroke that Richard is within Flint Castle.

SD *Enter:* The scene takes place on the approach to Flint Castle
  1 **intelligence:** news
  6 **hid his head:** both to take shelter and to keep from shame or discomfiture. Northumberland's use of this phrase emphasises his lack of respect in failing to use the King's title ('head') and provides York with a quibble on the word
 11 **The time hath been:** there was a time when
 14 **taking so the head:** omitting the title; going your own way. Note the continuing play on *take/mistake* and *head* in the next three lines
 17 **mistake: the heavens:** Neither the Folio nor Quarto punctuate after *mistake*, which emphasises the ambiguity of the line: *mistake* may mean either 'go astray' or 'misunderstand'

> • *Shakespeare ignores Holinshed and others, who record Richard's kidnap by Northumberland and his forcible removal to Flint. For what dramatic reasons do you think Shakespeare might have done this?*

That wounds me with the flatteries of his tongue.
Discharge my followers, let them hence away,
From Richard's night to Bolingbroke's fair day.

[*Exeunt*

Scene ③

Enter with drum and colours BOLINGBROKE, YORK,
NORTHUMBERLAND *and soldiers*

BOLINGBROKE   So that by this intelligence we learn
The Welshmen are dispersed, and Salisbury
Is gone to meet the King, who lately landed
With some few private friends upon this coast.

NORTHUMBERLAND   The news is very fair and good my lord,
Richard not far from hence hath hid his head.

YORK   It would beseem the Lord Northumberland
To say 'King Richard'. Alack the heavy day
When such a sacred king should hide his head.

NORTHUMBERLAND   Your grace mistakes; only to be brief   10
Left I his title out.

YORK   The time hath been,
Would you have been so brief with him, he would
Have been so brief with you to shorten you,
For taking so the head, your whole head's length.

BOLINGBROKE   Mistake not, uncle, further than you should.

YORK   Take not, good cousin, further than you should,
Lest you mistake: the heavens are over our heads.

BOLINGBROKE   I know it uncle, and oppose not myself
Against their will. But who comes here?

Enter PERCY

Welcome Harry. What, will not this castle yield?   20

PERCY   The castle royally is manned my lord,
Against thy entrance.

Bolingbroke sends Northumberland with a message of allegiance to Richard. He pledges support providing that his banishment is repealed: otherwise he threatens civil war. He commands his army to march in front of the castle so that the King can see the extent of his power. He imagines that he and Richard will meet like two great forces of nature.

25 lies: inhabits

26 lime: mortar

31 Noble lord: Northumberland – see lines 72 and 101, below

32 rude: strong but ill-shaped

32–34 rude ribs ... ruined ears: the comparison of the castle to a human body extends Richard's conceit (Act 3 scene 2 lines 167–170). The ribs are the walls with their buttresses and towers; the ears are the crenellations and loopholes. Bolingbroke's use of the pronoun *his* to refer to the castle may also indicate that his thoughts are preoccupied with Richard contained within

40–41 Provided that ... repealed: provided that my banishment is repealed and my lands unconditionally restored to me

42 the advantage of my power: my larger army

45–48 The which ... shall show: the main verb, *show*, is not apparent until the end of this clause which reads: My kneeling, submissively, shall gently demonstrate how far from my mind it is that the blood of a red tempest should drench the fresh green fields of King Richard's country. The inversion profoundly alters the impact of the words, stressing the violent vision above the conciliatory conclusion

52 tattered: This description of the battlements is consistent with the 'ruined ears' (line 34, above) but is essentially to make the contrast with the 'fair appointments'

53 Our fair appointments: our smart and well-kept equipment

55–57 the elements ... heaven: a thunderstorm. Bolingbroke is still playing with the image of lines 43–47

56 shock: Bolingbroke uses the word in the military sense of the engagement of two armies in battle and also alludes to the belief that thunder was caused by the collision of two opposing elements, fire (as lightning) and water

- *What do you think Bolingbroke's intentions are at this point in the play? Will Richard retain his crown?*
- *Look closely at Bolingbroke's speech. What do his rhetoric and tone reveal about his intentions, personality and state of mind?*

BOLINGBROKE   Royally?
                Why it contains no king.

PERCY   Yes, my good lord,
                It doth contain a king. King Richard lies
                Within the limits of yon lime and stone,
                And with him are the Lord Aumerle, Lord Salisbury,
                Sir Stephen Scroop, besides a clergyman
                Of holy reverence, who, I cannot learn.

NORTHUMBERLAND   O belike it is the Bishop of Carlisle.   30

BOLINGBROKE   Noble lord,
                Go to the rude ribs of that ancient castle,
                Through brazen trumpet send the breath of parley
                Into his ruined ears, and thus deliver:
                Henry Bolingbroke
                On both his knees doth kiss King Richard's hand,
                And sends allegiance and true faith of heart
                To his most royal person; hither come
                Even at his feet to lay my arms and power,
                Provided that my banishment repealed   40
                And lands restored again be fully granted;
                If not, I'll use the advantage of my power
                And lay the summer's dust with showers of blood
                Rained from the wounds of slaughtered Englishmen;
                The which, how far off from the mind of
                    Bolingbroke
                It is such crimson tempest should bedrench
                The fresh green lap of fair King Richard's land,
                My stooping duty tenderly shall show.
                Go signify as much while here we march
                Upon the grassy carpet of this plain.   50
                Let's march without the noise of threatening drum,
                That from this castle's tattered battlements
                Our fair appointments may be well perused.
                Methinks King Richard and myself should meet
                With no less terror than the elements
                Of fire and water when their thundering shock
                At meeting tears the cloudy cheeks of heaven.

Bolingbroke and York are impressed by the noble appearance of
Richard on the castle walls. Richard ignores them and scornfully
asks Northumberland why he has not bowed before him.

58 yielding: surrendering – arising from *shock* in line 56

59 rain: a quibble on reign. Perhaps Bolingbroke realises the
irony of what he has said and tries, unconvincingly, to correct
his presumptuousness in the next line

SD The trumpets ... within: The trumpets outside the castle
sound a call for peace. This is answered by the *trumpets* in the
castle. A fanfare follows

63 blushing: with the rosy colour of dawn. The word does not
imply embarrassment but rather the glory of Richard's
appearance. *Discontented* and *fiery* refer to the proverbial 'red sky
in the morning' which warns of approaching storms

64 portal: magnificent gateway. The image here is of
Phoebus/Apollo, the sun god, whose fiery chariot transports the
sun on its daily westward passage

65 envious: malicious; actively jealous

66–67 stain the track ... passage: darken the sky through which he
brightly passes

67 occident: west

68 Yet: still

69 the eagle's: the king of birds, whose acute sight was proverbial.
It was thought that if the eagle's eye began to fail he would fly
towards the sun. Its rays would renew his vision

69–70 lightens forth ... majesty: with his eyes flashing like
lightning he majestically controls

71 stain: York picks up Bolingbroke's word from line 66 and uses it
with its moral connotation of dishonour

72 We are amazed: Richard addresses himself solely to
Northumberland until line 126

73 To watch: expecting to see. It is ironic that Richard waits to
observe what Bolingbroke had twice said that he would do

76 awful duty: reverential homage

77 hand: signed document. The word inspires the quibble in lines
79 and 80

80 gripe: seize; control
sceptre: see Act 1 scene 1 line 118 and note

81 Unless ... usurp: without he commits sacrilege, steals and
wrongfully claims the crown

82 all: everyone else

83 torn their souls ... us: committed sin by breaking faith with
me. There is a play on *torn/turn*

85 my master: Richard emphasises his very personal relationship
with God
omnipotent: all-powerful

87 pestilence: fatal epidemic disease

88 unbegot: not yet conceived

89 Vassal: subservient. Richard emphasises the feudal relationship

Be he the fire, I'll be the yielding water;
The rage be his, whilst on the earth I rain
My waters – on the earth, and not on him.   60
March on, and mark King Richard how he looks.

The trumpets sound parley without, and answer
within. Then a flourish. KING RICHARD *appeareth on*
the walls with the BISHOP OF CARLISLE, AUMERLE,
SCROOP, *and* SALISBURY

BOLINGBROKE   See, see King Richard doth himself appear,
As doth the blushing, discontented sun
From out the fiery portal of the east,
When he perceives the envious clouds are bent
To dim his glory, and to stain the track
Of his bright passage to the occident.

YORK   Yet looks he like a king. Behold his eye,
As bright as is the eagle's, lightens forth
Controlling majesty. Alack, alack for woe   70
That any harm should stain so fair a show!

KING RICHARD   We are amazed, and thus long have we stood
To watch the fearful bending of thy knee,
Because we thought ourself thy lawful king.
And if we be, how dare thy joints forget
To pay their awful duty to our presence?
If we be not, show us the hand of God
That hath dismissed us from our stewardship;
For well we know no hand of blood and bone
Can gripe the sacred handle of our sceptre,   80
Unless he do profane, steal, or usurp.
And though you think that all, as you have done,
Have torn their souls by turning them from us,
And we are barren and bereft of friends,
Yet know, my master God omnipotent,
Is mustering in his clouds on our behalf
Armies of pestilence; and they shall strike
Your children yet unborn and unbegot,
That lift your vassal hands against my head,
And threat the glory of my precious crown.   90

Richard tells Northumberland that Bolingbroke is guilty of
treason by returning from exile, and warns him of the horrors of
civil war. Northumberland claims that Bolingbroke has come in
peace: he will stand his army down and serve Richard once his
rightful title and possessions have been granted to him. Richard
agrees to Bolingbroke's terms.

93 **treason:** since Bolingbroke is banished and, by his presence,
defies the king. For this reason Richard will not address him
directly

93–94 **open ... bleeding war:** write his bequest in purple by
making bloody war

95 **ere:** before

96 **crowns:** heads

97 **ill become ... face:** not suit England's beautiful land.
Shakespeare also refers to the young men as being the flowers of
England and their faces as being like flowers

98 **maid-pale peace:** the ideal of feminine beauty at this time was a
pale complexion

100 **pastures':** pastors' (shepherds) in both Quarto and Folio

102 **civil and uncivil arms:** the weapons of civil war and barbarous
weapons

103 **rushed upon:** surprised
thrice-noble: explained in the next seven lines as deriving from
his grandfather, Edward III, his father, John of Gaunt and from
his own *worth and honour*

105–108 **honourable tomb ... head:** Edward III's tomb is in
Westminster Abbey. He was the grandfather of both Richard and
Bolingbroke whose royal blood they thus share. The blood is
compared to two rivers flowing from one *spring* or *head*

112 **scope:** aim

113 **lineal royalties:** inherited rights (belonging to the king but
which he grants to a subject – see Act 2 scene 1 line 190, above)

114 **Enfranchisement:** (both) freedom from punishment and
admission to his rightful position

115 **on thy royal party ... once:** once conceded by you as a party to
the agreement

116 **commend to:** deliver over to

117 **barbed steeds:** war horses protected by armour

120 **credit:** believe

121 **returns:** replies

126 **kind commends:** greet him with expressions of kindness

---

- *What differences in tone do you notice between Richard
and Northumberland?*
- *How does Richard's choice of vocabulary tell us that he is
insincere in his reply to Northumberland (lines
122–126)?*

Tell Bolingbroke, for yon methinks he stands,
That every stride he makes upon my land
Is dangerous treason. He is come to open
The purple testament of bleeding war.
But ere the crown he looks for live in peace,
Ten thousand bloody crowns of mothers' sons
Shall ill become the flower of England's face,
Change the complexion of her maid-pale peace
To scarlet indignation, and bedew
Her pastures' grass with faithful English blood.   100

NORTHUMBERLAND   The King of heaven forbid our lord the King
Should so with civil and uncivil arms
Be rushed upon. Thy thrice-noble cousin
Harry Bolingbroke doth humbly kiss thy hand;
And by the honourable tomb he swears
That stands upon your royal grandsire's bones,
And by the royalties of both your bloods,
Currents that spring from one most gracious head,
And by the buried hand of warlike Gaunt,
And by the worth and honour of himself,   110
Comprising all that may be sworn or said,
His coming hither hath no further scope
Than for his lineal royalties, and to beg
Enfranchisement immediate on his knees;
Which on thy royal party granted once,
His glittering arms he will commend to rust,
His barbed steeds to stables, and his heart
To faithful service of your majesty.
This swears he as he is a prince and just,
And as I am a gentleman I credit him.   120

KING RICHARD   Northumberland, say thus. The King returns:
His noble cousin is right welcome hither,
And all the number of his fair demands
Shall be accomplished without contradiction.
With all the gracious utterance thou hast
Speak to his gentle hearing kind commends.

Richard privately asks Aumerle whether he has given away too much but is advised that he should make peace until he has more power on his side. Richard regrets that he has had to give into Bolingbroke and wonders whether he will now be deposed. He claims that he will accept whatever happens, and imagines living out his life in religious seclusion and being buried in an obscure grave.

128 look so poorly: act so humbly
fair: courteously
136 sooth: flattery – though ironically it can also mean 'truth'
140–141 scope: opportunity
146 A: in
147–149 a set of beads ... gown: Richard thinks of himself first as a beadsman (as described by Scroop in Act 3 scene 2 line 116), then living as a solitary hermit, dependent on charity (alms) and gowned in the uniform of a charitable foundation
set of beads: rosary
149 gay apparel: fine clothes
150 figured goblets: engraved drinking cups
151 palmer's: pilgrim's
152 carved saints: small wooden statues such as the pilgrim might have collected at a shrine
154 obscure: stress on first syllable
155 the King's highway: The formal rhetoric of the previous twelve lines gives way to macabre humour as Richard imagines being buried in the main highway to which his name and power are supposed to give security
156–158 trade/tread: a pun on two words which have the same etymological root
159 buried once: once I'm buried

                    [*To* AUMERLE] We do debase ourselves, cousin, do
                      we not,
                    To look so poorly and to speak so fair?
                    Shall we call back Northumberland and send
                    Defiance to the traitor, and so die?   130

AUMERLE   No, good my lord. Let's fight with gentle words,
                    Till time lend friends, and friends their helpful
                      swords.

KING RICHARD   O God, o God, that e'er this tongue of mine,
                    That laid the sentence of dread banishment
                    On yon proud man, should take it off again
                    With words of sooth! O that I were as great
                    As is my grief, or lesser than my name,
                    Or that I could forget what I have been,
                    Or not remember what I must be now!
                    Swellest thou, proud heart? I'll give thee scope to
                      beat,   140
                    Since foes have scope to beat both thee and me.

AUMERLE   Northumberland comes back from Bolingbroke.

KING RICHARD   What must the King do now? Must he submit?
                    The King shall do it. Must he be deposed?
                    The King shall be contented. Must he lose
                    The name of king? A God's name, let it go.
                    I'll give my jewels for a set of beads,
                    My gorgeous palace for a hermitage,
                    My gay apparel for an almsman's gown,
                    My figured goblets for a dish of wood,   150
                    My sceptre for a palmer's walking-staff,
                    My subjects for a pair of carved saints,
                    And my large kingdom for a little grave,
                    A little, little grave, an obscure grave;
                    Or I'll be buried in the King's highway,
                    Some way of common trade, where subjects' feet
                    May hourly trample on their sovereign's head;
                    For on my heart they tread now whilst I live;
                    And buried once, why not upon my head?
                    Aumerle thou weepest, my tender-hearted cousin.   160

When Aumerle weeps from sympathy, Richard makes him laugh. Northumberland returns and asks Richard to descend from the castle walls. Richard likens his descent to the fall of the sun from the heavens. Northumberland thinks Richard mad but Bolingbroke has his supporters kneel before the King.

162 **and they:** i.e the *despised tears*. The tears and sighs are emblems of rain and wind
   lodge: beat down by the wind and rain
163 **dearth:** famine
164 **play the wantons:** daily; trifle
165 **make some pretty match:** devise some clever game
166 **still:** always
167 **fretted us:** slowly worn away for us
168–169 **laid – there lies ... eyes:** 'laid' and the possibility of the rhyme suggests to Richard a customary form of words for a comic epitaph. This, the absurd image of the tear-eroded grave, and the play on ill/well in the next line, have the effect of cheering Aumerle
175 **make a leg:** bend the knee; make an obeisance or courtesy. Richard is remarking on the irony of Northumberland bowing to him and/or to Bolingbroke
176 **base-court:** the lower, outer courtyard of the castle, where the servants were quartered. An allusion to Richard's decline
178 **glistering:** glittering
   Phaethon: the son of Apollo who was destroyed when he failed to control the chariot of the sun as he struggled to drive it across the heavens. Richard is closely connected with the sun image throughout the play: note, for example Act 2 scene 4 lines 18–22 and lines 54–67 above
179 **Wanting the manage of:** lacking the horsemanship to control
   jades: horses – usually applied only to vicious and unruly animals
180 **grow base:** become inferior, degraded or worthless
181 **do them grace:** do them honour or favour
183 **night-owls:** the owl, a creature of darkness, was symbolic of evil and betrayal and thought to be a bird of ill-omen
   mounting larks: the lark sings beautifully while in flight and is an image of purity
SD *[Exeunt from above:* Richard and his companions leave the upper stage and descend through the tiring room to the main stage. The audience's viewpoint changes from outside to inside the castle
185 **fondly like a frantic man:** foolishly, like a lunatic
186 **Yet:** again
187 **Stand all apart:** make room; fall back
188 **show fair duty:** make obeisance; kneel

We'll make foul weather with despised tears;
Our sighs and they shall lodge the summer corn,
And make a dearth in this revolting land.
Or shall we play the wantons with our woes
And make some pretty match with shedding tears?
As thus to drop them still upon one place,
Till they have fretted us a pair of graves
Within the earth, and therein laid – there lies
Two kinsmen digged their graves with weeping eyes.
Would not this ill do well? Well well, I see   170
I talk but idly, and you laugh at me.
Most mighty prince my Lord Northumberland,
What says King Bolingbroke? Will his majesty
Give Richard leave to live till Richard die?
You make a leg, and Bolingbroke says 'Ay'.

NORTHUMBERLAND   My Lord, in the base-court he doth attend
To speak with you, may it please you to come down.

KING RICHARD   Down, down I come like glistering Phaethon,
Wanting the manage of unruly jades.
In the base-court? Base-court, where kings grow base 180
To come at traitors' calls, and do them grace.
In the base-court come down? Down court, down
     King,
For night-owls shriek where mounting larks should
sing.

                              [*Exeunt from above*

BOLINGBROKE   What says his majesty?

NORTHUMBERLAND   Sorrow and grief of heart
Makes him speak fondly like a frantic man.
Yet he is come.

Enter KING RICHARD *attended, below*

BOLINGBROKE   Stand all apart,
And show fair duty to his majesty.
                              [*Kneels*

My gracious lord.

Richard grants Bolingbroke's requests. He acknowledges that Bolingbroke has the power to do whatever he wishes and offers to make Bolingbroke heir to the throne. All depart for London.

190–191 debase, base: Richard continues to play on the word
192 Me rather had: I would rather
193 courtesy: kneeling in obeisance
195 Thus high at least: Richard indicates the crown he is wearing
198–199 So far be mine … love: be mine in so far – my respected lord – as my honest service will deserve your love
202 Uncle: the Duke of York
203 Tears show … remedies: tears demonstrate love but solve nothing
204 Cousin: Bolingbroke
205 you are old enough: both men were thirty-three

The Queen and her ladies are walking in a garden, trying to distract themselves from their worries.

3–5 bowls: the game was a popular Elizabethan pastime. A *rub* was any impediment to the true run of the bowl; the *bias* was the natural inclination of the weighted or shaped bowl to run in a curved path. The Queen thus suggests that, because of worldly difficulties, her life is unable to take the direction to which it would otherwise be destined

> • *Note the irony that Richard's words to York (lines 202–203) reflect the advice he was himself given earlier in the scene.*

KING RICHARD   Fair cousin, you debase your princely knee   190
                To make the base earth proud with kissing it.
                Me rather had my heart might feel your love
                Than my unpleased eye see your courtesy.
                Up cousin, up; your heart is up, I know,
                Thus high at least, although your knee be low.

BOLINGBROKE   My gracious lord, I come but for mine own.

KING RICHARD   Your own is yours, and I am yours and all.

BOLINGBROKE   So far be mine, my most redoubted lord,
                As my true service shall deserve your love.

KING RICHARD   Well you deserve. They well deserve to have   200
                That know the strongest and surest way to get.
                Uncle, give me your hands. Nay, dry your eyes;
                Tears show their love, but want their remedies.
                Cousin, I am too young to be your father,
                Though you are old enough to be my heir.
                What will you have, I'll give, and willing too;
                For do we must what force will have us do.
                Set on towards London, cousin, is it so?

BOLINGBROKE   Yea, my good lord.

KING RICHARD   Then I must not say no.
                                            [*Flourish. Exeunt*

Scene 4

Enter the QUEEN *and two* LADIES

QUEEN ISABEL   What sport shall we devise here in this garden
                To drive away the heavy thought of care?

FIRST LADY   Madam we'll play at bowls.

QUEEN ISABEL   'Twill make me think the world is full of rubs,
                And that my fortune runs against the bias.

SECOND LADY   Madam we'll dance.

The Queen can find nothing to distract her from grief.
Gardeners enter, intent upon binding up plants, pruning and
weeding to bring order to the garden.

> 7–8 **My legs can … grief:** I can't dance in joyful rhythm
> when my poor heart cannot grieve in moderation. (The
> Queen quibbles here on two meanings of 'to keep measure'
> – to be moderate or restrained in action and to keep in time
> to music)
>
> 13 **being altogether wanting:** since I entirely lack [joy]
> 14 **remember:** remind
> 15 **being altogether had:** since I am entirely possessed of
> [grief]
> 18 **it boots not to complain:** it does not help me to grieve
> for it
> 22–23 **And I could … thee:** I would be able to sing if only
> shedding a few tears would do me good – and if that were
> the case I wouldn't need to borrow tears from you
> 26 **My wretchedness … pins:** I'll bet my wretchedness
> against something trivial
> 27 **state:** political news; affairs of state
> 28 **Against a change:** when preparing for a change
> **forerun with:** prepared for; anticipated by
> 29 **young:** *yond* in the Folio but the Quarto's *young* suggests
> the *unruly children* and *prodigal* of the next lines
> **apricocks:** apricots
> 30–31 **their sire Stoop:** their tree bend – with reference to *sire*
> as father and king
> 31 **prodigal:** lavish; prodigious. The quibble emphasises the
> Gardener's personification of the apricots and begins the
> allegory of the garden as a little kingdom
> 34 **too fast-growing sprays:** the comparison of lofty plants to
> over-ambitious men was a common simile

> • *The image of the garden as a microcosm of human affairs*
> *is a literary convention. The words of the gardener should*
> *be seen as allegorical.*

QUEEN ISABEL	My legs can keep no measure in delight
	When my poor heart no measure keeps in grief.
	Therefore no dancing, girl. some other sport.
FIRST LADY	Madam we'll tell tales. 10
QUEEN ISABEL	Of sorrow or of joy?
FIRST LADY	Of either, madam.
QUEEN ISABEL	Of neither, girl.
	For if of joy, being altogether wanting,
	It doth remember me the more of sorrow;
	Or if of grief, being altogether had,
	It adds more sorrow to my want of joy;
	For what I have I need not to repeat,
	And what I want it boots not to complain.
SECOND LADY	Madam I'll sing.
QUEEN ISABEL	'Tis well that thou hast cause,
	But thou shouldst please me better wouldst thou
	weep. 20
SECOND LADY	I could weep madam, would it do you good.
QUEEN ISABEL	And I could sing would weeping do me good,
	And never borrow any tear of thee.

Enter GARDENER *and two* SERVANTS

But stay, here come the gardeners.
Let's step into the shadow of these trees
My wretchedness unto a row of pins
They'll talk of state; for everyone doth so
Against a change. Woe is forerun with woe.

[QUEEN *and* LADIES *stand apart*

GARDENER	[*to one man*]: Go bind thou up young dangling
	apricocks
	Which like unruly children make their sire 30
	Stoop with oppression of their prodigal weight;
	Give some supportance to the bending twigs.
	Go thou, and like an executioner
	Cut off the heads of too fast-growing sprays,

One of the men challenges the need to tidy the garden when the country has been left in such a state of disorder. The Gardener, unaware that the Queen overhears all he says, tells him that the King is captured and the favourites executed. He says that if the King had only cut back proud and unruly men they would have served him better and he would have gained from them.

35 **commonwealth:** the state and all its people. Compare Act 2 scene 3 lines 165–166 where the image of the commonwealth as a garden in need of care is first introduced by Bolingbroke and where *Bushy, Bagot and their complices* are caterpillars

36 **even:** of the same height; balance; in a state of equilibrium

38 **noisome:** harmful
without profit: i.e. they do not improve the garden, in the same way that harmful political forces damage the commonwealth

40 FIRST MAN: here and at line 54 Quarto prints *Man* and Folio *Ser*
in the compass of a pale: in ground surrounded by a fence

42 **firm:** stable

43 **our sea-walled garden:** compare John of Gaunt, Act 2 scene 1 lines 47–49

46 **knots:** knot gardens – flowerbeds laid out in intricate patterns, often symmetrical and separated by neat low hedges

47 **caterpillars:** see line 35, above, and note

48 **suffered:** allowed

49 **fall of leaf:** autumn – to balance *spring* in the previous line

51 **seemed in eating ... up:** seemed to support him when they were really devouring him

56 **trimmed and dressed:** pruned and fertilised

57 **at time of year:** in season

59 **overproud:** too full

60 **confound:** destroys; defeats

65 **crown:** a quibble on the crown or leafy top of a tree

> • *Consider the effect of the Gardener's words on the concealed Queen.*

That look too lofty in our commonwealth.
All must be even in our government.
You thus employed, I will go root away
The noisome weeds which without profit suck
The soil's fertility from wholesome flowers.

FIRST MAN   Why should we, in the compass of a pale,   40
Keep law and form and due proportion,
Showing as in a model our firm estate,
When our sea-walled garden, the whole land,
Is full of weeds, her fairest flowers choked up,
Her fruit trees all unpruned, her hedges ruined,
Her knots disordered, and her wholesome herbs
Swarming with caterpillars?

GARDENER   Hold thy peace.
He that hath suffered this disordered spring
Hath now himself met with the fall of leaf.
The weeds which his broad-spreading leaves did
          shelter,   50
That seemed in eating him to hold him up,
Are plucked up root and all by Bolingbroke –
I mean the Earl of Wiltshire, Bushy, Green.

FIRST MAN   What, are they dead?

GARDENER   They are; and Bolingbroke
Hath seized the wasteful King. O what pity is it
That he had not so trimmed and dressed his land
As we this garden. We at time of year
Do wound the bark, the skin of our fruit trees,
Lest being overproud in sap and blood,
With too much riches it confound itself.   60
Had he done so to great and growing men,
They might have lived to bear, and he to taste
Their fruits of duty. Superfluous branches
We lop away that bearing boughs may live.
Had he done so, himself had borne the crown,
Which waste of idle hours hath quite thrown down.

FIRST MAN   What, think you the King shall be deposed?

The Gardener is sure Richard will be deposed. The Queen
interrupts and berates him for talking of Richard's fall. The
Gardener maintains that the King's power cannot compare with
that of Bolingbroke. The Queen cannot understand why she is
the last to know what has happened. She decides to go to
London and curses the Gardener for breaking the bad news.

68 depressed: forced down

69 'Tis doubt: it's in the balance that

72 I am pressed to death ... speaking: my inability is killing me
– a reference to the torture used on prisoners who refused to
plead their guilt or innocence, which involved placing heavy
stones on the chest until the victim spoke or was crushed

73 Old Adam's likeness: Adam was put in the Garden of Eden
'to dress it' (Genesis Chapter 2 verse 15). See also Act 2
scene 1 line 42

75 suggested: tempted

75–76 What Eve, what serpent ... man: The devil, in the guise
of a serpent, tempted Eve with the fruit of the tree of
knowledge of good and evil. She, in turn, gave the fruit to
Adam. Their punishment – the *Fall* – was to be driven from
Eden and become mortal. Christ, *the second Adam,* was sent to
Earth to restore the possibility of immortality

79 Divine: prophesy

83 hold: stronghold; prison

84–89 Their fortunes ... down: For this image of the scales see
Daniel chapter 6 verses 26–28: 'God has numbered thy
kingdom and finished it ... Thou art weighed in the balance
and found wanting ... Thy kingdom is divided'. Compare also
Act 4 scene 1 lines 184–189, below

86 light: lacking in moral authority; frivolous; of little weight

89 odds: advantage

90 Post you: hurry; travel with speed

92 Nimble mischance: agile ill-chance. Chance was often
personified; here the Queen pictures it as a fleet-footed
messenger

93 Doth not ... me: doesn't your message concern me most

94–96 O, thou thinkest ... breast: O, you [mischance] intended
to deliver your message to me last so that I may keep the
sadness you inspire in my heart longer than anyone else

99 the triumph: here and in Act 5 the Queen compares
Richard's plight to that of prisoners who were paraded by
Roman emperors through the streets

GARDENER	Depressed he is already, and deposed
	'Tis doubt he will be. Letters came last night
	To a dear friend of the good Duke of York's 70
	That tell black tidings.
QUEEN ISABEL	O I am pressed to death through want of speaking.

[*She comes forward*]

Thou, old Adam's likeness act to dress this garden,
How dares thy harsh rude tongue sound this
   unpleasing news?
What Eve, what serpent hath suggested thee
To make a second Fall of cursed man?
Why dost thou say King Richard is deposed?
Darest thou, thou little better thing than earth,
Divine his downfall? Say, where, when, and how
Camest thou by this ill tidings? Speak thou wretch.   80

| GARDENER | Pardon me madam, little joy have I |

To breathe this news, yet what I say is true.
King Richard he is in the mighty hold
Of Bolingbroke. Their fortunes both are weighed.
In your lord's scale is nothing but himself,
And some few vanities that make him light.
But in the balance of great Bolingbroke
Besides himself are all the English peers,
And with that odds he weighs King Richard down.
Post you to London and you will find it so.   90
I speak no more than everyone doth know.

| QUEEN ISABEL | Nimble mischance that art so light of foot |

Doth not thy embassage belong to me,
And am I last that knows it? O thou thinkest
To serve me last that I may longest keep
Thy sorrow in my breast. Come ladies, go
To meet at London London's king in woe.
What, was I born to this that my sad look
Should grace the triumph of great Bolingbroke?
Gardener, for telling me these news of woe.   100
Pray God the plants thou graftest may never grow.

[*Exit* QUEEN *with her* LADIES

The Gardener is full of pity for the Queen and says that he will plant herbs to remind him of her sorrow.

102 so that thy state might: if it would ensure that your
    condition would
105–106 rue: an evergreen shrub with bitter, aromatic leaves
    used in medicine and symbolically associated with grief, pity
    (ruth) and repentance. Also called herb of grace

> • *The verse with which the scene closes emphasises that the*
>   *gardener is entirely symbolic and not intended to be seen*
>   *as naturalistic.*

GARDENER   Poor Queen, so that thy state might be no worse,
                I would my skill were subject to thy curse.
                Here did she fall a tear; here in this place
                I'll set a bank of rue, sour herb of grace.
                Rue, even for ruth, here shortly shall be seen,
                In the remembrance of a weeping queen.

                                              [*Exeunt*

CTIVITIES

Keeping track

Scene 1

1 What reason does Bolingbroke give for executing Bushy and Green?
2 What does Bolingbroke intend to do after leaving Bristol?

Scene 2

1 Why is Richard confident that he will defeat Bolingbroke?
2 Two messengers enter to confound Richard's hopes. Who are they and what news does each bring?
3 What does Richard decide to do at the end of this scene?

Scene 3

1 As Bolingbroke approaches Flint Castle, what does he say that his intention is?
2 In what way does Richard's entrance impress both Bolingbroke and York?
3 What is Richard's response to Northumberland's demands that Bolingbroke should be allowed his inheritance?
4 After Richard has descended to the base court, what further concessions does he make to Bolingbroke?

Scene 4

1 What emotional state is the Queen in at the beginning of this scene?
2 What information do the Gardener and his man reveal to the hidden queen?
3 What does the Queen decide to do at the end of this scene?

Characters

King Richard

1 Richard returns from Ireland but his world has changed and he seems a very different man from the one who left England after Act 2 scene 1. What are the main differences as they appear at the end of Act 3 scene 2?

2 Richard demonstrates a much greater range of emotion and expression during this Act than he has previously. The differences reflect his state of mind, whether or not he is playing a part in public and to whom he is speaking. Make notes on the variety of his forms of speech. How does this variety of expression change your reaction to Richard?

Bolingbroke

1 Look closely at Bolingbroke's first speech in Act 3 scene 1. What are his reasons for condemning Bushy and Green? How far has Shakespeare given us evidence to substantiate Bolingbroke's view?

2 If, at the end of this Act, Bolingbroke has the power to command a King, then he must himself be king in all but name. What qualities has Bolingbroke demonstrated in this Act which would seem to fit him for kingship?

Aumerle

• What role does Aumerle play in this Act? Why, dramatically, is he necessary to the plot?

Duke of York

• How does York continue to be consistent in his paradoxical role of supporting both his nephews?

Northumberland

• During this Act Northumberland emerges as the man who will do Bolingbroke's dirty work. Perhaps his most characteristic statement is when he dismisses Richard as speaking *'fondly like a frantic man'*. Look closely at the errands he does for Bolingbroke and the way in which he speaks. Is he just a stage villain or can you sympathise with his actions?

Queen Isabel

• The profound sense of sorrow which surrounds the Queen continues. Look at her final speech (scene 4 lines 92–101). How does it sum up both her role and that of other women in the society portrayed in this play?

Themes

1 **Fortune** Richard's fall is worked out very visually in this Act. Shakespeare uses the traditional image of the wheel of fortune. A man's life is compared to the turning of a wheel rim: though he may rise in power and success, it is inevitable that at the moment of his greatest achievement he will pass his peak and begin his descent. The Elizabethan theatre presents Shakespeare with the opportunity to act out this rise and fall. Richard begins scene 3 standing on the ground and, descending lower, talks of graves and the death of kings. He ascends the battlements of Flint Castle where he appears like the *'blushing discontented sun'* with *'eye as bright as is the eagle's'*. This is a false dawn, however; a mere reminder of greatness before he descends again to the 'base court'. The image dramatises a debate which is central to this play. Is the fall of a great man the consequence of his own failings, or the result of the random operation of fortune? How far do the events of this Act help answer that question?

2 **Order and Good Government** Look back to Act 2 scene 4 where the disordered state of the realm is presaged in the stars and, according to the Welsh Captain, because *'the bay-trees in our country are all withered'*. Political chaos, he believes, is reflected in the rest of creation. In Act 3 scene 4 the Gardener explains how effective government is chiefly concerned with the maintenance of good order. A popular style of garden in Shakespeare's time was the precisely ordered knot garden. This was laid out in a symmetrical pattern of small beds divided by closely cropped hedges. The beds contained flowers, fruit, herbs and medicinal plants but were so arranged as to be pleasing to the eye, like a finely worked piece of embroidery. The gardener needed to be constantly vigilant, paying attention both to detail and the total pattern.
   • Can you find other examples in this Act of images related to the garden and Richard's government?
   • Take each of the problems which the Gardener and his man list in lines 29–53 and relate it to a character or situation in the play.

3 **Dramatic irony** Irony exists when the audience (and perhaps some of the characters) know more about a situation on stage than the leading characters who are trying to cope with it. Sometimes dramatic irony is a great source of humour; sometimes, as here, it raises the anxiety and tension felt by the audience and this emphasises the tragic elements of the play. What examples of dramatic irony can you find in this Act and how do they contribute to the impact of the play?

Drama

1   **An interview in the condemned cell.** Northumberland arranges for
Green and Bushy to appear before the press to admit their guilt and
account for their actions. This proves to be a dangerous tactic! Stage the
scene:
- Read again Act 3 scene 1 lines 1–35.
- Remind yourself of the role of Bushy and Green in Act 1 scene 4, and
  in Act 2 scene 2.
- Consider what other characters have implied about their influence at
  court.
- Choose to be either Bushy or Green and prepare your press conference
  performance.
- The group as a whole hot-seats Bushy and Green one at a time.
- Review what you have learnt about the two men and about other key
  characters in the play such as Richard, Bolingbroke and
  Northumberland.

2   **Messenger.** Look again at scene 2. Establish all the pieces of information
and advice which are brought to Richard, divide these up between the
members of the class and report them one by one. Consider what the
cumulative impact of the bad news might be.

3   Consider the situation at the end of scene 3. Hot-seat Richard,
Bolingbroke, Aumerle and Northumberland to discover what they are
feeling and how they intend to act from now on. (Refer to the notes on
Hot Seating in Explorations page 233.)

4   **Act 3 scene 2 lines 144–177.** Divide the speech up between members of
the class – each section could end wherever there is a full stop, colon or
semi-colon. Learn your section(s) by heart. Stand in a circle and perform
the scene. Do this several times, until you are happy that you have found
the right rhythm and pace and are placing the climaxes appropriately. Your
aim is to end by making the feeling of grief and helplessness as strong as
possible, though you may wish to emphasise other emotions earlier in the
speech. (This activity will help you with the Close Study which follows.)

Close Study

Act 3 scene 2 lines 141–177

1 You should start by doing the drama activity **4** above.
2 Consider the context for this section: Richard has received a number of pieces of bad news. He has just accused his former favourites of betraying him, only to discover that they have been executed for supporting him. It is no surprise that his thoughts turn to his own death. Make a list of the words, both literal and metaphorical, which refer to death.
3 Contrast Richard's meditation on the 'barren earth' with what he had said about it in his first speech in this scene.
4 Throughout the play Richard has maintained a lofty view of monarchy: the king is God's anointed and His representative upon Earth. What contrasting view of monarchy does he express in this speech?
5 What images in the speech stress the vulnerability of human beings? In what ways does Richard emphasise the strength and inevitability of death?
6 What evidence is there within the speech that Richard is trying to excuse himself from responsibility for the predicament which he now faces?

Key scene

Act 3 scene 3 lines 62–end
The fall of Richard is portrayed through language and movement.

Keying it in

1   All the principal characters of the play are on stage (with the exception of
the Queen and those characters who are already dead). How would you
choose to stage this moment? Think in terms of a stage you know well
and draw a plan to indicate how you would position the characters.
Remember also to place Richard above the stage and towards the rear
(upstage) while Bolingbroke and York must be downstage, nearest the
audience. This will most closely represent the original staging. Richard
appeared on the gallery or upper stage while Northumberland,
Bolingbroke and their supporters were on the main stage which thrust into
the Pit.

The scene itself

2   **Lines 62–71**
Remind yourself of Richard's view of his own majesty. Look particularly at
Act 2 scene 1 lines 115–123 and Act 3 scene 2 lines 36–62. How do
Bolingbroke and York reflect images from both these speeches in their
words here?

3   **Lines 72–100**
   • Richard uses the royal plural to refer to himself, having earlier in the
scene used the singular 'I'. Why does he make this contrast? What
dramatic impact does it have?
   • Bolingbroke is clearly in earshot yet Richard refuses to address him
directly. Why is this? What is the dramatic effect upon the audience?
   • Richard continues the theme of political chaos being visible in the
natural world. What powerful image does he use?

4   **Lines 101–126**
   • Northumberland's words are uncharacteristically rhetorical. How does
he emphasise the truth of what he is saying? Do you believe him?
   • How do we know that Richard is insincere in his reply?

5   **Lines 127–171**
While Northumberland reports to Bolingbroke, Richard's 'private'
conversation with his cousin, Aumerle, contrasts with the previous sixty
lines.

- How does this section remind us that Richard is essentially an actor?
- How does Richard's treatment of Aumerle modify our view of his character?

6 Lines 172–186

Richard continues his comparison with the sun and his words also remind us of Salisbury's prophecy in Act 2 scene 4 lines 19–20:

> *Ah Richard! With the eyes of heavy mind*
> *I see thy glory like a shooting star*
> *Fall to the base earth from the firmament*

- How far do you agree with Northumberland's judgement? Is Richard foolish, mad or broken-hearted at this moment?

7 Lines 187–end

All kneel as Richard enters the base court but the King knows that this is sham courtesy.
- What words and actions demonstrate the extent of Bolingbroke's triumph?

Overview

Before Richard appears on the castle walls Bolingbroke says (lines 54–60):

> *Methinks King Richard and myself should meet*
> *With no less terror than the elements*
> *Of fire and water, when their thundering shock*
> *At meeting tears the cloudy cheeks of heaven.*
> *Be he the fire, I'll be the yielding water;*
> *The rage be his, whilst on the earth I rain*
> *My waters – on the earth and not on him.*

- How does Shakespeare use the four elements – earth, air, fire and water – to provide a linguistic and dramatic framework for the whole of this scene?
- How far are Bolingbroke's words (above) prophetic?

Writing

1　How have things ended up like this? None of the characters is very revealing about their ambitions or what motivates them, beyond a simple desire for what they see as justice and good government. Yet without a fight there seems to have been a coup and the King appears to be a prisoner of the new regime. Imagine that you were a foreign observer, trying to make sense of events for your government back home. Write a letter in which you explain the events of the play so far. Choose an appropriate tone: surprise, admiration for Bolingbroke, pity, disdain, or any other which you think could be appropriate.

2　What happens next? Whether or not you know how the play (or the real history) develops, predict the future for each of the main characters. Base your predictions both on the action of the play and on what each of the characters has revealed about themselves.

3　The role of Queen Isabel seems largely to be to comment on events and express grief and love for Richard. However, at the end of Act 3 she does exhibit some determination to take control. Can you round out her shadowy character by interviewing her? You could model your writing on the kind of celebrity interview which appears on the more serious television programmes or in broadsheet newspapers.

Bolingbroke holds court in London. Bagot is called to give evidence concerning the Duke of Gloucester's death. He implicates Aumerle in the plot and further suggests that Aumerle had plotted against Bolingbroke.

4 **wrought it:** worked it; i.e. collaborated
5 **office:** duty
 timeless: untimely
9 **unsay what ... delivered:** take back words you have already spoken
10 **dead time:** fatal; dark – as in 'the dead of night'
13 **Calais:** where Gloucester died: see Act 1 scene 1 line 100 and note
14 **that very time:** on the same occasion. Either Shakespeare's chronology is wrong – Bolingbroke was not banished until much later – or he intends us to note the anachronism and judge Bagot's behaviour accordingly
18 **withal:** besides; moreover
19 **your cousin's:** i.e. Bolingbroke's
20 **my fair stars:** the stars which shone to signify his noble birth
22 **chastisement:** correction; punishment

• *What aspects of Bolingbroke's opening speech emphasise his assumption of complete power?*

Act four

Scene 1

Enter as to Parliament BOLINGBROKE *with the* LORDS
AUMERLE, NORTHUMBERLAND, HARRY PERCY,
FITZWATER, SURREY, *the* BISHOP OF CARLISLE, *the*
ABBOT OF WESTMINSTER, *another* LORD, HERALD, *and*
OFFICERS *with* BAGOT

BOLINGBROKE   Call forth Bagot.
Now Bagot, freely speak thy mind
What thou dost know of noble Gloucester's death,
Who wrought it with the King, and who performed
The bloody office of his timeless end.

BAGOT   Then set before my face the Lord Aumerle.

BOLINGBROKE   Cousin, stand forth, and look upon that man.

BAGOT   My Lord Aumerle, I know your daring tongue
Scorns to unsay what once it hath delivered.
In that dead time when Gloucester's death was
    plotted   10
I heard you say 'Is not my arm of length,
That reacheth from the restful English court
As far as Calais to mine uncle's head?'
Amongst much other talk that very time
I heard you say that you had rather refuse
The offer of an hundred thousand crowns
Than Bolingbroke's return to England,
Adding withal, how blest this land would be
In this your cousin's death.

AUMERLE   Princes and noble lords,
What answer shall I make to this base man?   20
Shall I so much dishonour my fair stars
On equal terms to give him chastisement?

Aumerle contemptuously dismisses the charges and challenges
Bagot. Bolingbroke forbids Bagot from taking up the challenge
but Fitzwater, Percy, and another lord repeat the charge and
throw down their gages.

24 **attainder:** accusation of crime and dishonour
25 **gage:** pledge. He obviously throws down a gauntlet since it is
 a *manual seal* – a pun on 'hand' and the manual sign or
 autograph used to give authority to a contract. (Holinshed says
 that hoods were used by Fitzwater and other lords)
27–28 **maintain ... heart-blood:** defend myself against your lies
 by killing you
29 **temper:** the hard surface; quality. Aumerle also alludes to his
 own angry temper
31–32 **Excepting one ... so:** I wish that the man who had made
 me so angry were the most noble here apart only from one
 [Bolingbroke]
33 **If that thy ... sympathy:** if your courage insists/depends on
 being matched by someone of the same rank
34 **in gage:** by exchanging pledges they become bound to resolve
 their dispute in personal combat (the phrase gives us the
 modern 'engage')
36 **tauntingly:** boastfully
39 **turn:** return
40 **rapier:** a long, pointed, double-edged sword – unknown in
 England before the sixteenth century. Fitzwater's conceit
 ('forged') matches Aumerle's ten lines earlier
45 **appeal:** accusation
 all: entirely
47–48 **the extremest ... breathing:** my (or your) last breath; to
 the death
49 **And if:** if indeed
52–59 **I task ... you:** These lines are not in the Folio: perhaps
 they (and 'Another Lord') were a customary performance cut
 or represent an early draft of the play
52 **I task ... like:** I give the earth the same task – of bearing my
 gage
54 **hollowed:** shouted; hallooed – a hunting cry to urge on
 hounds, it follows from 'spur' in the previous line
55 **pawn:** pledge; security
56 **Engage it to the trial:** accept this challenge to trial by
 combat

• *It is important to remember that Aumerle and*
 Bolingbroke are both nephews of the dead Gloucester.
• *In what ways does this scene mirror the first scene of the*
 play?

Either I must, or have mine honour soiled
With the attainder of his slanderous lips.
There is my gage, the manual seal of death,
That marks thee out for hell. I say thou liest,
And will maintain what thou hast said is false
In thy heart-blood, though being all too base
To stain the temper of my knightly sword.

BOLINGBROKE   Bagot, forbear, thou shalt not take it up.   30

AUMERLE   Excepting one, I would he were the best
In all this presence that hath moved me so.

FITZWATER   If that thy valour stand on sympathy,
There is my gage Aumerle, in gage to thine.
By that fair sun which shows me where thou
    standest,
I heard thee say, and vauntingly thou spakest it,
That thou wert cause of noble Gloucester's death.
If thou deniest it twenty times, thou liest,
And I will turn thy falsehood to thy heart,
Where it was forged, with my rapier's point.   40

AUMERLE   Thou darest not, coward, live to see that day.

FITZWATER   Now by my soul, I would it were this hour.

AUMERLE   Fitzwater, thou art damned to hell for this.

PERCY   Aumerle, thou liest, his honour is as true
In this appeal as thou art all unjust;
And that thou art so, there I throw my gage
To prove it on thee to the extremest point
Of mortal breathing. Seize it if thou darest.

AUMERLE   And if I do not, may my hands rot off,
And never brandish more revengeful steel   50
Over the glittering helmet of my foe.

ANOTHER LORD   I task the earth to the like, forsworn Aumerle,
And spur thee on with full as many lies
As may be hollowed in thy treacherous ear
From sun to sun. There is my honour's pawn;
Engage it to the trial if thou darest.

Surrey supports Aumerle and challenges Fitzwater, who accuses Aumerle of being in league with Mowbray. Aumerle requests that Mowbray be recalled from banishment so that he can answer the charge. Bolingbroke agrees.

57 **Who sets ... all:** Who else bets against me? By heaven I'll cast my dice against all comers. Aumerle probably throws down a second glove here: see line 83, below

62 **in presence:** present

65 **boy:** servant – in this context a considerable insult

66 **lie so heavy on:** give right to – with a play on lie

72 **fondly:** foolishly
forward: eager – Fitzwater refers to himself

74 **in a wilderness:** i.e. in the most inhospitable of places, where no one else could come between them (see Act 1 scene 1 line 64)

76 **my bond of faith:** his gage which he has thrown down earlier

77 **tie thee ... correction:** commit you to my harsh punishment

78 **in this new world:** i.e. under the rule of Bolingbroke

79 **appeal:** accusation

80 **Norfolk:** i.e. Thomas Mowbray

83 **trust me with a gage:** if Aumerle throws down his gloves at lines 25 and 57 then he needs to borrow a third. Alternatively, Shakespeare is now thinking of Holinshed and the use of hoods as gages (see note to line 25, above)

83–84 **trust me ... this:** the Quarto and Folio both have a comma after *gage* so the line either means 'trust me: Norfolk lies; lend me a gage' or 'I throw down this borrowed gage to pledge that I will prove that Norfolk lies'

85 **repealed:** recalled from exile
try: test

86 **rest under gage:** remain to be resolved according to the pledges made

89 **signories:** territories; estates

90 **we:** for the first time Bolingbroke uses the royal plural

> • *Who is telling the truth? Why is it so difficult to know?*

AUMERLE	Who sets me else? By heaven, I'll throw at all.
	I have a thousand spirits in one breast
	To answer twenty thousand such as you.

| SURREY | My Lord Fitzwater, I do remember well 60 |
| | The very time Aumerle and you did talk. |

| FITZWATER | 'Tis very true, you were in presence then, |
| | And you can witness with me this is true. |

| SURREY | As false, by heaven, as heaven itself is true. |

| FITZWATER | Surrey thou liest. |

SURREY	Dishonourable boy,
	That lie shall lie so heavy on my sword
	That it shall render vengeance and revenge
	Till thou, the lie-giver, and that lie do lie
	In earth as quiet as thy father's skull
	In proof whereof there is my honour's pawn; 70
	Engage it to the trial if thou darest.

FITZWATER	How fondly dost thou spur a forward horse.
	If I dare eat, or drink, or breathe, or live,
	I dare meet Surrey in a wilderness,
	And spit upon him whilst I say he lies,
	And lies, and lies. There is my bond of faith
	To tie thee to my strong correction.
	As I intend to thrive in this new world,
	Aumerle is guilty of my true appeal.
	Besides, I heard the banished Norfolk say 80
	That thou Aumerle didst send two of thy men
	To execute the noble Duke at Calais.

AUMERLE	Some honest Christian trust me with a gage.
	That Norfolk lies, here do I throw down this,
	If he may be repealed to try his honour.

BOLINGBROKE	These differences shall all rest under gage
	Till Norfolk be repealed. Repealed he shall be,
	And though mine enemy, restored again
	To all his lands and signories. When he is returned
	Against Aumerle we will enforce his trial. 90

The Bishop of Carlisle reports that, following courageous
service in the Crusades, Mowbray has died in Venice.
Bolingbroke says that he will appoint a time for all the charges
to be tried. York enters and announces that Richard has
abdicated and adopted Bolingbroke as his heir. He invites the
Duke to ascend the throne but the Bishop of Carlisle intervenes.
He maintains that the rightful king owes his power to God
alone and that no subject can judge the monarch.

92–100 Many a time ... long: Holinshed records Mowbray's
death in Venice but the remaining detail appears to be dramatic
invention in order to set up Bolingbroke's reaction

93 in glorious Christian field: i.e. in the crusader battles against
the Moslem occupation of Jerusalem

95 Saracens: Moslem Arabs

96 toiled: wearied

103–104 the bosom ... Abraham: heaven – a biblical image: see
Luke Chapter 16 verse 22

108 plume-plucked: stripped bare; humbled. The phrase alludes
both to falconry – the bird of prey is allowed to *plume*, or
remove the feathers of, its victim – as well as to the feathers on
the helmet of a king or nobleman which signified his dignity.
There may also be a reference to Aesop's fable of the crow who
dressed himself in stolen feathers and was finally unmasked

109 sceptre: the jewelled rod symbolising the King's authority

111 descending now ... him: which you have inherited from him
(see Act 3 scene 3 lines 204–208)

112 And long live ... name: either Henry has three syllables or
the Folio is correct: 'And long live Henry, of that Name the
Fourth'. The latter is a better metrical match for Bolingbroke's
next line

114 Marry: an exclamation or mild oath derived originally from
'by the Virgin Mary'

115 Worst: least worthy

116 Yet best beseeming me: it is most fitting for me (as a bishop)

119 noblesse: nobility

120 Learn him forbearance: teach him to refrain
so foul a wrong: i.e. to sit in judgement upon God's anointed
King

123 but they are by: unless they are present

124 apparent: clear and obvious

125 figure: image

BISHOP OF CARLISLE   That honorable day shall ne'er be seen.
Many a time hath banished Norfolk fought
For Jesu Christ in glorious Christian field,
Streaming the ensign of the Christian cross
Against black pagans, Turks, and Saracens,
And toiled with works of war, retired himself
To Italy, and there at Venice gave
His body to that pleasant country's earth,
And his pure soul unto his captain Christ,
Under whose colours he had fought so long.   100

BOLINGBROKE   Why Bishop, is Norfolk dead?

BISHOP OF CARLISLE   As surely as I live my lord.

BOLINGBROKE   Sweet peace conduct his sweet soul to the bosom
Of good old Abraham. Lords appellants,
Your differences shall all rest under gage
Till we assign you to your days of trial.

Enter YORK

YORK   Great Duke of Lancaster I come to thee
From plume-plucked Richard, who with willing soul
Adopts thee heir, and his high sceptre yields
To the possession of thy royal hand.   110
Ascend his throne, descending now from him,
And long live Henry, fourth of that name!

BOLINGBROKE   In God's name I'll ascend the regal throne.

BISHOP OF CARLISLE   Marry God forbid.
Worst in this royal presence may I speak,
Yet best beseeming me to speak the truth.
Would God that any in this noble presence
Were enough noble to be upright judge
Of noble Richard. Then true noblesse would
Learn him forbearance from so foul a wrong.   120
What subject can give sentence on his king?
And who sits here that is not Richard's subject?
Thieves are not judged but they are by to hear,
Although apparent guilt be seen in them;
And shall the figure of God's majesty,

Carlisle predicts that if Richard is deposed, civil war will follow. Northumberland arrests the Bishop for treason. Bolingbroke requests the presence of Richard in order for him to abdicate in public.

126 captain ... elect: see Act 1 scene 2 line 38. Carlisle describes Richard as God's chosen (elect) instrument to direct His earthly army, care for His creation and exercise judgement on His behalf

127 planted: established

128 subject and inferior breath: creatures who are subject to his rule and inferior to him

129 forfend it, God: God forbid, prevent

130 refined: purified; civilised. See Malachi (chapter 3) where God refines his people so that they are fit to worship Him

131 heinous: hateful; odious

134 Lord of Herford: Carlisle pointedly avoids using the title Bolingbroke has returned to claim: 'I was banished Herford/But as I come, I come for Lancaster.' (Act 2 Scene 3 lines 112–113)

135 proud Herford's king: i.e. Richard

136 let me prophesy: compare the Captain in Act 2 scene 4 lines 10–11 and John of Gaunt (Act 2 scene 1 line 33ff)

139 Turks and infidels: see lines 93–95 above, and notes

141 Shall kin ... confound: shall ensure the mutual destruction of families and the nation

144 Golgotha: the place of Christ's crucifixion and, in Hebrew, 'the place of the skull'. The suggestion here is that to depose Richard and bring about civil war would be to crucify Christ once again

145 this house against this house: The house of Anjou (the Plantagenets) was the one house from which both the houses of Lancaster and York descended. Richard II was the last Plantagenet king. Carlisle foresees the long civil war which Shakespeare had already chronicled in the three parts of *Henry VI* and *Richard III*.

148 Prevent it ... so: the line is metrically uneven, which may be an intentional rhetorical device; however, the Folio and later Quartos all have 'and let it', while Alexander Pope suggested 'Prevent, resist it ... '

151 Of: on a charge of
capital: i.e. crime for which the death penalty applies

154–318: This section is omitted from the first three Quarto editions

154 the commons' suit: on 22 October 1399, the House of Commons requested that, since Richard had resigned his own crown a decree should be published which explained the reasons for his abdication

156 surrender: the crown, i.e. abdicate

157 conduct: escort – to ensure his safe conduct

159 sureties: bail, or a person who will ensure that the lords return to court to answer the charges laid against them

160 beholding: obliged; indebted

His captain, steward, deputy elect,
Anointed, crowned, planted many years,
Be judged by subject and inferior breath,
And he himself not present? O forfend it God,
That in a Christian climate souls refined   130
Should show so heinous, black, obscene a deed!
I speak to subjects, and a subject speaks,
Stirred up by God thus boldly for his king.
My Lord of Herford here, whom you call king,
Is a foul traitor to proud Herford's king;
And if you crown him, let me prophesy
The blood of English shall manure the ground,
And future ages groan for this foul act.
Peace shall go sleep with Turks and infidels,
And in this seat of peace tumultuous wars   140
Shall kin with kin, and kind with kind confound.
Disorder, horror, fear, and mutiny
Shall here inhabit, and this land be called
The field of Golgotha and dead men's skulls.
O if you raise this house against this house,
It will the woefullest division prove
That ever fell upon this cursed earth.
Prevent it, resist it, let it not be so,
Lest child, child's children, cry against you woe.

NORTHUMBERLAND   Well have you argued sir, and for your pains,   150
Of capital treason we arrest you here.
My Lord of Westminster, be it your charge
To keep him safely till his day of trial.
May it please you, lords, to grant the commons'
    suit?

BOLINGBROKE   Fetch hither Richard, that in common view
He may surrender so we shall proceed
Without suspicion.

YORK   I will be his conduct. [*Exit*

BOLINGBROKE   Lords, you that here are under our arrest,
Procure your sureties for your days of answer.
Little are we beholding to your love,   160

Richard arrives, angry that he has to appear in public and in front of those who have betrayed him. York invites him to abdicate. Richard tells Bolingbroke to seize the crown which he holds in his hands. He taunts the Duke and expresses his grief.

161 **little looked for at:** expected little from

SD *regalia:* the symbols of monarchy – crown, orb and sceptre

165 **insinuate:** worm my way into the king's favour by stealthy and subtle means

168 **favours:** faces; friendly behaviour (a quibble)

170 **So Judas did to Christ:** ' ... he came to Jesus, and said, Hail master; and kissed him' Matthew Chapter 26 verse 49. Compare also Act 3 scene 2 lines 129–132
twelve: the twelve disciples of Jesus, of whom Judas was one

173 **both priest and clerk:** the clerk spoke the responses – such as 'Amen' – to the priest's prayers

176–7 **service, office:** quibbles on 'church service' and 'duty'

178 **tired:** exhausted, but with a pun on 'attired', referring to the regalia which is now on the stage

184 **owes:** owns; possesses
two buckets: the system of winding two buckets on a spindle so that as the empty bucket was lowered it assisted in drawing up the full one was used proverbially to describe fortune favouring one person at the expense of another

185 **emptier:** compare Act 3 scene 3 lines 84–86. Richard reverses the image, claiming that it is Bolingbroke whose vanity makes him *light*

190 **still:** always

> • *How does Richard seize the initiative and become the centre of attention?*

And little looked for at your helping hands.

Enter RICHARD *and* YORK *and officers bearing the regalia*

RICHARD
Alack, why am I sent for to a king
Before I have shook off the regal thoughts
Wherewith I reigned? I hardly yet have learned
To insinuate, flatter, bow, and bend my knee.
Give sorrow leave awhile to tutor me
To this submission. Yet I well remember
The favours of these men. Were they not mine?
Did they not sometime cry 'All hail!' to me?
So Judas did to Christ. But he in twelve   170
Found truth in all but one; I, in twelve thousand,
    none.
God save the King! will no man say amen?
Am I both priest and clerk? Well then, amen
God save the King, although I be not he;
And yet amen, if Heaven do think him me.
To do what service am I sent for hither?

YORK
To do that office of thine own good will
Which tired majesty did make thee offer:
The resignation of thy state and crown
To Henry Bolingbroke.

RICHARD
                              Give me the crown.   180
Here, cousin – seize the crown. Here, cousin –
On this side my hand, and on that side thine.
Now is this golden crown like a deep well
That owes two buckets, filling one another,
The emptier ever dancing in the air,
The other down, unseen, and full of water.
That bucket down, and full of tears am I,
Drinking my griefs, whilst you mount up on high.

BOLINGBROKE
I thought you had been willing to resign.

RICHARD
My crown I am, but still my griefs are mine.   190
You may my glories and my state depose,
But not my griefs; still am I king of those.

Richard reluctantly abdicates. Having conquered his grief he declares in formal and rhetorical terms the full extent of what he does. Northumberland tells Richard that he must read aloud the accusations which are the basis for his deposition.

194–198 cares: a series of quibbles on *care* as personal worry, grief, thoroughness and as the heavy responsibilities of kingship. The rhymed couplets and balance of each line around a central caesura (see Glossary p. 243) continues the image of Richard and Bolingbroke's fortunes balancing each other

194 Your cares ... down: The establishment of your responsibilities does not do away with my cares

195 by old care done: which happened through my caring (for the wrong things)

198 'tend: attend upon; always accompany

200 Ay, no..be: the quibbles here become clearer if we note that *Ay* and *I* are homophones (see Glossary p 244) and *nothing* is no-thing. The actor playing Richard has many possible ways of infuriating Bolingbroke with this reply

202 undo: ruin, perhaps accompanied by a literal undoing of robes

205 sway: sovereign power

206 balm: oil used in anointing as king (see Act 3 scene 2 line 55)

209 release all duteous oaths: release all those who have sworn to obey me

211 manors: estates
revenues: stress on second syllable

212 deny: declare to be untenable, unforceable

213 all oaths: Richard had previously emphasised the sacred nature of the feudal oath of fealty. See Act 1 scene 3 lines 178–192 where Bolingbroke made an oath he has now broken

214 are made: that are made

215 Make me: God make me
with nothing grieved: with no cause of grief – though the words are ambiguous

218 an earthy pit: the grave. The word also had connotations of prison and was synonymous with Hell

220 sunshine: Richard bequeaths to Bolingbroke the symbol of his own kingship

221 What more remains?: though understood by Northumberland to mean 'is there anything further to do here and now?' the question is again ambiguous – a rhetorical realisation of the extent of Richard's loss
read: read aloud

227 ravel out: disentangle; make plain – the word was weavers' jargon

BOLINGBROKE	Part of your cares you give me with your crown.
RICHARD	Your cares set up do not pluck my cares down.
	My care is loss of care by old care done;
	Your care is gain of care by new care won.
	The cares I give, I have, though given away,
	They 'tend the crown, yet still with me they stay.
BOLINGBROKE	Are you contented to resign the crown?

RICHARD   Ay, no; no, ay; for I must nothing be.   200
           Therefore no 'No', for I resign to thee.
           Now, mark me how I will undo myself.
           I give this heavy weight from off my head,
           And this unwieldy sceptre from my hand,
           The pride of kingly sway from out my heart.
           With mine own tears I wash away my balm,
           With mine own hands I give away my crown,
           With mine own tongue deny my sacred state,
           With mine own breath release all duteous oaths.
           All pomp and majesty I do forswear;   210
           My manors, rents, revenues I forgo;
           My acts, decrees, and statutes I deny.
           God pardon all oaths that are broke to me;
           God keep all vows unbroke are made to thee.
           Make me, that nothing have, with nothing grieved,
           And thou with all pleased, that hast all achieved.
           Long mayst thou live in Richard's seat to sit,
           And soon lie Richard in an earthy pit.
           God save King Henry, unkinged Richard says,
           And send him many years of sunshine days.   220
           What more remains?

NORTHUMBERLAND   No more, but that you read
           These accusations, and these grievous crimes
           Committed by your person and your followers
           Against the state and profit of this land;
           That by confessing them, the souls of men
           May deem that you are worthily deposed.

RICHARD   Must I do so? And must I ravel out
           My weaved-up follies? Gentle Northumberland,

Richard objects to the demand to read aloud his offences, reminding Northumberland that if he were to read an account of his faults it would include deposing a king. Northumberland insists, but Richard's eyes are tearful and he cannot read the paper. Richard claims that he has become a traitor to himself by abdicating. He berates Northumberland for his insulting behaviour, and ask for a mirror so that he can see what he has now become.

229 **record:** accented on the second syllable
232 **heinous article:** infamous, highly criminal statement
234 **oath:** the oath of allegience sworn by all the nobility at Richard's coronation
235 **Marked with a blot ... heaven:** a reference to Revelation Chapter 3 verse 5: 'I will not blot his name out of the book of life'. See also Act 1 scene 3 lines 202–203
237 **bait:** persecute (as in bear or badger-baiting)
238 **Pilate:** see Matthew 27 verse 24 where Pilate washed his hands before the multitude saying, 'I am innocent of the blood of this just person', before delivering Christ to be crucified. Bolingbroke has already compared himself to Pilate in ordering the death of Bushy and Green (Act 3 scene 1 lines 5–6)
239 **Pilates:** a quibble on 'pilots' who 'deliver' by 'water' (line 242). The water becomes, in Richard's mind, the waters of the Jordan in which John the Baptist washed away sin, and then his tears (244)
240 **sour:** bitter, and referring specifically to the vinegar given to Christ to drink on the cross
245 **a sort:** pack; an assortment – and a pun on *salt* as in his tears
249 **T'undeck the pompous body:** To undress and remove the decoration from the magnificent person
251 **state:** high rank; power; magnificence
253 **haught:** haughty: arrogant
255 **that name ... font:** his baptismal name; his most basic identity and the name by which he is known to God
256–257 **Alack the heavy day ... out:** Shame on the day when I have struggled to live so long
260 **the sun:** the transfer of the image to Bolingbroke is complete (see line 221 above)
263 **An if:** if indeed
sterling: of value; current (currency)
yet: still

- *In what ways does Richard's language reveal the emotional turmoil he is experiencing?*

If thy offences were upon record,
Would it not shame thee, in so fair a troop,   230
To read a lecture of them? If thou wouldst,
There shouldst thou find one heinous article,
Containing the deposing of a king,
And cracking the strong warrant of an oath,
Marked with a blot, damned in the book of heaven.
Nay, all of you that stand and look upon me,
Whilst that my wretchedness doth bait myself,
Though some of you, with Pilate, wash your hands.
Showing an outward pity – yet you Pilates
Have here delivered me to my sour cross,   240
And water cannot wash away your sin.

NORTHUMBERLAND   My lord dispatch, read o'er these articles.

[*Offers a paper*]

RICHARD   Mine eyes are full of tears, I cannot see.
And yet salt water blinds them not so much
But they can see a sort of traitors here.
Nay, if I turn mine eyes upon myself,
I find myself a traitor with the rest.
For I have given here my soul's consent
T'undeck the pompous body of a king;
Made glory base, and sovereignty a slave;   250
Proud majesty, a subject; state, a peasant.

NORTHUMBERLAND   My lord –

RICHARD   No lord of thine, thou haught insulting man;
Nor no man's lord. I have no name, no title,
No, not that name was given me at the font,
But 'tis usurped. Alack the heavy day,
That I have worn so many winters out,
And know not now what name to call myself.
O that I were a mockery king of snow,
Standing before the sun of Bolingbroke,   260
To melt myself away in water-drops!
Good king, great king, and yet not greatly good,
An if my word be sterling yet in England,
Let it command a mirror hither straight

Bolingbroke says that Richard need not read the accusations aloud. Richard looks in the mirror and sees neither the sorrow nor the kingly glory he expects. He breaks the mirror and suggests to Bolingbroke that it demonstrates the ease with which he can be destroyed. Bolingbroke refuses to accept the analogy – a mirror shows an image, not reality.

266 **bankrupt:** suggested by *sterling*, above and the images of poverty in lines 250–252

267 **some of you:** somebody; some one of you

273 **the very book:** the one particular book – a further reference to *the book of heaven* (see line 236, above and note), though by the end of the next line – *and that's myself* – Richard's thoughts have once more turned upon himself and his own unadorned appearance as the present sign of his guilt

275 **Give me that ... read:** The looking-glass is a frequent symbol in poetry of the period, used to represent both truth and vanity. See, for example, Shakespeare's *Sonnet 77*: 'Thy glass will show thee how thy beauties wear.'

280 **beguile:** delude; deceive

280-282 **Was this the face ... men?:** An apparent, ironic, reference to Marlowe's *Dr Faustus* (c. 1588) in which Faustus greets the beautiful Helen with 'Was this the face that launched a thousand ships/And burnt the topless towers of Ilium?' (Act 5 scene 1 lines 99–100)

283 **wink:** blink

284 **faced:** countenanced; covered over (referring to his own stupidity) – though it is possible that he is also referring to the folly of his favourites or to the Peasant's Revolt which, as a boy king, he had faced down

285 **outfaced:** overcome; put to shame

288 **shivers:** splinters

291-292: **The shadow of ... face:** your apparent despair has merely destroyed the image of your face. Is Bolingbroke dismissive of Richard's play-acting or does he speak kindly?

> • *How does Richard emphasise that it is not just his royal status that he has lost?*
> • *What, do you think, are Richard's purposes in his scene with the mirror?*

That it may show me what a face I have,
Since it is bankrupt of his majesty.

BOLINGBROKE   Go some of you, and fetch a looking-glass.

[*Exit* ATTENDANT

NORTHUMBERLAND   Read o'er this paper while the glass doth come.

RICHARD   Fiend, thou torments me ere I come to hell.

BOLINGBROKE   Urge it no more, my Lord Northumberland   270

NORTHUMBERLAND   The commons will not then be satisfied.

RICHARD   They shall be satisfied. I'll read enough
When I do see the very book indeed
Where all my sins are writ, and that's myself.

[*Enter* ATTENDANT *with a glass*]

Give me that glass, and therein will I read.
No deeper wrinkles yet? Hath sorrow struck
So many blows upon this face of mine
And made no deeper wounds? O flattering glass,
Like to my followers in prosperity,
Thou dost beguile me. Was this face the face   280
That every day under his household roof
Did keep ten thousand men? Was this the face
That like the sun did make beholders wink?
Is this the face which faced so many follies,
That was at last outfaced by Bolingbroke?
A brittle glory shineth in this face;
As brittle as the glory is the face,

[*He throws the glass down*

For there it is, cracked in an hundred shivers.
Mark, silent King, the moral of this sport,
How soon my sorrow hath destroyed my face.   290

BOLINGBROKE   The shadow of your sorrow hath destroyed

The shadow of your face.

RICHARD   Say that again.
'The shadow of my sorrow' – ha, let's see.
'Tis very true, my grief lies all within,

Richard asks to be allowed to go. Bolingbroke sends Richard to the Tower and appoints his own coronation date. He departs with his retinue, leaving only the Abbot of Westminster, the Bishop of Carlisle and Aumerle who begin to plot against Bolingbroke.

295 **external manners of laments:** expressions of grief
298 **the substance:** see Act 2 scene 2 line 14 and note. *Substance* is a philosophical and theological term describing the real, eternal essence of a thing and is often contrasted with the *shadow* by which it is perceived by mortals. Thus Richard turns Bolingbroke's dismissive phrase into an affirmation that his grief is in fact profoundly real. To Bolingbroke's exasperation Richard continues, mockingly, to thank him
301 **boon:** favour
307 **to:** as
314 **your sights:** i.e. of the whole court
316 **Convey:** transport: Richard seizes on the word to play on its other meanings of to steal or to make away with by stealth
317 **nimbly:** quickly – but the word often has pejorative connotations of immorality and slyness
320 **pageant:** spectacle; piece of drama
322 **as sharp ... thorn:** a further reference to Christ who was crowned with thorns at his crucifixion. The language of the remainder of this scene is strongly religious

> • *On his exit Richard makes his feelings clear: what emotions do you think Bolingbroke is experiencing at this moment?*

And these external manners of laments
Are merely shadows to the unseen grief
That swells with silence in the tortured soul.
There lies the substance; and I thank thee King,
For thy great bounty, that not only givest
Me cause to wail, but teachest me the way   300
How to lament the cause. I'll beg one boon,
And then be gone and trouble you no more.
Shall I obtain it?

BOLINGBROKE   Name it, fair cousin.

RICHARD   'Fair cousin'? I am greater than a king;
For when I was a king my flatterers
Were then but subjects; being now a subject
I have a king here to my flatterer.
Being so great, I have no need to beg.

BOLINGBROKE   Yet ask.

RICHARD   And shall I have?   310

BOLINGBROKE   You shall.

RICHARD   Then give me leave to go.

BOLINGBROKE   Whither?

RICHARD   Whither you will, so I were from your sights.

BOLINGBROKE   Go some of you, convey him to the Tower.

RICHARD   O good, convey? Conveyors are you all,
That rise thus nimbly by a true king's fall.

                    [*Exeunt* RICHARD *and* GUARD

BOLINGBROKE   On Wednesday next we solemnly set down
Our coronation. Lords, prepare yourselves.

                    [*Exeunt all except the* ABBOT OF WESTMINSTER,
                          the BISHOP OF CARLISLE, *and* AUMERLE

ABBOT OF WESTMINSTER   A woeful pageant have we here beheld.   320

BISHOP OF CARLISLE   The woe's to come; the children yet unborn
Shall feel this day as sharp to them as thorn.

AUMERLE   You holy clergymen, is there no plot

324 pernicious: destructive; ruinous. The word was also a rare synonym for nimble. Aumerle's use of *blot* is a further reminder of Richard's words (see line 236, above)

327–8 take the sacrament ... intents: take the sacraments of Holy Communion with me as a solemn pledge not to reveal my intentions. He may also intend an oath to be taken on the sacramental bread and wine. Holy Communion is symbolic of the Last Supper of Christ and his disciples and the reference here is a further link to Richard as well as lending gravity to the supper which the Abbot offers the conspirators (line 333 below)

          To rid the realm of this pernicious blot?

ABBOT OF WESTMINSTER   My lord,
          Before I freely speak my mind herein,
          You shall not only take the sacrament
          To bury mine intents, but also to effect
          Whatever I shall happen to devise.
          I see your brows are full of discontent,   330
          Your hearts of sorrow, and your eyes of fears.
          Come home with me to supper, I will lay
          A plot shall show us all a merry day. [*Exeunt*

ACTIVITIES

Keeping track

Scene 1

1 Who appears to have changed his allegiance at the beginning of this scene?
2 Why is it not possible for Aumerle's alibi to be corroborated by Thomas Mowbray, Duke of Norfolk?
3 Why is the Bishop of Carlisle arrested for treason?
4 Why is Richard brought before Bolingbroke and the nobles?
5 Who are compared to a pair of buckets at a well?
6 What is the cause of Richard's anger against Northumberland?
7 Why does Richard ask for a looking-glass?
8 Who is involved in the plot against Bolingbroke?

Characters

King Richard

• Despite the fact that this scene includes Richard's abdication and conveyance to prison, he seems to dominate it. He is, in several senses, the scene's leading actor.
1 How do other character and events prepare for his entrance?
2 What aspects of Richard's characters are not visible in this scene? Do we observe his real feelings and character or do you think we are more aware of Richard as an actor and poet?

Bolingbroke

• Bolingbroke is a usurper. The Bishop of Carlisle and Richard both condemn him during the scene, yet what aspects of his behaviour may lead us to feel more sympathetic towards him by the end of the scene?

Aumerle

• In a scene whose early action mirrors the interchange of challenges of Act 1 scene 1, Aumerle is cast in a heroic role. This will become important in the light of events in the last Act. What is significant in what Aumerle says and the way he behaves in this Act?

Duke of York
- York invites Bolingbroke to become king. To what extent is this a surprise and to what extent is it an inevitable consequence of previous events and his reaction to them?

Northumberland
- What does Northumberland do in this Act which continues to make him invaluable to Bolingbroke?

Themes

1 **Honour and chivalry.** This Act returns to the public display of chivalric values evident in Act 1 scene 1. Through Mowbray a specific link is made between the two scenes.
   - What elements are the same?
   - How does Bolingbroke handle things differently from Richard?
   - Considered from a modern perspective, what are the strengths and weaknesses of the noble code of honour demonstrated here?

2 **Kingship and human identity.** This is a scene of transition: as Bolingbroke seeks to achieve the crown, Richard is discovering what it is to be a common man. Both demonstrate how kings have to act a part. The king's appearance marks him out as different. People address him in particular ways. Yet at one point in the scene, as Richard demonstrates, no one seems certain just who the king is. When Richard abdicates he symbolically and poetically strips himself of power. His assumption of common humanity seems to him to lead directly to death (lines 202–218).
   - What do we learn from the debate between Richard and Bolingbroke about kingship?

Drama

1 **Lines 1–85.** This passage has the potential to be comic, with gages flying across the stage as one challenge follows another.
   - Try performing the scene yourselves and working out movements which will retain a sense of gravity. You might start, for example, in a circle in order to create a greater threat to Aumerle.
   - Lines 52–59 are omitted in the Folio, suggesting that the practice in Shakespeare's company was to make a cut in performance. Try your version with and without these lines: can you use them to increase the sense of menace or are they better cut?

2 **The abdication of the King (lines 154–317).** Work in groups of four or five. One of you (or your teacher) is a reporter while the other four represent Bolingbroke, Northumberland, York and Richard. As the characters enter Westminster Hall for the abdication, the reporter interviews each in turn to discover what outcome they expect. Then each character reveals what he is really thinking – which may be very different.

3 In pairs, as Richard and Bolingbroke, read lines 180–203. If possible, learn them by heart. Make a cardboard crown or borrow some suitably firm piece of headgear (such as a crash helmet – a soft hat will not work). Play the scene as Shakespeare wrote it. Work out who is holding the crown at each moment of the scene. Consider how the crown needs to be handled – remember that it is an object with sacred and symbolic power. Discuss the feelings which each of the men experiences as they pass the crown between them. How strongly do they feel the urge to grab and hang on to it?

Close study

Act 4 scene 1 lines 114–149
This speech combines a key statement of principle with a forthright prophecy of future chaos.

1 What do we already know about the Bishop of Carlisle and the values he holds? Where do you think his loyalties lie? (He is a minor character but you can read the advice he gives to Richard in Act 2 scene 2. In Act 3 scene 3 line 20 Northumberland seems scornful of him. Note also his praise of Mowbray earlier in this scene, lines 91–102.)
2 Lines 115–116 clearly show Carlisle's unease. Why does he feel compelled to speak? Why does he speak of being in 'this royal presence' when Richard is not present and he is about to deny Bolingbroke's right to be king?
3 Lines 117–133. Carlisle's argument is based on two principles, one of which is familiar to us today. What are they?
4 Lines 134–149. The second part of the speech is Carlisle's prophecy of civil war. The two houses (line 145) are of York and Lancaster and, as Shakespeare's audience knew, the reigns of Henry VI and Richard III were beset by 'tumultuous wars' between them.

- What similar prophecies of war have been made during the play?
- How does Carlisle use carefully chosen verbs, other metaphorical language and figures of speech for rhetorical effect in this section?

5   Carlisle is a Christian Bishop. How is his right to speak as a messenger of God emphasised linguistically in this passage?

Key scene

Act 4 scene 1 lines 154–317

This section is not in the three quarto editions of the play. Since it is concerned with the abdication of the king, it was considered too sensitive to publish during Queen Elizabeth I's lifetime. However, Heminge and Condell, Shakespeare's actor colleagues who edited the First Folio of 1623, included it. It is known that the scene was performed on 7 February 1601, the day before the Earl of Essex's abortive rebellion, and that Elizabeth remarked, 'I am Richard II, know ye not that?'

It is interesting to consider why Shakespeare chose to stage this scene. In Holinshed's historical account on which the play is based, Richard simply signs a document. Shakespeare allows the characters to reveal more of themselves and to deepen our sympathy for them. He also creates a dramatically satisfying conflict. Though we know Bolingbroke now has all the power, it is Richard who manipulates the situation.

Keying it in

1   What is the motivation for Richard and Bolingbroke at the start of this scene? (You may find it useful to do drama activity 2, on page 164, as preparation.)

The scene itself

2   **Lines 154–157**
- Why is it important for Northumberland and Bolingbroke to have Richard abdicate and confess his failures publicly?

3   **Lines 162–180**
- How does Richard express his bitterness towards his former courtiers? What aspect of their behaviour does he draw attention to?
- Why does no one say 'Amen' to Richard's 'God save the king!'?
- How does Richard's speech confuse the court and help Richard to seize the initiative?

4 **Lines 177–220**
Movement is very important here. Richard manipulates Bolingbroke
into becoming an unwilling actor in this scene. (You may find it helpful
to do drama activity 3, on page 164.)
- How is the crown used by Richard to demonstrate both his difficulty
  in relinquishing power and Bolingbroke's desire for it?
- The scene is striking for its symmetry, both in movement and
  language. What examples can you find of the way Shakespeare
  balances the rise and fall of the two men and the glory and grief
  belonging to the crown?
- Refer to Act 3 scene 3 lines 142–159. It almost seems as though
  those lines are a private rehearsal for the public renunciation of lines
  203–218. What similarities can you find between the two speeches?

5 **Lines 221–274**
- In what ways has this section been prepared for by the Bishop of
  Carlisle (lines 117–133)?
- How does Richard's language reflect his belief that he has been
  uniquely ordained by God as his representative on earth?
- In lines 256–266 Richard's abdication is affirmed by his reversal of
  the image of the sun which has been applied to him throughout the
  play. What does this tell us about Richard's state of mind and the
  nature of kingship?

6 **Lines 275–317**
- Richard calls for the mirror in order to view his own grief. In what
  ways is the mirror symbolic of other aspects of the drama of this
  scene?
- When Bolingbroke says that *'The shadow of your sorrow hath
  destroyed/The shadow of your face'* he pointedly suggests that he has
  seen through Richard's acting: his grief is not real. How do you
  think the actor playing Richard should deliver the remainder of this
  scene? Do the lines suggest anger or grief? Is Richard acting or
  being himself?

Overview
What would be the dramatic consequence of following the censored Quarto
text and omitting this scene?

Writing

1 Write an account of how you would produce this Act on a stage or other performance area known to you. (This might be a theatre you have visited, or your school or college drama studio, for example.) Use a diagram of your chosen acting area to show the movements, exits and entrances which you would recommend for this Act. Include any essential scenery and props. You will need to offer opportunities for formal ceremony as well as for Carlisle and Richard to dominate during their main speeches. At the end of the scene Carlisle, Westminster and Aumerle must be able to conspire together.

2 Discuss the way in which Shakespeare uses Christian references in this act. What is the dramatic effect of relating so much of the language to the Bible and to Christian history?

3 Conspiracy: imagine you were one of the conspirators at the end of this Act. Write the manifesto that seeks to persuade others of the rightness of your cause. You could do this in the form of a leaflet or poster to be left in public places, so aim for maximum impact and a succinct argument.

The Queen meets Richard on his way to imprisonment in the Tower. She is full of pity for her husband. He tries to comfort her, telling her to look on their happy past as merely a dream, and instructs her to retreat to a French convent.

1–2 **This way the king ... tower:** The scene picks up from Act 3 scene 4 where the Queen decides to meet Richard in London (line 97) and alludes to Bolingbroke's Roman triumph (line 99). According to legend, Julius Caesar built the forerunner of the Norman Tower of London following his invasion of Britain in 55BC

2 **ill-erected:** built for evil purposes

3 **flint:** hard-hearted; built from flint

5 **rebellious earth:** a transferred epithet in which the earth is made to stand for the state of the country and the behaviour of its people

8 **fair rose:** Richard is 'that sweet, lovely rose' according to Hotspur in *1 Henry 4* (Act 1 scene 3 line 173). Symbolically the word represents both purity and love

11–15 **Ah, thou ... guest?:** You are like the ruin of a great city, an image of honour, the symbol of your own death, not the real King Richard. You are like a beautiful inn: why should you house ugly grief when that common alehouse, Bolingbroke, is thought suitable for the entertainment of triumph? The Queen alludes to the tradition that London was built by the descendants of Aeneas and other who fled from Troy and that the kings of Britain can thus trace their lineage back to him

17 **make my end too sudden:** kill me too soon

18 **state:** condition; splendour

20 **but this:** only this, i.e. that we are what we now appear to be. Perhaps Richard emphasises the point by gesture to his clothes. The Quarto has a colon after *this*.

21 **necessity:** the constraining power of circumstance; inevitability

22 **keep a league:** join together in a solemn covenant

23 **religious house:** convent

24 **a new world's crown:** immortal life; a heavenly reward

25 **Which our profane ... down:** which we have cast away in this life through our wicked behaviour

- *What images does Shakespeare use to underline the feeling of decline and decay here?*

Act five

Enter the QUEEN *and* LADIES

QUEEN ISABEL   This way the King will come; this is the way
To Julius Caesar's ill-erected tower,
To whose flint bosom my condemned lord
Is doomed a prisoner by proud Bolingbroke.
Here let us rest, if this rebellious earth
Have any resting for her true King's Queen.

Enter RICHARD *and* GUARD

But soft, but see, or rather do not see,
My fair rose wither. Yet look up, behold,
That you in pity may dissolve to dew,
And wash him fresh again with true-love tears.   10
Ah thou the model where old Troy did stand,
Thou map of honour, thou King Richard's tomb,
And not King Richard; thou most beauteous inn,
Why should hard-favoured grief be lodged in thee,
When triumph is become an alehouse guest?

RICHARD   Join not with grief, fair woman, do not so,
To make my end too sudden. Learn, good soul,
To think our former state a happy dream,
From which awaked, the truth of what we are
Shows us but this. I am sworn brother, sweet,   20
To grim necessity, and he and I
Will keep a league till death. Hie thee to France,
And cloister thee in some religious house.
Our holy lives must win a new world's crown
Which our profane hours here have thrown down.

QUEEN ISABEL   What, is my Richard both in shape and mind
Transformed and weakened? Hath Bolingbroke

The Queen begs Richard to demonstrate greater anger against Bolingbroke. He tells her to reconcile herself to his death and to repeat the story of his fall to anyone who will hear. Northumberland enters with orders to take Richard to Pomfret Castle in Yorkshire and for the Queen's swift journey to France.

29–34 The lion: the monarch of the animal kingdom and used as a symbol of the English crown. The lion was also associated with Christ. Traditionally the lion only became angry when wounded

31 To be: at being

31–34 wilt thou … beasts: will you, like a school pupil, accept punishment, kiss the stick with which you are beaten, flatter those who rage at you by your utter humility, when you are a lion, the king of all animals

35 if aught but beasts: had my subjects been anything other than beasts

37 sometimes: former; sometime

40–50 In winter's … king: compare Act 3 scene 2 lines 155–175

42 betid: happened

43 quite: require; return; repay

46–47 For why … tongue: because even the inanimate firewood will sympathise with the sad tone of your emotional voice

49 some: i.e. of the brands which will seem to bear the traditional signs of mourning – ash or black funeral clothes

52 Pomfret: Pontefract in Yorkshire

53 there is order ta'en for you: arrangements have been made for you

55–65 Northumberland … usurped throne: The history of the relationship between Northumberland and Bolingbroke is a major element of the two *Henry IV* plays. In *2 Henry 4* Act 3 scene 1 lines 67–79 Bolingbroke, as Henry IV, ruefully recalls these prophetic words of Richard

58–59 foul sin … corruption: the image is of a boil coming to a head

60 Though he: even if he were to

61 helping him to all: since you helped him to the whole kingdom

Deposed thine intellect? Hath he been in thy heart?
The lion dying thrusteth forth his paw
And wounds the earth, if nothing else, with rage   30
To be o'erpowered; and wilt thou pupil-like
Take the correction mildly, kiss the rod,
And fawn on rage with base humility,
Which art a lion and the king of beasts?

RICHARD   A king of beasts indeed; if aught but beasts
I had been still a happy king of men.
Good sometimes queen, prepare thee hence for
    France.
Think I am dead, and that even here thou takest,
As from my deathbed, thy last living leave.
In winter's tedious nights sit by the fire   40
With good old folks, and let them tell thee tales
Of woeful ages long ago betid;
And ere thou bid goodnight, to quite their griefs
Tell thou the lamentable tale of me,
And send the hearers weeping to their beds;
For why, the senseless brands will sympathize
The heavy accent of thy moving tongue,
And in compassion weep the fire out;
And some will mourn in ashes, some coal-black,
For the deposing of a rightful king.   50

Enter NORTHUMBERLAND

NORTHUMBERLAND   My lord, the mind of Bolingbroke is changed.
You must to Pomfret, not unto the Tower.
And madam, there is order ta'en for you:
With all swift speed you must away to France.

RICHARD   Northumberland, thou ladder wherewithal
The mounting Bolingbroke ascends my throne,
The time shall not be many hours of age
More than it is, ere foul sin gathering head
Shall break into corruption. Thou shalt think,
Though he divide the realm and give thee half,   60
It is too little, helping him to all.
He shall think that thou, which knowest the way

Richard predicts that Northumberland and Bolingbroke will soon distrust each other. He notes that Northumberland has now divorced him from both his country and his wife. Richard and Isabel prepare, with great tenderness, to part.

66 of: between

68 worthy: well-deserved

69 and there an end: let that be the end of it; enough

70 forthwith: immediately

75 with a kiss 'twas made: since it was a kiss which sealed their marriage vows an *unkiss* should end the marriage, but Richard realises that a kiss can never be unkissed: to kiss now could only confirm the oath of loyalty made between them

77 pines the clime: torments the region

78 set: she set. Queen Isabel was the daughter of the King of France and her marriage was celebrated with great splendour. (Shakespeare chooses to ignore the fact that she was only aged ten at the time of Richard's deposition and the marriage had never been consummated)

79–102: Note the heroic couplets

79 May: emblematic of love and new life

80 Hallowmas: All Saint's Day – the day following Hallowe'en, the first of November and thus the opposite end of the year to May Day. It is the day on which Christians think of those who have died in the faith

shortest of day: mid-winter – another symbol of death.

84 little policy: poor politics. Some editors follow the Folio in giving this line to Northumberland

86–87 So two ... here: Richard suggests that the grief will be doubled if they grieve apart, and it is appropriate that the grief at their condition should be great

88 Better far off ... nearer: it is better to be far from each other than to be near yet not nearer than we are now

89 count thy way: measure your journey

92 piece the way out: lengthen the journey

93 in wooing sorrow let's be brief: let us not talk about sorrow any more

95 dumbly part: their speech is stopped by a kiss, following Richard's command in line 93

96 mine: my heart

To plant unrightful kings, wilt know again,
Being ne'er so little urged, another way
To pluck him headlong from the usurped throne.
The love of wicked men converts to fear,
That fear to hate, and hate turns one or both
To worthy danger and deserved death.

NORTHUMBERLAND   My guilt be on my head, and there an end.
Take leave and part, for you must part forthwith.   70

RICHARD   Doubly divorced! Bad men, you violate
A two-fold marriage – 'twixt my crown and me,
And then betwixt me and my married wife.
Let me unkiss the oath 'twixt thee and me;
And yet not so, for with a kiss 'twas made.
Part us, Northumberland; I towards the north,
Where shivering cold and sickness pines the clime;
My wife to France, from whence set forth in pomp
She came adorned hither like sweet May,
Sent back like Hallowmas or shortest of day.   80

QUEEN ISABEL   And must we be divided? Must we part?

RICHARD   Ay, hand from hand, my love, and heart from heart.

QUEEN ISABEL   Banish us both, and send the King with me.

RICHARD   That were some love, but little policy.

QUEEN ISABEL   Then whither he goes, thither let me go.

RICHARD   So two together weeping make one woe.
Weep thou for me in France, I for thee here
Better far off than, near, be ne'er the near.
Go count thy way with sighs, I mine with groans.

QUEEN ISABEL   So longest way shall have the longest moans.   90

RICHARD   Twice for one step I'll groan, the way being short,
And piece the way out with a heavy heart.
Come come, in wooing sorrow let's be brief,
Since wedding it, there is such length in grief.
One kiss shall stop our mouths, and dumbly part;
Thus give I mine, and thus take I thy heart.

[They kiss

97–98 Give me … heart: return my heart to me since it would not be a good role for me to play to keep your heart and kill it (because I shall soon die of grief). This conceit of lovers keeping each other's hearts, and of exchanging them in a kiss, was common – see, for example, Shakespeare's *Sonnet 133*

101 We make woe … delay: we play games with grief through this foolishly loving delay

The Duke of York tells his wife about the entry of Bolingbroke and Richard into London. The people had thrown rubbish on Richard's head but cheered Bolingbroke. Banners on the walls welcomed Bolingbroke and he humbly thanked the crowds.

3 our two cousins': her nephews, Bolingbroke and Richard. Cousin was used generally at the time to describe kinship

5 rude: unkind; violent
misgoverned: unruly; unrestrained

9 Which his … know: [The horse] seemed to know his rider and his aspirations

14 Through casements … eyes: through windows devouring him with their eyes

15–16 and that all … said: all the walls, covered with painted cloths, seemed to say. Paintings, with words and slogans issuing from characters' mouths, were hung on walls during pageants and celebrations

16 at once: all together

18–21 Whilst he … along: this description mirrors that of Bolingbroke's departure in Act 1 scene 4 lines 23–36

19 Bare-headed, lower: doffing his hat and bowing lower

- *What is the effect of the heroic couplets in lines 79–102?*
- *How does the beginning of scene 2 develop dramatically from the previous scene?*

QUEEN ISABEL   Give me mine own again; 'twere no good part
               To take on me to keep and kill thy heart.

                                        [*They kiss*
               So, now I have mine own again, be gone,
               That I may strive to kill it with a groan.   100

RICHARD   We make woe wanton with this fond delay.
               Once more adieu, the rest let sorrow say.

                                        [*Exeunt*

Scene ②

Enter DUKE OF YORK *and the* DUCHESS

DUCHESS OF YORK   My lord, you told me you would tell the rest,
                  When weeping made you break the story off,
                  Of our two cousins' coming into London.

YORK   Where did I leave?

DUCHESS OF YORK   At that sad stop, my lord,
               Where rude misgoverned hands from windows' tops
               Threw dust and rubbish on King Richard's head.

YORK   Then, as I said, the Duke, great Bolingbroke,
               Mounted upon a hot and fiery steed
               Which his aspiring rider seemed to know,
               With slow but stately pace kept on his course,   10
               Whilst all tongues cried 'God save thee, Bolingbroke'
               You would have thought the very windows spake,
               So many greedy looks of young and old
               Through casements darted their desiring eyes
               Upon his visage, and that all the walls
               With painted imagery had said at once
               'Jesu preserve thee, welcome Bolingbroke'.
               Whilst he from the one side to the other turning,
               Bare-headed, lower than his proud steed's neck,
               Bespake them thus, 'I thank you countrymen'.   20
               And thus still doing, thus he passed along.

York reports that Richard bore his abuse with grief and
patience. He claims that what has happened must be the will of
God and that henceforth he will faithfully serve Bolingbroke.
Aumerle enters. He has been reduced in rank because of his
support for Richard.

24 **well-graced:** full of grace
27 **Even:** the metre suggests the word was pronounced *e'en*
32 **still:** constantly
33 **badges:** i.e. the tears and smiles were the outward signs of his
   grief and patience
   patience: endurance of suffering
34 **for some strong purpose:** having some greater intention (not
   understood by human beings)
   steeled: hardened
35 **perforce:** by physical violence:
   melted: the conceit recognises that the high emotion of the
   occasion would normally have caused sympathy for Richard –
   hearts would have melted – but that because God purposed
   otherwise people hardened against him. Steel requires intense
   heat, the melting of iron and physical force
36 **barbarism itself have:** even savages would have
38 **bound our calm contents:** calmly and contentedly pledge
   ourselves
40 **for aye allow:** acknowledge for ever
43 **Rutland:** Earl of Rutland; Bolingbroke deprived him of the
   greater title, Duke of Aumerle, because of his part in the
   events enacted in Act 4 scene 1 lines 1–90
44 **I am in ... truth:** I have offered myself as surety for his good
   faith, in front of all my peers in the royal council
45 **fealty:** fidelity; loyalty
46–47 **Who are the violets ... spring?:** who are the early, sweet-
   smelling favourites in the inexperienced king's new court?
49 **as lief be none:** rather not be one of them
50 **bear you well:** take care; watch your step
51 **cropped:** cut down
   prime: maturity
52 **Do these justs and triumphs hold?:** will the jousts and
   tournaments be held? These celebrations at Oxford had been
   designed by the Abbot of Westminster and others (see Act 4
   scene 1 lines 323–333) as an opportunity to assassinate Henry
   IV and reinstate Richard

- *What are the indications that Aumerle's mood has*
  changed significantly from earlier appearances in the
  play?

DUCHESS OF YORK   Alack poor Richard, where rode he the whilst?

YORK   As in a theatre the eyes of men,
                    After a well-graced actor leaves the stage,
                    Are idly bent on him that enters next,
                    Thinking his prattle to be tedious;
                    Even so, or with much more contempt, men's eyes
                    Did scowl on gentle Richard. No man cried 'God
                       save him'.
                    No joyful tongue gave him his welcome home;
                    But dust was thrown upon his sacred head,   30
                    Which with such gentle sorrow he shook off,
                    His face still combating with tears and smiles,
                    The badges of his grief and patience,
                    That had not God for some strong purpose steeled
                    The hearts of men, they must perforce have melted,
                    And barbarism itself have pitied him.
                    But heaven hath a hand in these events,
                    To whose high will we bound our calm contents.
                    To Bolingbroke are we sworn subjects now,
                    Whose state and honour I for aye allow.   40
                    Enter AUMERLE

DUCHESS OF YORK   Here comes my son Aumerle.

YORK   Aumerle that was,
                    But that is lost for being Richard's friend;
                    And madam, you must call him Rutland now.
                    I am in Parliament pledge for his truth
                    And lasting fealty to the new-made King.

DUCHESS OF YORK   Welcome, my son, who are the violets now
                    That strew the green lap of the new-come spring?

AUMERLE   Madam, I know not, nor I greatly care not.
                    God knows I had as lief be none as one.

YORK   Well, bear you well in this new spring of time,   50
                    Lest you be cropped before you come to prime.
                    What news from Oxford? Do these justs and
                       triumphs hold?

AUMERLE   For aught I know, my lord, they do.

Aumerle's father, York, notices a sealed document partially concealed in his clothes, which he is reluctant to show. The Duchess tries to protect her son but York seizes the document and finds it to be evidence of the Abbot of Westminster's plot against Bolingbroke. Chaos ensues as York prepares to take the document to Bolingbroke, who is now King Henry IV.

55 **prevent:** the word was used specifically to describe God's intervention in human affairs, anticipating human need. Aumerle, thinking of the plot and assuming God's desire to reinstate Richard, uses the word in both the general and special senses

56 **What seal:** the red wax seal would hang from ribbon or string attached to the document
   without thy bosom: outside your doublet

66 **'gainst:** in preparation for

67 **Bound to himself?:** Had he entered into such a contract, involving clothes being made on credit, it would be the other party who kept the sealed copy

75 **by my troth:** by my pledge of faith

79 **appeach:** inform against

> • *In what way does Shakespeare use dramatic irony here?*

YORK	You will be there, I know.
AUMERLE	If God prevent not, I purpose so.
YORK	What seal is that that hangs without thy bosom? Yea, lookest thou pale? Let me see the writing.
AUMERLE	My lord, 'tis nothing.
YORK	No matter then who see it. I will be satisfied, let me see the writing.
AUMERLE	I do beseech your grace to pardon me. 60 It is a matter of small consequence, Which for some reasons I would not have seen.
YORK	Which for some reasons sir, I mean to see I fear, I fear –
DUCHESS OF YORK	What should you fear? 'Tis nothing but some bond that he is entered into For gay apparel 'gainst the triumph day.
YORK	Bound to himself? What doth he with a bond That he is bound to? Wife, thou art a fool. Boy, let me see the writing.
AUMERLE	I do beseech you pardon me, I may not show it. 70
YORK	I will be satisfied, let me see it I say.
	[*He plucks it out of his bosom, and reads it*
YORK	Treason, foul treason! Villain, traitor, slave!
DUCHESS OF YORK	What is the matter my lord?
YORK	Ho, who is within there? Saddle my horse. God for his mercy, what treachery is here!
DUCHESS OF YORK	Why what is it my lord?
YORK	Give me my boots I say. Saddle my horse. Now by mine honour, by my life, by my troth, I will appeach the villain.
DUCHESS OF YORK	What is the matter?
YORK	Peace foolish woman. 80
DUCHESS OF YORK	I will not peace. What is the matter Aumerle?

The Duchess tries to persuade York not to betray their son. York is determined to reveal all to the new King. He sets off for the Court.

83 answer: pay for

85–87 Strike him ... I say: the Duchess tells her son to strike the servant; Aumerle is too stunned (amazed) by the turn of events to act, the Duchess rounds on the servants and York repeats his command

91 teeming date: reproductive period. Since *to teem* was to empty or pour out, she sees time as drinking up her life

95 fond: foolish

97 ta'en the sacrament: taken an oath on the holy sacrament – the blood and body of Christ – to conspire against Bolingbroke (see above, Act 4 scene 1 lines 326–330)

98 interchangeably set down their hands: signed equally and reciprocally: each would have had an identical copy of the bond and all would have signed each one

99 be none: not be one of them

100 what is that to him: the bond and the plot it signifies

102 groaned for him: i.e. in giving birth to him

103 thou wouldst: possibly pronounced 'thou'dst'

> • *Why does York propose to betray his son to King Henry?*

AUMERLE   Good mother be content, it is no more
                    Than my poor life must answer.

DUCHESS OF YORK   Thy life answer?

YORK   Bring me my boots. I will unto the King.

Enter SERVANT *with his boots*

DUCHESS OF YORK   Strike him Aumerle. Poor boy thou art amazed.

                    [*To* SERVANT] Hence, villain, never more come in
                      my sight.

YORK   Give me my boots I say.

DUCHESS OF YORK   Why York what wilt thou do?
                    Wilt thou not hide the trespass of thine own?
                    Have we more sons? Or are we like to have?   90
                    Is not my teeming date drunk up with time?
                    And wilt thou pluck my fair son from mine age,
                    And rob me of a happy mother's name?
                    Is he not like thee? Is he not thine own?

YORK   Thou fond mad woman,
                    Wilt thou conceal this dark conspiracy?
                    A dozen of them here have ta'en the sacrament
                    And interchangeably set down their hands
                    To kill the King at Oxford.

DUCHESS OF YORK   He shall be none;
                    We'll keep him here, then what is that to him?   100

YORK   Away fond woman, were he twenty times my son
                    I would appeach him.

DUCHESS OF YORK   Hadst thou groaned for him
                    As I have done, thou wouldst be more pitiful.
                  But now I know thy mind, thou dost suspect
                  That I have been disloyal to thy bed,
                  And that he is a bastard, not thy son.
                  Sweet York, sweet husband, be not of that mind.
                  He is as like thee as a man may be,
                  Not like to me, or any of my kin,
                  And yet I love him.

YORK   Make way unruly woman. [*Exit*   110

The Duchess tells Aumerle to take York's horse and reach King
Henry before his father.

112 **Spur post:** ride quickly, using a relay of horses
116 **never will I ... ground:** I will lay prostrate before King Henry
and not get up

King Henry is bemoaning the fact that he hasn't seen his son for
three months. The young man is rumoured to be living with thieves
and rogues. Percy provides evidence of Prince Henry's dissolute
behaviour.

1 **me:** omitted in the Folio and some other editions
my unthrifty son: Prince Hal, later King Henry V, the chief
protagonist of *1 Henry IV*, *2 Henry IV* and *Henry V*. Hal's
delinquent youth, in the company of Sir John Falstaff and various
low-life hangers on, is the major element of *1 Henry IV*. The
activities described in the next dozen lines reflect events in that play
unthrifty: wasteful; immoral
3 **If any plague hang over us:** see Richard's prophecy in Act 3
scene 3 lines 85–90 which Bolingbroke seems to have in his mind.
The plague is a symbol of any calamity and 'hangs' because it was
believed to be air-borne
7 **loose:** immoral
9 **watch:** night-watchmen
our passengers: those passing along the king's highway
10 **While:** 'which' in the Quarto and Folio but usually emended.
Lines 10–12 may be corrupted text
young wanton: unruly child
effeminate: unmanly; weak; soft
13 **PERCY:** a further precursor of *1 Henry IV* in which Hal and Percy
will become rivals
15 **the gallant:** chivalrous and fashionable young gentleman (ironic)
16 **the stews:** the brothels
17 **the commonest creature:** i.e. a prostitute
18 **a favour:** gift from a lady worn by her knight in combat
19 **lustiest:** strongest, heartiest – but with sexual overtones: Hal
compares the tournament to sexual conquest
20 **As dissolute as desperate:** He is as immoral as he is hopeless
through both: i.e. 'dissolute' and 'desperate'
21 **I see ... hope:** these lines foreshadow Henry's legendary
reformation

• *King Henry introduces the subject of his unruly son. This*
character does not appear in the play, so why does
Shakespeare tell us about him?

DUCHESS OF YORK   After, Aumerle. Mount thee upon his horse,
Spur post, and get before him to the King,
And beg thy pardon ere he do accuse thee.
I'll not be long behind – though I be old,
I doubt not but to ride as fast as York;
And never will I rise up from the ground
Till Bolingbroke have pardoned thee. Away, be gone.

[Exeunt

Scene 3

Enter BOLINGBROKE *now* KING HENRY, PERCY, *and
other* LORDS

KING HENRY   Can no man tell me of my unthrifty son?
'Tis full three months since I did see him last.
If any plague hang over us, 'tis he.
I would to God, my lords, he might be found.
Inquire at London 'mongst the taverns there,
For there, they say, he daily doth frequent
With unrestrained loose companions,
Even such, they say, as stand in narrow lanes
And beat our watch, and rob our passengers,
While he, young wanton, and effeminate boy,   10
Takes on the point of honour to support
So dissolute a crew.

PERCY   My lord, some two days since I saw the Prince,
And told him of those triumphs held at Oxford.

KING HENRY   And what said the gallant?

PERCY   His answer was, he would unto the stews,
And from the commonest creature pluck a glove,
And wear it as a favour, and with that
He would unhorse the lustiest challenger.

KING HENRY   As dissolute as desperate. Yet through both   20
I see some sparks of better hope, which elder years

Aumerle arrives and begs a private audience with the King, behind locked doors. He gains a pardon from Henry before disclosing what he has done. York arrives and shouts a warning to Henry, who lets him in.

29 **my knees grow to the earth:** Aumerle kneels
30 **My tongue cleave ... mouth:** Quoted from Psalm 137 verse 6
    cleave: stick fast
33–34 **If on the first ... thee:** If your fault was of the first kind – intention – however wicked it is I pardon you in order to secure your love in the future
40 **safe:** harmless
42 **secure:** over-confident
43–44 **Shall I ... face?:** Must I/will you let me, because of my love for you, speak (of) treason to you face to face?

> • *What significant details are revealed here about Henry's behaviour as king?*

	May happily bring forth. But who comes here?
	Enter AUMERLE *amazed*
AUMERLE	Where is the King?
KING HENRY	What means our cousin, that he stares and looks so wildly?
AUMERLE	God save your grace. I do beseech your majesty To have some conference with your grace alone.
KING HENRY	Withdraw yourselves, and leave us here alone. [*Exeunt* PERCY *and* LORDS What is the matter with our cousin now?
AUMERLE	For ever may my knees grow to the earth, My tongue cleave to my roof within my mouth, Unless a pardon ere I rise or speak.
KING HENRY	Intended or committed was this fault? If on the first, how heinous e'er it be, To win thy after-love I pardon thee.
AUMERLE	Then give me leave that I may turn the key, That no man enter till my tale be done.
KING HENRY	Have thy desire.
	[*The* DUKE OF YORK *knocks at the door and crieth*
YORK	[*within*] My liege beware, look to thyself, Thou hast a traitor in thy presence there.
KING HENRY	Villain, I'll make thee safe.
	[*Draws his sword*]
AUMERLE	Stay thy revengeful hand, thou hast no cause to fear.
YORK	Open the door, secure foolhardy King. Shall I for love speak treason to thy face? Open the door, or I will break it open.
	KING HENRY *opens the door. Enter* YORK
KING HENRY	What is the matter uncle? Speak, recover breath, Tell us how near is danger, That we may arm us to encounter it.

30

40

King Henry reads the sealed paper while Aumerle reminds him of the pardon already given. Henry commends York's loyalty. When Henry says that he will spare Aumerle because of his father's virtue, York objects. The Duchess arrives to plead for her son, not knowing that he has already been pardoned.

49 **that my haste forbids me show:** because I am out of breath

52 **is not confederate with my hand:** does not share the intentions implied by my signature

53 **it:** the signature

56 **Forget to pity:** ignore your impulse to forgive him

57 **a serpent:** compare Act 3 scene 3 line 131

60–66 **Thou sheer ... son:** This is a further development of the image first used by the Duchess of Gloucester (Act 1 scene 2 lines 11–21) and by Northumberland (Act 3 scene 3 line 108) and once more emphasises the kinship between the principal characters of the play

60 **sheer:** pure
immaculate: unblemished

61 **through muddy passages:** through corruption

62 **his:** i.e. the sheer fountain's

63 **overflow of good:** outpouring of goodness
converts to bad: is changed to bad [in Aumerle]

65 **digressing:** deviant

66 **So:** If so
be his vice's bawd: serve only to procure his immorality

67–68 **An he shall spend ... gold:** if his shameful behaviour shall waste my honourable reputation in the same way that spendthrift sons waste the wealth accumulated by their careful fathers. Some editions have 'And' for 'An' (Folio and first Quarto)

78 **Our scene is altered:** King Henry sees the humour of the situation, which is perhaps emphasised by the mock-heroic verse from here until line 130

79 **'The Beggar and the King':** Probably a reference to the ballad of King Cophetua who fell in love with a beggar maid. The title, not the subject, inspires the reference

80 **dangerous:** said, at least partly, ironically

> • *How does this scene help to establish Henry in the role of king?*

YORK	Peruse this writing here, and thou shalt know
	The treason that my haste forbids me show.
AUMERLE	Remember, as thou readest, thy promise passed. 50
	I do repent me, read not my name there,
	My heart is not confederate with my hand.
YORK	It was, villain, ere thy hand did set it down.
	I tore it from the traitor's bosom, King.
	Fear, and not love, begets his penitence.
	Forget to pity him lest thy pity prove
	A serpent that will sting thee to the heart.
KING HENRY	O heinous, strong, and bold conspiracy!
	O loyal father of a treacherous son!
	Thou sheer, immaculate and silver fountain 60
	From whence this stream through muddy passages
	Hath held his current and defiled himself.
	Thy overflow of good converts to bad,
	And thy abundant goodness shall excuse
	This deadly blot in thy digressing son.
YORK	So shall my virtue be his vice's bawd,
	An he shall spend mine honour with his shame,
	As thriftless sons their scraping fathers' gold.
	Mine honour lives when his dishonour dies,
	Or my shamed life in his dishonour lies. 70
	Thou killest me in his life – giving him breath,
	The traitor lives, the true man's put to death.
DUCHESS OF YORK	[*within*] What ho, my liege, for God's sake let
	me in.
KING HENRY	What shrill-voiced suppliant makes this eager cry?
DUCHESS OF YORK	A woman, and thy aunt, great King – 'tis I.
	Speak with me, pity me, open the door,
	A beggar begs that never begged before.
KING HENRY	Our scene is altered from a serious thing,
	And now changed to 'The Beggar and the King'.
	My dangerous cousin, let your mother in, 80
	I know she is come to pray for your foul sin.

After the Duke and Duchess argue about Aumerle's fate all three kneel before King Henry. The Duke still demands that his son be sentenced. The Duchess denies that her husband means what he says.

82–83 If thou do pardon ... may: If you pardon him, regardless of who prays (for his death), more wickedness is likely to be encouraged by your forgiveness

84–85 This festered joint ... confound: If this festering limb (Aumerle), is cut off (executed) the rest of the limbs (i.e. the nation) will remain healthy, but if you do nothing it (he) will destroy the whole body

87 Love loving ... can: a love which does not love itself (and the children which its love begets) cannot love anyone else. She implies that York's love for Bolingbroke should not be trusted

88 what does thou make here?: what are you trying to achieve/doing here?

89 shall thy ... rear?: Do you intend your dry breasts to feed this traitor for a second time?

93 never see ... sees: live in misery. There is a deliberate comparison made by the Duchess between her situation, asking forgiveness of the King, and that of the penitent who lives a life of prayer and cannot share in eternal life (the 'day that the happy sees') until forgiven by God

96 Unto: joining

102 and would be denied: and wishes to be refused

103 and all beside: and everything else

105 still: will always

- *Often in performance the scene changes abruptly from a serious to a comic tone with the arrival of the Duchess. Why might Shakespeare wish to make such a change of mood?*
- *What is the dramatic effect of the rhyming couplets here?*

Enter DUCHESS

YORK   If thou do pardon, whosoever pray,
                More sins for this forgiveness prosper may.
                This festered joint cut off, the rest rest sound;
                This let alone will all the rest confound.

DUCHESS OF YORK   O King, believe not this hard-hearted man.
                Love loving not itself, none other can.

YORK   Thou frantic woman, what dost thou make here?
                Shall thy old dugs once more a traitor rear?

DUCHESS OF YORK   Sweet York be patient. Hear me gentle liege   90
                                    [*Kneels*]

KING HENRY   Rise up good aunt.

DUCHESS OF YORK   Not yet, I thee beseech.
                For ever will I walk upon my knees,
                And never see day that the happy sees
                Till thou give joy, until thou bid me joy
                By pardoning Rutland my transgressing boy.

AUMERLE   Unto my mother's prayers I bend my knee.

                                    [*He kneels*]

YORK   Against them both my true joints bended be.

                                    [*He kneels*]

                Ill mayst thou thrive if thou grant any grace.

DUCHESS OF YORK   Pleads he in earnest? Look upon his face.
                His eyes do drop no tears, his prayers are in jest,   100
                His words come from his mouth, ours from our
                    breast.
                He prays but faintly, and would be denied,
                We pray with heart and soul, and all beside.
                His weary joints would gladly rise I know,
                Our knees still kneel till to the ground they grow.
                His prayers are full of false hypocrisy,
                Ours of true zeal and deep integrity.
                Our prayers do outpray his – then let them have
                That mercy which true prayer ought to have.

The Duchess wants to hear the King say 'pardon'. Even when he does, she makes him repeat the word. The Duchess is as extravagant in her thanks as she was in her pleading. King Henry orders York to seize the other conspirators and threatens their deaths.

112 **An if:** supposing that

116 **short as sweet:** she plays on 'short and sweet' which was proverbial in the sixteenth century

117 **No word like ... meet:** there is no word so appropriate for kings to say than 'pardon'

118 **Pardonne-moi:** pardon me – said in refusing a request.

120 **sour:** bitter – suggested as the antithesis of sweet in line 116, above

121 **That sets the word ... word:** that makes the word contradict itself

123 **chopping:** broken

124–125 **Thine eye ... ear:** I can see what you want to say in your eyes: say it aloud. Listen to what your sympathetic heart says. This couplet is particularly ludicrous – close to Bottom's 'I see a voice' (*A Midsummer Night's Dream* Act 5 scene 1 line 190)

127 **rehearse:** speak aloud

128–129 **I do not sue ... hand:** I do not ask to stand up: my only plea at the moment is for pardon. There is a play on 'suit in hand' as in a game of cards

133 **Twice saying ... twain:** Saying pardon twice does not weaken the pardon by dividing it in two *or* does not pardon two people. While the Duchess intends the former meaning, it inspires Bolingbroke to think of the other conspirators

135 **A god on earth thou art:** though this may seem extravagant, it emphasises both that Bolingbroke's exercise of mercy reflects God's grace to humanity and that he has assumed the mantle of God's anointed associated previously with Richard

136 **our trusty brother-in-law:** Richard II's half-brother, John Holland, Duke of Exeter, husband of Bolingbroke's sister. He is referred to in passing in Act 2 scene 1 line 281. 'Trusty' is ironic

   the abbot: of Westminster. See Act 4 scene 1 lines 321–end

137 **consorted crew:** conspiracy; gang

138 **straight:** immediately

   dog them at the heels: follow them closely; track them down

139 **several powers:** various forces

KING HENRY   Good aunt stand up.

DUCHESS OF YORK   Nay, do not say 'Stand up'.   110
Say 'Pardon' first, and afterwards, 'Stand up'.
An if I were thy nurse thy tongue to teach,
'Pardon' should be the first word of thy speech.
I never longed to hear a word till now.
Say 'Pardon', King, let pity teach thee how.
The word is short, but not so short as sweet.
No word like 'Pardon' for kings' mouths so meet.

YORK   Speak it in French, King, say 'Pardonne-moi'.

DUCHESS OF YORK   Dost thou teach pardon pardon to destroy?
Ah, my sour husband, my hard-hearted lord,   120
That sets the word itself against the word.
Speak 'Pardon' as 'tis current in our land,
The chopping French we do not understand.
Thine eye begins to speak, set thy tongue there;
Or in thy piteous heart plant thou thine ear,
That hearing how our plaints and prayers do pierce,
Pity may move thee 'Pardon' to rehearse.

KING HENRY   Good aunt stand up.

DUCHESS OF YORK   I do not sue to stand.
Pardon is all the suit I have in hand.

KING HENRY   I pardon him, as God shall pardon me.   130

DUCHESS OF YORK   O happy vantage of a kneeling knee,
Yet am I sick for fear. Speak it again.
Twice saying 'Pardon' doth not pardon twain,
But makes one pardon strong.

KING HENRY   With all my heart
I pardon him.

DUCHESS OF YORK   A god on earth thou art.

KING HENRY   But for our trusty brother-in-law and the abbot,
With all the rest of that consorted crew,
Destruction straight shall dog them at the heels.
Good uncle, help to order several powers
To Oxford, or where'er these traitors are.   140

142 **if I once:** when I
145 **make thee new:** free you from sin; make you reborn.
Aumerle inherited his father's title, served King Henry and
his son loyally, and died at the battle of Agincourt where
'with blood he sealed A testament of noble-ending love'
Henry V Act 4 scene 6 lines 26–27

Sir Piers Exton enters. He has heard the King speaking of his
desire for Richard's death. Exton believes that Henry was
suggesting that he should murder him. He decides to go to
Pomfret and kill Richard as a mark of his friendship with
Henry.

  1 **mark:** hear and attend to
  5 **urged it twice together:** said it insistently, twice over
  6 **wishtly:** wistfully; intently; steadfastly; longingly
11 **rid his:** rid him of his

> • *Scene 3 ends with a further sudden change of tone, and*
> *scene 4 introduces an entirely new character to the play.*

> They shall not live within this world, I swear,
> But I will have them if I once know where.
> Uncle farewell, and cousin adieu.
> Your mother well hath prayed, and prove you
> true.

DUCHESS OF YORK   Come my old son, I pray God make thee new.

[*Exeunt*

Scene 4

Enter SIR PIERS EXTON *and* SERVANT

EXTON   Didst thou not mark the King what words he
spake?
'Have I no friend will rid me of this living fear?'
Was it not so?

SERVANT   These were his very words.

EXTON   'Have I no friend?' quoth he. He spake it twice,
And urged it twice together, did he not?

SERVANT   He did.

EXTON   And speaking it, he wishtly looked on me,
As who should say 'I would thou wert the man
That would divorce this terror from my heart' –
Meaning the King at Pomfret. Come let's go.   10
I am the King's friend, and will rid his foe.

[*Exeunt*

In prison and alone Richard imagines populating his cell with thoughts created by his soul and brain. He thinks of heaven, of escape and of happiness.

1 **studying:** here and at line 15 below Richard may refer to a Bible
2 **This prison:** Pontefract (Pomfret) Castle
3 **for because:** because
5 **hammer it out:** work it out; puzzle it out
6 **prove:** put to the test to be
8 **A generation of still breeding thoughts:** offspring in the form of thoughts which will themselves breed other thoughts
10 **In humours:** in their various temperaments
11 **For no thought is contented:** my thoughts are not happy (and neither are the people of the real world)
12 **As:** such as
13 **scruples:** spiritual doubts
the word: the word of God: the Bible, from which the quotations in the next lines come
15–17 **'Come, little ... needle's eye:** The verses on which these words are based can be found in close proximity in Matthew chapter 19 verses 14 and 24 (and in Mark 10 and Luke 18). The verses deal with the ease with which a child may come to God and the difficulty faced by a rich man. Shakespeare's adaptation of the verse seems to suggest that he was aware that *camel* could refer to the animal or to a thick rope and the *needle's eye* was both the hole in the head of the needle and a small entrance for pedestrians – a postern – within a city gate
17 **needle's:** probably pronounced 'neelds' or 'neeles'
18 **tending to ambition:** the ambition of eternal life, but also to escape from prison
20 **flinty ribs:** the walls – compare Act 3 scene 3 line 32
22 **for:** because
in their pride: in their prime of life
23 **content:** happiness
24 **That they are ... slaves:** by accepting that they are not the first to be subject to the whims of fortune
25 **silly:** foolish; simple-minded
26 **refuge their shame:** find protection from the shame they feel
27 **many have:** i.e. many have sat
29–30 **Bearing their ... like:** finding consolation for their suffering in the fact that others before them have suffered in the same way

Scene 5

Enter RICHARD *alone*

RICHARD   I have been studying how I may compare
This prison where I live unto the world;
And for because the world is populous,
And here is not a creature but myself,
I cannot do it. Yet I'll hammer it out.
My brain I'll prove the female to my soul,
My soul the father, and these two beget
A generation of still-breeding thoughts,
And these same thoughts people this little world,
In humours like the people of this world.   10
For no thought is contented. The better sort,
As thoughts of things divine, are intermixed
With scruples, and do set the word itself
Against the word,
As thus: 'Come, little ones'; and then again,
'It is as hard to come as for a camel
To thread the postern of a small needle's eye'.
Thoughts tending to ambition, they do plot
Unlikely wonders: how these vain weak nails
May tear a passage through the flinty ribs   20
Of this hard world, my ragged prison walls;
And for they cannot, die in their own pride.
Thoughts tending to content flatter themselves
That they are not the first of fortune's slaves,
Nor shall not be the last; like silly beggars,
Who sitting in the stocks refuge their shame,
That many have, and others must sit there;
And in this thought they find a kind of ease,
Bearing their own misfortunes on the back
Of such as have before endured the like.   30
Thus play I in one person many people,
And none contented. Sometimes am I king,

Richard realises that he is playing characters in a play of his own invention, but whatever role he takes, he is always mortal. He hears music and thinks of the unharmonious nature of his life. The music's broken rhythm reminds him that he has failed to use time well. Though Richard wants the music to stop, he recognises that it is a gift from someone who still loves him.

34 penury: poverty

39 Nor I ... man is: neither I nor any mere human

40 With nothing shall be pleas'd: shall be happy with having nothing *or* shall be pleased with anything

40–41 eased With being nothing: released by death

43 time is broke and no proportion kept: there is no rhythm and the notes are not held for their correct lengths

45 the daintiness of ear: sufficiently acute hearing

46 check: criticise; rebuke
string: stringed instrument

47–48 for the concord ... broke: in respect of the harmony of my nation during my reign I could not hear how my disorderliness (lack of rhythm) destroyed it

49 wasted, waste: laid waste and disrupted; diminished morally; squandered; allowed to pass; waste away: all senses are present

50 numbering clock: a mere instrument to count the hours

51–54 My thoughts ... tears: This section is impossible to paraphrase but concerns his thoughts which, sad, are heard in his sighs and seen in his tears. His finger wipes the tears away. The thoughts are represented in the clock by the counting of the minutes, his sighs by the jarring noise of the pendulum, his tearful eyes by the face of the clock and the hand that wipes the tears away by the hand of the clock

52 watches, watch: intervals of time; vigils; the clock face

55 Now sir: having peopled his cell with thoughts, Richard imagines himself lecturing them

58 times: periods of time

58–59 But my time ... joy: But my time, like a traveller riding rapidly into a new country, has run into Bolingbroke's proud and joyful era

59 posting on: very rapidly

60 jack of the clock: a figure of a man which strikes the bell on the outside of a clock. Richard sees himself as Bolingbroke's puppet

62 have holp: may have helped. Music restored harmony to disordered minds

66 strange brooch: rare thing of value

Then treasons make me wish myself a beggar,
And so I am. Then crushing penury
Persuades me I was better when a king,
Then am I kinged again; and by and by
Think that I am unkinged by Bolingbroke,
And straight am nothing. But whate'er I be,
Nor I, nor any man that but man is,
With nothing shall be pleased, till he be eased   40
With being nothing. Music do I hear.

[*The music plays*]

Ha, ha; keep time! How sour sweet music is
When time is broke, and no proportion kept.
So is it in the music of men's lives.
And here have I the daintiness of ear
To check time broke in a disordered string,
But for the concord of my state and time,
Had not an ear to hear my true time broke.
I wasted time, and now doth time waste me;
For now hath time made me his numbering clock;   50
My thoughts are minutes, and with sighs they jar
Their watches on unto mine eyes, the outward watch
Whereto my finger like a dial's point,
Is pointing still, in cleansing them from tears.
Now sir, the sound that tells what hour it is
Are clamorous groans which strike upon my heart,
Which is the bell; so sighs, and tears, and groans
Show minutes, times, and hours. But my time
Runs posting on in Bolingbroke's proud joy,
While I stand fooling here, his jack of the clock.   60
This music mads me. Let it sound no more;
For though it have holp madmen to their wits,
In me it seems it will make wise men mad.
Yet blessings on his heart that gives it me,
For 'tis a sign of love; and love to Richard
Is a strange brooch in this all-hating world.

Enter a GROOM *of the stable*

A groom, one of Richard's former servants, visits him. He pities Richard but tells him that even his favourite horse has become Bolingbroke's proud servant. Richard wishes that his horse had thrown Bolingbroke and killed him. A gaoler, the keeper of the prison, enters with food and the groom leaves.

67 **peer:** equal; nobleman – both senses are present since the groom is now as much a nobleman as Richard is a royal prince

68 **ten groats:** a groat was worth 4d (4 old pence). A royal was a coin worth ten shillings (120d) and a noble was worth six shillings and eight pence (80d) – the difference between the two therefore being ten groats (three shillings and fourpence or 40d). However, 'royal' Richard values his life less than that of the 'noble' groom

69 **What art thou?:** who are you?

70 **no man never:** the double negative construction is used for emphasis
dog: 'a worthless, despicable, surly or cowardly fellow' (OED)

71 **make misfortune live:** force me to stay alive in my misfortune

75 **sometimes royal master's face:** the face of my formerly-royal master

76 **earned:** grieved

78 **roan Barbary:** a Barbary was a valuable breed of horse as well perhaps as the name of his specific horse. *Roan* describes the coat in which the main colour – usually chestnut – is mixed with white or grey. The significance of the groom's account is to indicate the extent to which Richard's supporters have deserted him

80 **dressed:** groomed

85 **jade:** nag; worthless beast
eat: eaten. Probably pronounced *et*

86 **clapping him:** i.e. slapping or patting him as he was riding

89 **usurp his back:** wrongfully mount him. 'Usurp' is most often used to describe the act of seizing power from a rightful authority

90 **rail on:** abuse

91 **awed by:** in awe of

94 **galled:** blistered and made sore by hard riding
jauncing: prancing

SD *meat:* food

95 **here is no longer stay:** you cannot stay here any longer

> • *What, do you think, is the dramatic purpose of the groom's appearance?*

GROOM	Hail royal prince.
RICHARD	Thanks noble peer.

The cheapest of us is ten groats too dear.
What art thou, and how comest thou hither,
Where no man never comes but that sad dog   70
That brings me food to make misfortune live?

GROOM	I was a poor groom of thy stable, King,

When thou wert king; who travelling towards York
With much ado at length have gotten leave
To look upon my sometimes royal master's face.
O how it earned my heart when I beheld
In London streets, that coronation day,
When Bolingbroke rode on roan Barbary,
That horse that thou so often hast bestrid,
That horse that I so carefully have dressed.   80

RICHARD	Rode he on Barbary? Tell me gentle friend.

How went he under him?

GROOM	So proudly as if he disdained the ground.

RICHARD	So proud that Bolingbroke was on his back?

That jade hath eat bread from my royal hand,
This hand hath made him proud with clapping him.
Would he not stumble, would he not fall down –
Since pride must have a fall – and break the neck
Of that proud man that did usurp his back?
Forgiveness, horse – why do I rail on thee,   90
Since thou, created to be awed by man,
Wast born to bear? I was not made a horse,
And yet I bear a burden like an ass,
Spurred, galled, and tired by jauncing Bolingbroke.

Enter KEEPER *to* RICHARD *with meat*

KEEPER	Fellow, give place, here is no longer stay.

RICHARD	If thou love me, 'tis time thou wert away.

GROOM	What my tongue dares not, that my heart shall say.

[*Exit*

The gaoler has been instructed by Exton not to taste
Richard's food for poison. When Richard strikes the gaoler
Exton and his men enter and assault Richard. Richard kills
some of Exton's men but is himself struck down. Exton is
immediately shocked by what he has done.

99 **taste of it first:** the King's food was tasted, or assayed, as a
precaution against poison
as thou art wont to do: as you usually do

103 **is stale:** has lost its novelty or interest

SD *strikes the* KEEPER: according to Holinshed he attacked the
keeper with a carving knife

105 **what means death ... assault:** While this could be
rhetorical and indicate 'what does Death mean by assaulting
me so barbarously' the word 'means' could be addressed to
the murderers and the line could be very fragmented,
accompanied as it is by violent action: 'What meanest
thou ... '
rude: barbarous; violent – the word had stronger
connotations then than now

106 **Villain ... instrument:** according to Holinshed Richard
was attacked by Sir Pierce Exton and eight men. They were
armed with bills – very long shafts bearing axe heads or
blades. Richard wrung the bill from the hands of the first to
attack him and killed four of the others with it before Sir
Pierce, hiding in Richard's own chair, pole-axed him as he
passed

SD The stage directions here are not in the Folio or Quarto
and are conjectural

109 **staggers thus my person:** that causes my body to totter
and reel. Here and in the next three lines Richard makes a
final assertion of his royalty: by talking to himself in the
third person he emphasises the separation between his
earthly, fallible body and his immortal, consecrated soul

112 **gross:** impure; earthly (as opposed to the spiritual)

114 **O would:** if only

118 **the rest:** the men that Richard had killed, this line being an
instruction to the surviving murderers.

> • *What is the dramatic effect here of the various entrances
> and exits, and Richard's attack on the Keeper?*
> • *How do you react to Richard's final speech? Some critics
> consider it weak and merely conventional. Even if it is,
> does this matter?*

KEEPER	My lord, will't please you to fall to?
RICHARD	Taste of it first as thou art wont to do.
KEEPER	My lord I dare not. Sir Piers of Exton, 100 Who lately came from the King, commands the contrary.
RICHARD	The devil take Henry of Lancaster, and thee! Patience is stale, and I am weary of it. <div align="right">[*Strikes the* KEEPER</div>
KEEPER	Help, help, help! *Enter the murderers,* EXTON *and* SERVANTS
RICHARD	How now, what means death in this rude assault? Villain, thy own hand yields thy death's instrument. [*He snatches a weapon from a* SERVANT *and kills him*] Go thou and fill another room in hell. [*He kills another* SERVANT. *Then* EXTON *strikes him down*]
RICHARD	That hand shall burn in never-quenching fire That staggers thus my person. Exton, thy fierce hand Hath with the King's blood stained the King's own land. 110 Mount, mount, my soul, thy seat is up on high, Whilst my gross flesh sinks downwards here to die. <div align="right">[*Dies*</div>
EXTON	As full of valour as of royal blood. Both have I spilled. O would the deed were good! For now the devil, that told me I did well, Says that this deed is chronicled in hell. This dead King to the living King I'll bear. Take hence the rest, and give them burial here. <div align="right">[*Exeunt*</div>

King Henry is dealing with the conspiracy against him. The rebels seem to be having some success, but Northumberland and Fitzwater report that the revolt has been put down. Percy reports that the Abbot of Westminster has died and he brings the Bishop of Carlisle to be sentenced. King Henry is merciful and orders him only to find a monastery in which to live out his life.

 2 **the rebels:** i.e. those involved in the Abbot of
   Westminster's conspiracy
 3 **Ciceter:** Cirencester, which was (and sometimes still is)
   pronounced like this
 8 **The heads ... Kent:** according to Holinshed the heads of
   the conspirators were set upon poles on London Bridge.
   The Quarto inaccurately includes 'Oxford' in this list of
   rebels
 9 **manner of their taking:** way they were captured
10 **at large discoursed:** described in detail
14 **Brocas:** Sir Leonard Brokas
15 **Consorted:** associated; conspiring
18 **I wot:** I know
20 **With clog of:** weighed down by the burden of
   sour melancholy: bitter black bile – one of the humours
   which, in excess, gave rise to depression
22 **Carlisle:** brought to answer for his speech in Act 4 scene 1
   lines 114–152
   abide: await submissively. The remainder of the scene is in
   rhyming couplets
23 **doom:** judgement
25–26 **some reverend room ... life:** some monastic cell, more
   worthy than the prison cell you now live in, and enjoy it as
   best you can

> • *Our attitude towards Henry as King is governed not only*
>   *by the way in which he behaves but by the attitude of the*
>   *nobles towards him. How do they behave towards him*
>   *here?*

Scene 6

Flourish. Enter KING HENRY, *the* DUKE OF YORK,
other LORDS, *and* ATTENDANTS

KING HENRY   Kind uncle York, the latest news we hear
Is that the rebels have consumed with fire
Our town of Ciceter in Gloucestershire,
But whether they be ta'en or slain we hear not.

Enter NORTHUMBERLAND

Welcome my lord. What is the news?

NORTHUMBERLAND   First, to thy sacred state wish I all happiness.
The next news is, I have to London sent
The heads of Salisbury, Spencer, Blunt, and Kent.
The manner of their taking may appear
At large discoursed in this paper here.   10

KING HENRY   We thank thee gentle Percy for thy pains;
And to thy worth will add right worthy gains.

Enter FITZWATER

FITZWATER   My lord, I have from Oxford sent to London
The heads of Brocas and Sir Bennet Seely,
Two of the dangerous consorted traitors
That sought at Oxford thy dire overthrow.

KING HENRY   Thy pains Fitzwater shall not be forgot.
Right noble is thy merit well I wot.

Enter PERCY *with the* BISHOP OF CARLISLE, *guarded*

PERCY   The grand conspirator Abbot of Westminster
With clog of conscience and sour melancholy   20
Hath yielded up his body to the grave.
But here is Carlisle living to abide
Thy kingly doom and sentence of his pride.

KING HENRY   Carlisle, this is your doom:
Choose out some secret place, some reverend room
More than thou hast, and with it joy thy life.

Exton enters with the body of Richard. King Henry is not grateful, realising that the murder of Richard will damage his reputation. He banishes Exton from his sight, promising to mourn Richard and to go on a pilgrimage to the Holy Land in order to purge his guilt.

27 **So as thou ... strife:** the more peacefully you can live, the more peaceful will be your death

31 **Thy buried fear:** compare Act 5 scene 4 line 2, where Exton quotes Bolingbroke's references to Richard as his 'living fear'

33 **of Bordeaux:** the title by which he was known before his accession to the throne, from the place of his birth

35 **A deed of slander:** a shameful and discreditable act; something of ill-repute

38 **They love not ... need:** related to a proverb 'Kings may love treason but hate the traitor'

43 **Cain:** Having murdered his brother Abel, Cain was cursed by God to be 'a fugitive and vagabond' (Genesis 5, verse 12). Compare also Bolingbroke's accusation that Mowbray's murder of Gloucester was 'like sacrificing Abel's', and Mowbray's opinion of his banishment that he would 'dwell in solemn shades of endless night' (Act 1 scene 3 line 177)

48 **sullen:** solemn; gloomy
    incontinent: immediately

49 **I'll make ... Holy Land:** a further link to *1 Henry IV* which begins with Bolingbroke repeating his intention to go on a Crusade – an intention which is not fulfilled

50 **To wash ... hand:** compare Act 3 scene 1 lines 5–6

51 **grace my mournings here:** honour me by joining me in mourning

52 **bier:** literally, the stand on which a coffin is placed but used here as a figure of speech (synecdoche) to represent death

---

- *Henry's words are less an obituary for Richard than an expression of his own guilt. What emotions do you think we are expected to feel at the end of the play?*

So as thou livest in peace, die free from strife;
For though mine enemy thou hast ever been,
High sparks of honour in thee have I seen.

Enter EXTON *with the coffin*

EXTON   Great King, within this coffin I present   30
           Thy buried fear. Herein all breathless lies
           The mightiest of thy greatest enemies,
           Richard of Bordeaux, by me hither brought.

KING HENRY Exton, I thank thee not, for thou hast wrought
           A deed of slander with thy fatal hand
           Upon my head and all this famous land.

EXTON   From your own mouth my lord, did I this deed.

KING HENRY They love not poison that do poison need,
           Nor do I thee. Though I did wish him dead,
           I hate the murderer, love him murdered.   40
           The guilt of conscience take thou for thy labour,
           But neither my good word nor princely favour.
           With Cain go wander thorough shades of night,
           And never show thy head by day nor light.
           Lords, I protest my soul is full of woe
           That blood should sprinkle me to make me grow.
           Come mourn with me for what I do lament,
           And put on sullen black incontinent.
           I'll make a voyage to the Holy Land
           To wash this blood off from my guilty hand.   50
           March sadly after, grace my mournings here
           In weeping after this untimely bier.   [*Exeunt*

Keeping track

Scene 1

1 What advice does Richard give Isabel to help her to cope with their fall from power?
2 How, according to Isabel, should Richard behave in response to his humiliation?
3 What news does Northumberland bring to Richard and Isabel?
4 How is Richard now 'doubly divorced'?

Scene 2

1 In what contrasting ways does the crowd react to Richard and to Bolingbroke on their entry into London?
2 Why has Aumerle been deprived of his title?
3 What is the intention of the conspiracy of which Aumerle (Rutland) is part?

Scene 3

1 Why is King Henry concerned about his son?
2 Why does Henry forgive Aumerle?
3 What sentence does Henry pass on the rest of the conspirators?

Scene 4

1 What phrase has Henry used which convinces Exton that he should kill Richard at Pomfret?

Scene 5

1 What does the groom tell the imprisoned Richard which only emphasises the extent of his betrayal?
2 What does the Keeper refuse to do?
3 What is uncharacteristic about Richard's behaviour from line 102 until his death?

Scene 6

1 Why does Henry save Carlisle from execution?
2 Why does Henry lament Richard's murder?

Characters

King Richard

- As Richard approaches death he becomes aware of the extent to which he has contributed to his downfall. What is the evidence for this?
- Richard is portrayed as being less self-obsessed in this last Act. How is his growing awareness of others exemplified?

Bolingbroke

- Bolingbroke begins to confront the realities of being a king, and one who has attained the throne by questionable means.
1 What are the signs in this Act that King Henry IV will be more successful than his predecessor?
2 What personal and spiritual price is the new king already beginning to pay at the end of the play?

Aumerle

- Aumerle first conspires against Henry on Richard's behalf but soon betrays his fellow conspirators in order to save his own skin. How would you characterise his behaviour? Is he either politically astute or cynical, or just a dutiful young man doing as his parents tell him, or would you make some other judgement on him?

Duke of York

- In this Act York is entirely loyal to Bolingbroke. Review his actions and suggest why you think that he behaves in the way that he does.

Northumberland

- Richard suggests that Northumberland is bound to be dissatisfied with Bolingbroke as King.
1 What is characteristic about Northumberland's reply (scene 1 lines 69–70)?
2 How does his response differ from that of either Bolingbroke or Richard when they consider the effects of their actions at various points during this Act?

Queen Isabel
- We are familiar with the 'weeping queen' from earlier Acts, but what other aspects of her character are introduced or emphasised in scene 1?

Themes

1 **Consequences** In the **Explorations** which follow this section we will consider the theme of causation and what the play has to say about this. By way of preparation, and as we review this last Act, make a list of all the ways in which things have changed between the beginning and the end of the play. Start by listing all the characters and noting what has happened to them. Then describe the political and psychological changes that have taken place.

2 **Vanity** Richard tells his wife to *'think our former state a happy dream'* and much of Act 5 is concerned with ways in which life offers only a passing happiness. The word 'vanity' was used rather differently in Elizabethan times from today. It implied that human ambition for power, wealth, glory or beauty was vain because everything passes and human life is all too brief.
- What other references to this theme of the vanity of human life and behaviour can you find in Act 5?
- How far do you think Bolingbroke is affected by the realisation of his own mortality?

Drama

1 **Scene 3 lines 22–145** The aim here is to consider how far this scene has a serious purpose and how far it is a comic interlude. Work in groups of five. One person is the narrator and the others are Bolingbroke, Aumerle, York and the Duchess. While the narrator reads the scene the cast mimes the action. Pause at intervals and ask the characters, especially Bolingbroke, to say what they are thinking. Good places to pause would be lines 24, 39, 72, 81, 110 and 136. At each point also consider what the tone of the scene is and what emotion you would wish to communicate to the audience.

2 **Scene 6 lines 30–52** Exton enters the court with the body of Richard. Use the whole group to create a tableau of this moment. Cast the named characters – everyone else can be the 'other Lords and attendants'.

- Ask each person to say in one word or a short phrase what their feelings are at the moment when Exton appears with the body and says his first sentence.
- Read the scene to line 38 – does anyone feel any different about the situation now?
- Read to the end of the scene. Ask each person again to express their feelings.
- Improvise some dialogue as the King exits. Does anyone speak to Exton or attempt to argue with the King? Who might be planning what?

Close study

Act 5 scene 1
At the end of Act 3 scene 4 (the Garden scene) the Queen resolved to go to London to meet Richard.

1 What is the significance of the Queen's references to Richard as her *'fair rose'* and as a *'model'*, *'tomb'* and *'inn'* (lines 8–15)? How do these images contrast with those she uses in lines 29–34?
2 Richard offers Isabel words of consolation (lines 16–50). What does he suggest she should do? His advice is largely conventional – the type of consolation offered in many Christian books from antiquity onwards. What are the indications that his advice is, however, deeply felt and motivated by his love for her?
3 Richard prophesies Northumberland's future behaviour. How does this relate to the prophecy of Carlisle in the previous Act?
4 Lines 78–102 are rhyming couplets and the verse is characterised by end-stopped lines and *stychomythia* (see Glossary page 246).
 - Why are these appropriate here?
 - What actions accompany the lines?
5 How does Shakespeare acknowledge the emotional intensity of this scene by the way he begins the next?

Key scene

Act 5 scene 5
Shakespeare's audience will have been familiar with the story of the murder of Richard, and the previous brief scene with Exton ensures that the events here come as no surprise. Scene 5 concludes a process by which all the trappings of kingship have been stripped from Richard. He is bereft of power, freedom, friends and relatives.

Keying it in

1   Remind yourself of Richard's speech and behaviour in Act 1 scene 1.
    Read lines 1–30 and 190–205. What mood and tone characterise these
    lines? Are there any apparent differences with the way in which he
    speaks in act 5 scene 5?

The scene itself

2   **Lines 1–41**
    Richard has acted a series of parts throughout the play. Here, where he
    is his only audience, he imagines a whole cast of characters in his mind
    (line 31).
    • This speech is dominated by one *conceit* (see Glossary). What is the
      comparison Richard makes?
    • He notes that neither his thoughts nor the people of the world are
      happy (lines 10–11). What are the two ways in which, he says,
      people may find *ease*?

3   **Lines 41–66**
    When Richard hears music we are reminded that, conventionally, this
    was a symbol of harmony and order both on earth and in heaven.
    Remind yourself of Gaunt's statement about music in Act 2 scene 1 line
    6. Music was used to restore the minds of the distressed and to
    represent a return to normality. The music here suits his condition by
    being disordered. It is the rhythm which is wrong, reminding him of
    the way in which time has mistreated him and that he has himself
    wasted time.
        Why, despite the inadequacy of the music, does he welcome it? How
    does Shakespeare use the music to show that Richard is not entirely self-
    obsessed?

4   **Lines 67–97**
    The episode with the groom may seem an irrelevance. The groom
    means well but his tale of Barbary is misplaced. He does however serve
    to distract Richard from his grief.
    • How does he do this?
    • How does the groom further extend our sympathy for Richard?

5   **Lines 98–118**
    In a play which chronicles a revolution, and in which so many people
    die, this is the one moment of violent action and death on stage. Earlier
    in the Act Isabel complains that Richard has not thrust 'forth his paw'
    like the enraged lion. Now he is roused, first by the groom's story, then
    by the Keeper and his refusal to taste the food.

- How does the imagery of Richard's final speech continue references with which we have become familiar throughout the play?
- What is the dramatic impact of Exton's immediate guilt at the death of Richard?

Overview

6 If Richard is a failure as a king, on the personal level there seem to be qualities to admire in him.
   - What characterises his behaviour in this scene?
   - How far is the Richard with which we are presented in this scene a believable development of the man we have witnessed previously?

Writing

1 Write Aumerle's account of events in Act 5. Try to suggest what his motivation is for his change of loyalties and have him reflect upon the characters of the two kings and the behaviour of his parents.

2 What happens next? This play is the beginning of a cycle of eight plays – four of which Shakespeare had already written when he started *Richard II*. Whether or not you know any of these subsequent plays, show what you think will happen to three of the key characters.
   - Choose from Bolingbroke, York, Aumerle, Queen Isabel and Northumberland.
   - Write your account in the first person.
   - Make your characters recount the things which may have happened to them after the end of Shakespeare's play.
   - Have them reflect upon the ways in which the reign of Richard II influenced their lives.
   - Make them comment on anything they regret in their own behaviour and in that of others.

3 *Sir Piers of Exton and the mark of Cain.*
   In old age Sir Piers writes his autobiography, seeking to explain his life and influences upon it. In your account you could develop some of the themes explored by Richard in Act 5 scene 5 lines 1–40. He might, for example, have had 'thoughts tending to ambition' which were later replaced by 'thoughts divine'. He might now be considering whether his life has led to contentment or whether he 'with nothing shall be pleased till he be eased with being nothing'. You could also refer to Act 1 to see how Bolingbroke and Mowbray faced the prospect of exile. In conclusion, Sir Piers could reflect upon whether the murder of a king is ever justified, and whether the murderer can find forgiveness in this world or the next.

Explorations

A question of approach

As you study this play you will find that you begin to understand it from several different perspectives simultaneously.

- At first, you are likely to have been concerned most about the narrative.
- Then you will have begun to think about the thoughts and feelings of the various characters.
- You will have started to consider the writer's purpose through thinking about some of the themes and issues of the play.
- You will have become aware of the technical aspects of dramatic construction.
- You will have been considering how language is the raw material from which the play and its dramatic effect is fashioned.
- You may have considered some of the contexts in which the play exists and how its performance and meaning have changed over time.

The *Explorations* that follow will allow you to consider each of these perspectives. They will also help you to make clear your understanding in the context of examinations and coursework essays.

A play is essentially an audio-visual experience

No two members of the audience see quite the same play and no two performances are ever exactly the same. Two important lessons follow from this:

- The printed text is not the play; the play is what you see when you go to the theatre. The text is a set of instructions to be interpreted by the director and actors, artists and technicians.
- There is no one 'right answer' to the play, but rather a range of possible interpretations. Your view can be just as valid as anyone else's, but only if you can present it clearly and support it by valid arguments derived from the text.

Thinking about the play

By the time you have discussed the text carefully and seen or visualised a performance, you should be beginning to clarify and organise your response to the play as a whole. Most examination questions concentrate on *content* and *form,* and these are useful terms which offer you an approach and a framework within which you can prepare to write successfully.

- Establish clearly in your mind the broad issues raised by the text and the possible areas for discussion.
- Consider and discuss some of the possible views and interpretations of these issues.
- Be clear about your personal view and lay down a sensible framework of knowledge and argument within which your personal response can be convincing.
- Identify the key incidents, scenes and quotations which will form the basis of an essay.
- Make notes and organise them so that the appropriate textual evidence and illustrations are easily available when you come to write an essay.

Character

Judging a character can never simply be a case of putting together all the evidence of the written word and drawing conclusions. It is more complicated than that.

Characters are revealed by:

- What they say to other characters
- How they behave.

Problems

Characters are rarely consistent.

1 Major characters (such as Richard and Bolingbroke) are subject to change because the events in which the action of the play is based are significant enough to affect the main protagonists: the more important the character, the closer to the action, the greater the reaction.
2 Characters might say or do things for effect: they might be seeking to impress or mislead someone else and not mean what they say at all. We may have to consider whether a character is being sincere or has an ulterior motive. For example, consider the behaviour of Richard during Act 1.
   - In what ways is he neither open nor honest in his dealings with Mowbray and Bolingbroke in scenes 1 and 3?

Characters are also revealed by:

- What other characters say about them
- How other characters behave towards them.

Problems

As in life, whether you accept A's opinion of B depends on how you feel about A. If you believe that A is untrustworthy or has a perverse sense of values, then A's criticism of B might prove to be a glowing character reference. Alternatively, an opinion might either be based on false information or be deliberately misleading. It is essential not to accept one character's opinion of another on face value. For example, Gaunt is savagely critical of Richard, but we need to consider whether the reason for this is entirely of Richard's making. Another tricky character is Northumberland.

- Are there examples of moments when Northumberland's words and actions are apparently dishonest?

Characters are also revealed by:

- Soliloquies
- Asides.

This may be the best way to assess a character's personality since he or she is sharing thoughts and feelings with the audience. All pretence is dropped because other characters are not involved. For example, Richard's soliloquy in Act 5 scene 5 is one of the most revealing moments in the play.

- What revealing asides can you find in Act 4?

Critical moments

At critical moments in the play you can begin to gain insight into character by seeking answers to certain questions. There is no formula that will apply to every situation, but these questions can start you off and might lead you to consider other questions of your own:

- What has the character said or done?
- What is significant about the way in which the character speaks?
- Why has the character said or done this?
- What will happen as a result of this speech or action?
- Could or should these reactions have been avoided?
- What does this incident tell us about the character?
- How does the character change as a result of this incident?

You could try the 'Critical moment' approach by applying these questions, and others which may suggest themselves to you, to Act 1 scene 3 line 139 – the moment at which Richard banishes Bolingbroke and Mowbray.

Characters in Richard II

Richard

Commenting on 'Mine ear is open and my heart prepared' (Act 3 scene 2 line 93), Dr Johnson wrote in 1765:

> It seems to be the design of the poet to raise Richard to esteem in his fall and consequently to interest the reader in his favour. He gives him only passive fortitude, the virtue of a confessor rather than of a king. In his prosperity we saw him imperious and oppressive; but in his distress he is wise, patient and pious.

Several questions follow from this.
- In what ways does Richard lack the qualities that would make him an effective monarch? Would you characterise him as 'imperious and oppressive'?
- Is Richard 'raised to esteem in his fall'? What qualities, if any, do you find admirable in him as he falls?
- Is his fortitude merely passive? If it is, do you consider that a weakness? Consider what Queen Isabel says about this in Act 5 scene 1.
- How far is Richard 'wise, patient and pious' at the end of the play? What is the evidence that he acquires these characteristics in the course of the action of the play?
- What elements of Richard's character are not summarised by Dr Johnson's comments? For example, is it true that Richard demonstrates a love of the poetic in his speech? What is the evidence that he is more concerned with striking public poses than acting in a judicous and effective manner?

Bolingbroke

Bolingbroke becomes King Henry IV, and his reign is Shakespeare's subject for two further plays. On his death bed, at the end of *2 Henry IV* (Act 4 scene 3 lines 312–324) he tells his son:

> *God knows, my son,*
> *By what bypaths and indirect and crooked ways*
> *I met this crown; and I myself know well*
> *How troublesome it sat upon my head ...*
> *   It seemed in me*
> *But as an honour snatched with boisterous hand;*
> *And I had many living to upbraid*
> *My gain of it by their assistances,*
> *Which daily grew to quarrel and to bloodshed,*
> *Wounding supposed peace.*

- Summarise the evidence that Bolingbroke 'met this crown' by 'indirect and crooked ways'. How far does Shakespeare present Bolingbroke as actively seeking the crown? Is is true that the best evidence of Bolingbroke's success as a political schemer is that he never seems to be ambitious for the crown?
- Bolingbroke attains the crown unlawfully. The abdication is little more than a legal fiction and Henry becomes king by right of conquest. There is evidence within the play that he will make a more decisive king than Richard and that his subjects welcome him. To approve a monarch who, without apparent rightful title to the throne, succeeds by a coup was, however, politically unacceptable in Shakespeare's time. Where do you think the playwright's sympathies lie: for Bolingbroke or against him?

In Act 4 scene 1 line 196 Richard says 'Your care is gain of care, by new care won'. By the end of *2 Henry IV* Bolingbroke is aware that the dire prophecies of Richard (and Carlisle) have come true. On the political level the *Henry IV* plays are concerned largely with '*quarrel ... bloodshed, Wounding supposed peace*'. Bolingbroke never makes pilgrimage to Jerusalem to expiate his guilt at the death of Richard. His spiritual state, like his kingdom, is doomed to disorder because he engineers the death of God's anointed king.

John of Gaunt

Gaunt's speech in Act 2 scene 1 is one of the most common Shakespearean quotations, though often used out of context. He appears to offer an uncomplicated paean of praise to his country but, as a recent critic has suggested, Gaunt 'is not a disinterested apologist for England. He has an agenda of his own'. (*The Genius of Shakespeare*, J Bate, 1997). It is worth remembering that Gaunt was a son of Edward III, a rival to his brother, Edward the Black Prince and, following his brother's death, the most powerful man in England.

What is Gaunt's 'agenda' in *Richard II*? What does he wish to achieve for his family? What does he have to lose by Richard's reign? How far is there evidence that he really cares for England at all?

Aumerle

- Review the role of Aumerle in the play. Summarise his appearances on stage. You should find that he appears in a large number of scenes, but what dramatic purpose does he fill? One way of determining this is to consider what would happen if his role were missing entirely. Richard would be without a confidant at several important moments in the play. Nor would he have a supporter who is both likeable and motivated to act.
- What qualities do you find in Aumerle's character?
- Does he sacrifice principle for personal survival at the end of the play? Do you approve of his actions?

  Aumerle reappears briefly in *Henry V*. He is by then the Duke of York, in succession to his father. He is 'brave York', and dies in the service of Bolingbroke's son, leading the vanguard at the Battle of Agincourt.

The Duke of York

York represents the political and familial dilemmas that run throughout the play. As a son of Edward III and an elder statesman he is pictured as having the safety of both family and realm at heart. He feels for his brother, John of Gaunt, but we see him attempting to pour oil on troubled waters in Act 2 scene 1 when Gaunt harangues Richard. He wants everyone in the family to get along together. He is moved by Gaunt's death: 'Be York the next that must be bankrupt so!' he reflects, seeming to have a premonition of the disinheriting of Bolingbroke. Though he complains bitterly to Richard about this injustice, the king makes him Governor of England when he leaves for Ireland 'For he is just and always loved us well.'

- Catalogue York's reactions to the events of the play.
- What would you say are the principles by which he lives? When these principles conflict with each other, which take precedence?
- Do you think Shakespeare intended us to view York as 'just' and as a man to be admired?
- The way in which York is played can have a significant effect upon the impact of the play. Should York be portrayed as ineffectual and weak, or as a skilled politician who survives, and ensures the survival of this family, by having greater foresight at every twist and turn of events?

Northumberland

Northumberland is perhaps the closest the play comes to having a villain. We have noted on several occasions the role he plays in respect of Bolingbroke. There is no doubt that he wishes to see Richard removed and Bolingbroke on the throne. When there are disagreeable things to be said, especially to Richard himself, Northumberland is sent to say them. Thus Shakespeare deflects some of the antipathy we might otherwise feel towards Bolingbroke.

Subsequently, as Richard prophesies in Act 5 scene 1 lines 55–68, Northumberland rebels against Bolingbroke. The two parts of *Henry IV* are dominated by the civil war he engenders. Shakespeare certainly had this in mind while writing *Richard II*. In 2 *Henry IV* Warwick reminds the King – the former Bolingbroke – that:

King Richard might create a perfect guess
That great Northumberland, then false to him,
Would of that seed grow to a greater falseness,
Which should not find a ground to root upon
Unless on you.

(Act 3 scene 1 lines 83–87)

However, Northumberland is persuaded to quit the rebellion and thus betrays his own side. Henry hears of Northumberland's final defeat just as his own mortal illness takes hold. The fates of both Northumberland and Bolingbroke are thus bound together through three plays.

• How does Shakespeare prepare his audience for the future scheming and dishonesty of Northumberland by the way that he portrays him in *Richard II*?

Queen Isabel

Richard II may seem a very masculine play to the modern audience. Almost all the characters are male and the few female characters are given no opportunity to influence events. Apart from the plot, which revolves entirely round the desires of its principal male characters, two other reasons present themselves.

First, the Elizabethan theatre did not use female actors – modesty and social expectation forbade it – so female roles were played by young men. Secondly, the drama is essentially one of political intrigue and chivalric action, neither of which allowed much opportunity (in the context of the time) for women to make their mark on events. Yet in the two parts of *Henry IV* women play a much greater part, partly because Shakespeare creates a moving relationship between Henry Percy and his wife and because the plays are dominated by Falstaff who is given a female foil in Mistress Quickly.

In *Richard II* the Duchesses of Gloucester and of York have brief, angry, outbursts while Isabel's several appearances climax in a moving final scene with her husband. However, her language rarely rises above conventional speech.

- What dramatic purpose is served by the character of Queen Isabel?
- In theory the Queen is superfluous to the action. Even the Garden scene could be played without her. What would be missing from the play if it were staged without Isabel?

The minor characters
The play has a large number of minor characters who may speak little or have only one major scene. The list includes Bushy, Green and Bagot, Salisbury, Thomas Mowbray, the Gardener, the Bishop of Carlisle, Sir Piers of Exton, and the Duchesses of Gloucester and of York. Shakespeare has a number of reasons for including these characters:

- They are essential to the narrative (perhaps because they were key historical characters)
- They offer a contrasting opinion of the major characters
- They articulate a point of view which would otherwise be unheard
- They have symbolic significance.

Though they are not fully developed characters and may show little or no development during the course of the play, they do offer alternative ways of looking at the world of the play and the values of its protagonists.

- Show why each of the minor characters listed above has a significant role in the play. What would be missing if Shakespeare had not included each of the characters? If you were producing the play with a very small company of actors, which if any of them would you choose to cut, and why?

Themes

Causation

Are we the authors of our own lives? All the principal characters have to face this question. Death, separation, a change of status, new alliances, exile and spiritual desolation are all personal consequences of the events of the play and the main characters are left with the question of how far they have control over events.

The play starts in a world of apparent certainties. Formal chivalry and a strong sense of law dominate the first Act and the speeches of John of Gaunt. By the end, however, a king and several other characters are dead while others believe national disaster awaits.

- Make a list of all the major changes that take place during the course of the play.
- How far do consequences flow from human decisions and will, how far are they the result of chance and accident? Consider the list you have made and indicate which of the changes are examples of purpose and which are examples of humanity being 'fortune's slaves'.
- Where do you think Shakespeare's sympathies lie: does he regard his characters as victims of fate or the authors of their own downfall or triumph, or both?

Time

While in some respects the play is based on classical models of tragic drama, it also refers back to an English tradition of morality plays. We have referred on several occasions to the way in which it is about good government. Another moral aspect with which it is concerned is the notion of using time well.

'I wasted time and now doth time waste me' says Richard, in his moving soliloquy about time in Act 5 scene 5 (lines 41–60) and we are often reminded of the significance of time in the play.

- Sometimes there is ironically bad timing: the news of Bolingbroke's return arrives just after Richard has departed for Ireland, for example.
- For some characters time simply runs out: this happens to both Mowbray and the Duchess of Gloucester.

- Richard fails to seize the appropriate time. The Gardener notes that he and his fellows do their tasks 'at time of year' while Richard's fall has been the consequence of 'waste of idle hours' (Act 3 scene 4 lines 55–66).
- It is all the more ironic, therefore, that the symbol with which Richard most associates himself is the sun, the great enumerator of human time.
- Bolingbroke, on the other hand, demonstrates the capacity to seize the time and profit from each unforgiving moment. He notes what can be achieved by 'the breath of kings' and never seems to hesitate.

1 Collect together references in the play to time and the consequences of human subjugation to time.
2 What lessons do the major characters, and by extension the audience, learn about the use of time?

The language of the play

Verse

The first linguistic challenge which the play offers the reader or performer is that, unusually for Shakespeare, it is written entirely in verse. Much of the play is blank verse (see Glossary) but it also contains a large number of heroic couplets (rhyming iambic pentameters), and some sections of verse are structured like fragments of a sonnet. The style of this verse is rhetorical: highly artificial and designed for emotional impact. Richard's verse in Acts 3 and 5 demonstrates the power of Shakespeare's poetry, especially in his monologues and soliloquies. At other moments the verse may seem less flexible, particularly in dialogue. Some of the rhyming couplets in Act 5 scene 3, for example, seem very weak.

- Look at the short Act 2 scene 4. Rhyming couplets, which have an almost inevitable sense of finality, are used to mark the departure of each of the characters. Most of the lines in this scene are end-stopped. That is, the sense of a line does not run over into the next line, and each line is a complete phrase or clause. These two features make the scene lack naturalism: it feels artificial and is rather difficult to speak as dialogue. However, the very strong rhythm does lend a sense of gravity to the moment.
- Consider Act 1 scene 3 lines 208–248. What is the dramatic impact of Shakespeare's use of blank verse and heroic couplets in this section? How does he use rhythmical variation to increase the emotional impact?

Shakespeare makes little distinction between characters through their mode of speech: this was an aspect of his writing which he was to develop in his later plays. The Gardener and the Groom speak in verse forms which have nothing to differentiate them from that of the play's Dukes and Duchesses.

Imagery

We have noted several recurring images in the play. In performance we may gradually become tuned in to the power of metaphor. We become aware that we are being asked to view the world of the play through a particular linguistic perspective:

> *Like perspectives, which rightly gazed upon*
> *Show nothing but confusion, eyed awry*
> *Distinguish form*
> (Act 2 scene 2 lines 18–20)

Three perspective pictures (among others) which colour the world of the play are:
- biblical imagery
- the sun
- the garden.

1 Biblical imagery

The language and stories of the Bible and the theology flowing from them, were more familiar to the audience of Shakespeare's time than to our own. The choice of reference in *Richard II* is significant.

- Read the story of Adam, the Garden of Eden, and Cain and Abel contained in Genesis chapters 2, 3 and 4. These stories are concerned with the Judaeo-Christian explanation of human suffering. God created humanity to live in happiness in a perfect world, but temptations, human greed, and jealousy led to exclusion from the Garden. Adam and Eve and their descendants are doomed to wander the Earth in pain and suffering.
- What parallels can you find between these stories and those of Richard, Bolingbroke, Mowbray and Exton?
- How does the language of the play reflect that of Genesis? (Look particularly at Act 1 scene 1 lines 84–108, Act 1 scene 2, Act 1 scene 3 lines 148–177, Act 3 scene 4, and the last speech of the play.)
- There are also New Testament images in *Richard II*. In what ways is Richard compared to Christ?

2 The sun

The frame of the contemporary state portrait of Richard II in Westminster Abbey is embellished with animals, birds and sunbursts. They serve to remind the viewer that the king is the source of prosperity and glory to his country. The sun is the creative power which drives the universe, but it may also dazzle and destroy.

- Consider the use of the word 'sun' at the following moments: Act 1 scene 3 line 145; Act 2 scene 1 line 12; Act 2 scene 4 line 21; Act 3 scene 3 line 63; Act 4 scene 1 lines 254–283. What associations does the word have and what does its use tell us about kingship?
- How does Act 3 scene 3 lines 176–183 represent the fall of Richard both in dramatic and figurative terms?

3 The Garden

The Garden scene (Act 3 scene 4), which compares Richard and his government of the country to a gardener's control of a garden, is central to the imagery of the play. It is not the only moment at which characters compare human life and behaviour in this way.

- Look at the image used by Queen Isabel to describe Richard in Act 5 scene 1 lines 7–10, and compare them with Act 1 scene 2 lines 13–21, and Act 2 scene 1 lines 134 and 153. How do these lines continue and develop the image used by the Gardener?
- The Gardener talks of 'the soil's fertility' which it is his duty to protect (Act 3 scene 4 line 39). Soil, earth and ground are words which also reverberate throughout the play. Look, for example, at how the word 'ground' is used in Act 1 scene 3 lines 306–309, Act 2 scene 3 line 90 and generally in Act 3 scene 2. How do all these uses develop the vision of England contained in John of Gaunt's speech in Act 2 scene 1?

All three groups of images – Biblical, sun and garden – are related. The sun and the garden are themselves religious images; all remind us that Richard knows his 'master, God omnipotent' has given him a sacred trust, though other characters doubt his ability to fulfil that trust. The web of imagery in the play draws us in to its framework of belief and action.

Contexts

We do not experience literature (or any art form) in a vacuum. Our approach to the work is conditioned by our own knowledge and experience as well as by the circumstances under which the work was produced. Other, less individual, contexts also condition our response to the text. In the case of *Richard II* we shall consider:
- the play as a theatrical experience
- the audience's response to the play.

To do this we will discuss features of *Richard II* both as a tragedy and a history play, and how our response to the play might differ from that of the original audience.

1 **The play as a theatrical experience**
   Detailed study of a complex and interesting play may lead one away from the experience of the play in performance. It is important to remember that the author's prime intention is not to indulge in philosophical arguments, impress with linguistic flair or develop a sociological critique (though all these may be present in the text) but to entertain. When we are in the theatre we are more concerned to engage with an experience than to question what it all means.
   - In what ways is *Richard II* theatrical? Despite the fact that Shakespeare largely avoids physical conflict, do you consider the play a dramatic experience?
     Among the points you may consider are:
     – sharply differentiated characters
     – a succession of conflict situations
     – dramatic irony
     – trial scenes
     – moments of high emotion

- political intrigue which affects the government of the nation
- highly rhetorical poetry
- one fight and many deaths.

The plot was probably well known to Shakespeare's audience which would have been most interested in what the play says about the characters and how the narrative is developed theatrically. We know that the play was a popular success but it is something of a surprise that Shakespeare seems to ignore some dramatic opportunities.

- Imagine that you are a modern film producer about to make a film of *Richard II*. List any events reported in the play but not shown on the stage and which you feel would contribute to the drama of your film.
- Suggest reasons why Shakespeare does not attempt to show any of these scenes.

Among your considerations might be that some of the potential action – Bolingbroke's entry into London, for example – is beyond the capacity of the Elizabethan (or any) stage to show convincingly. More significantly, scenes such as the deaths of Gaunt or of Bushy, Green and Wiltshire would provide emotional climaxes at points which would alter the dramatic development of the play.

- Draw a graph of the emotional temperature of the play. To do this you will need a sheet of paper on which the 'x' axis is divided equally between the scenes of the play and the 'y' axis represents the dramatic tension of the play. Mark on the page events and moments of emotional tension. When you join the tension points you will probably finish with a graph which rises, perhaps in a rather uneven manner, from just above zero at the very beginning of the play to a high point towards the end of Act 5 scene 5. It will probably fall back in the final scene. Compare your graph with that of other students to consider just how high an emotional temperature the play generates and whether you agree on the dramatic hot spots.

2 The play as tragedy

The title of the play when it was first published was *The Tragedie of King Richard the Second*. Tragedy has a specific meaning in dramatic literature and more than any other of Shakespeare's English history plays (with the exception of *Richard III*) this play has many of the hallmarks of dramatic tragedy.

Elizabethan playwrights looked back to the writings of Aristotle and Seneca for a model of tragic drama and *Richard II* has the following features of classical tragedy:

- a hero of high rank who comes to a tragic end
- the hero's fall is the consequence of a combination of a tragic flaw in his nature and ill fortune
- hubris – overweening pride – is a key element in the protagonist's fall
- elaborate, rhetorical language.

Some elements are largely, though not entirely, present:

- the action of the play is tragic throughout – though there are a few moments of comedy and emotional relief
- violent action occurs off-stage – until the penultimate scene.

Some elements of classical tragedy, for example the unities of time and place described by Aristotle, are absent from this play, as they are generally in English tragedy.

The aim of tragic writing was not to frighten or depress the audience. Aristotle wrote of tragic drama cleansing the emotions, providing what he called *catharsis*. Members of the audience should leave the theatre feeling relieved and invigorated by the emotional journey they have experienced.

1 What elements of the language, characterisation and action of *Richard II* suggest that it should continue to be considered one of Shakespeare's tragedies?
2 Do we care enough about Richard for us to feel him to be a tragic hero?

3 How far do you think the audience is likely to experience *catharsis* as a result of seeing *Richard II*? How might certain elements – for example the prominent role played by Bolingbroke, and the varying emotional tone, especially in Act 5 – prevent the play becoming an overwhelming emotional experience?

3 The play as history

1 What was Shakespeare's intention in writing *Richard II*? He had already written four plays about the consequences of Richard II's reign – three parts of *Henry VI* and *Richard III*. These plays were celebratory in that they demonstrated how Henry VII, the first Tudor monarch and grandfather of Elizabeth I, had come to power at the end of the War of the Roses. Shakespeare's audience was asked to consider its good fortune in having had a century of successful Tudor government and of being spared the disaster of civil war – perhaps the most appalling condition to befall any society.
   • What did Shakespeare consider to be the hallmarks of good government, according to the commentary he provides in *Richard II*?

2 When Shakespeare wrote *Richard II* he probably had in mind that he was completing a sequence which had started with *Edward III* – an anonymous play to which he had almost certainly contributed in about 1589 – and would continue with plays about Henry IV and Henry V. This project would have an air of artistic completeness about it which may have appealed to the playwright, though more important would have been the simple commercial reason that history plays were popular, especially those which allowed the acting company to flatter the monarch and other noble patrons.
   • What aspects of the play do you think are calculated to please the Elizabethan audience?

3 *Richard II* deals with dangerous material: the abdication and murder of a king. It is only able to do so because it affirms so strongly the divine right by which English monarchs ruled and the dangers attendant on defying God's law.

- Consider the statements about monarchy and the prophecies about England's future made by various characters during the play. How does Shakespeare ensure that *Richard II* is a warning that 'worldly men cannot depose/The deputy elected by the Lord'? How does the Biblical imagery of the play help to affirm the sanctity of the monarch? (See 'The Language of the Play' on page 225.)

4 Another factor which must concern us in the writing of history is the standpoint of the writer. Some critics have argued that *Richard II* and the other three plays of the second tetralogy are written from the point of view of the House of Lancaster. Shakespeare is thought to have had strong Lancastrian connections in his 'missing years' and Queen Elizabeth is descended from the House of Lancaster through John of Gaunt's third wife. Gaunt's memorable praise of England,

This precious stone set in the silver sea,
Which serves it in the office of a wall,
Or as a moat defensive to a house,
Against the envy of less happier lands;

would chime with all who saw Elizabeth as the leader who had defended the country against the Spanish Armada only seven years before.

- Though Elizabeth is said to have disliked the popular association of her with Richard II, are there any elements of the play which might have pleased her?

4 The play and the audience today

Finally, it is important to bear in mind our own preconceptions in approaching this play. We are four hundred years away from the time of Shakespeare and a further two hundred from the reign of Richard II. We receive entertainment in a different way. We have different expectations of family, morality and social class. We view the world from different scientific, religious and geographical perspectives.

- Make a list of what you think are the ten most important differences between our time and that of Shakespeare. Compare your list with those of other students. Collate the top three differences. Apply these differences to your experience of *Richard II*. How do they ensure that the way we will experience the play is bound to be different from that of the original audience?

How does a modern audience receive the play? The language causes difficulty, but is often less of a problem in performance than when we read the play on our own. The actors and production will tell us much about the action and relationships which we otherwise struggle to work out from the printed text. The values and behaviour of the characters may also be a problem. Their adherence to a chivalric code and semi-feudal relationships seems odd to us who live with democratic institutions and different shared moral values.

- List the values and behaviours presented in the play and which now seem out of date or alien. If you had to write the rule book for the nobility of the world of *Richard II*, what would it contain? (Write the chapter headings as well as a few entries in greater detail.)

Drama activities

In the Activities sections we suggest a number of ways in which you can explore the play using drama. The notes that follow explain how the different types of activity can be organised. Most of the suggestions in the book fall into one of these groups:
- improvisation
- hot seating
- stopping the action
- forum theatre.

Improvisation

Improvisation is a form of theatre in which the actors do not have a written script, but make it up as they 'go along'. When you improvise, you need to know:
- **who** you are
- **when** and **where** the scene takes place
- **what** happened before the scene takes place
- **why** the scene is happening (for example if there is a conflict between the characters or a problem they are faced with).

How you improvise depends upon how much planning and polishing you want to do. Some people like just to launch into the situation without any planning at all. This is a good way of working if you want to find out about the characters, relationships and emotions involved. Others like to discuss the situation and the main things that will happen before they begin to improvise. This is useful if you are working towards a scene, so that it becomes more confident and 'polished' – especially if you are preparing for a performance. Which approach you use depends upon the situation you are working on and what you want to get out of it.

Hot seating

This is a good way of examining very closely the thoughts and feelings of one character at a key moment in the play.

For example, you might choose Bolingbroke at the moment in Act 1 scene 1 when he accuses Mowbray of treason. If you wanted to explore this situation through hot seating, this is what you would do:

1 Choose one member of the group to be Bolingbroke.
2 That person sits 'in the hot seat', with the rest of the group around him.
3 Other members of the group ask Bolingbroke about how he feels and why he acted in the way that he did.
4 Bolingbroke must reply in character, and without pausing too long to think about his answer.
5 The rest of the group keep the questions going, picking up the replies that Bolingbroke gives.
6 At the end you can discuss what came out of the questioning and whether Bolingbroke's replies agree with the way other people see his character.

Variations

• The people in the group can become characters themselves: Richard, Mowbray and John of Gaunt.
  Then each one has to ask questions from the point of view of that character.
• The questioners can take on different styles of questioning. One might be sympathetic, while a second would be aggressive, and a third sneering, for example.

Stopping the action

This is a different way of focusing on a particular moment in the play. Instead of choosing a particular character, you choose a particular moment. There are two main ways in which you can do this.

Photographs

A photograph is based on the idea that you freeze a particular moment in the play. You can do it in different ways:

- *Freeze Frame* Have one member in the group act as the photographer. The rest of the group act the scene and at the moment the photographer says 'Freeze!', everyone must stay absolutely still.
- Choose the moment in the scene you want to photograph. Discuss how the photograph should look and then take up the positions you have agreed.
- Choose the moment in the scene you want to photograph. Give each member of the group a number. Number 1 takes up position as his/her character and freezes. Number 2 then joins Number 1 and freezes. Number 3 does the same and so on until everyone is in the photograph.

Once you have made your photograph you can come out of it one at a time and make suggestions about how it could be improved. You can also build on the photograph by one of the following:

- Make up a caption for the photograph.
- Let each character speak his or her thoughts at that moment in the play.

Statues/Paintings

For these you choose one member of the group to be the artist. Then choose:

- a moment in the play
- a title you have made up
- a quotation.

The artist then arranges the members of the group, one by one, into a group statue or pose of the chosen subject. Different members of the group can take it in turn to be the artist.

Forum theatre

Another way of exploring a key moment in the play is called 'forum theatre'. The group divides in two:

- a small number of actors take on roles
- the rest are theatre directors.

You then work as follows:

1 Choose the moment in the play you are going to work on. (For example, the moment in Act 2 scene 1 when Northumberland says, 'Well, lords, the Duke of Lancaster is dead.)

2 Choose someone to be Northumberland.

3 Arrange the space you are working in, agree where the characters are, where people enter and exit and so on.

4 Start by asking Northumberland to say what he thinks about where he should be and how he should move.

5 Then the rest of the group, the 'directors', try out different ways of presenting that moment. For example:
   • they can ask him to speak his lines in a particular way
   • they can suggest he uses certain moves or gestures.

6 The short extract from the play can be tried in several different ways until the group have used up all their ideas.

7 Then you should discuss what worked and what didn't work and why.

Preparing for an examination

You will be expected to have a detailed and accurate knowledge of your set texts. You must have read your set texts several times and you need to know the sequence of events and the narrative of a text. The plot summaries in this edition should help you with this. It may seem rather unfair but you will get little credit in the final examination for merely 'telling the story'; simply 'going through' the narrative is seen as particularly worthless in an open-book examination. However, you will be in no position to argue a convincing case or develop a deep understanding unless you have this detailed knowledge.

The questions

A-level questions are demanding but they should always be accessible and central, a fair test of your knowledge and understanding. They are rarely obscure or marginal. There is a relatively small number of questions which can be asked on any text, even though the ways in which they can be worded are almost infinite. They tend to fall into quite straightforward categories or types, as outlined below.

Character

You may be asked to discuss your response to a particular character, to consider the function or presentation of a character or perhaps to compare and contrast characters.

Society

You may be asked to consider the kind of society depicted by the text or perhaps the way in which individuals relate to that society.

Themes

You may be asked to discuss the ideas and underlying issues which are explored by a text, and the author's concerns and interests.

Attitudes

You may be asked to consider what views or values are revealed by the text, what is valued and what is attacked.

Style or technique

You may be asked to look at the methods a writer uses to achieve particular effects. In essence, you are being asked to examine how a text achieves its effects and you need to consider such matters as diction, imagery, tone and structure.

Personal response

You may be asked to give your own view of the text but this must be more than just unsupported assertion. You need to move beyond 'I think...' to a well-considered evaluation based on close reading and textual evidence. It is worth remembering that there are a limited number of sensible responses to a text.

'Whole text' questions

These questions require you to consider the text as a whole. You need a coherent overview of the text and the ability to select appropriate detail and evidence.

'Specific' passages

These questions require close reading and analysis but sometimes the specific passage has to be related to another passage or perhaps to the whole text.

Conclusion

A critical essay attempts to construct a logical argument based on the evidence of the text. It needs a clear sense of direction and purpose; it is better to start with a simple, coherent attitude than to ramble aimlessly or produce a shapeless answer which never gets into focus. Each paragraph should be a step in a developing argument and should engage in analysis of textual detail which is relevant to the question. You must answer the question set – as opposed to the question you wanted to be set – and you must be prepared to discuss a specific aspect of the text or approach it from a slightly new or unexpected angle. You will need to be selective and choose the material which is appropriate to the actual question. An essay which deals only in sweeping generalisations may be judged to lack detail and substance, while one which gets too involved in minor details may lack direction and a conceptual framework. The ideal balance is achieved when overview and detailed knowledge combine to allow easy movement from the general to the particular, and back again.

Although different examination boards and syllabuses have their own ways of expressing them, there are basically three criteria against which your work will be judged. They are:
- knowledge and understanding
- answering the question relevantly
- written expression.

Practice questions

1   Dr Johnson, who edited *Richard II* in his collected edition
    of Shakespeare in 1765 wrote:

> *This play is one of those which Shakespeare has apparently
> revised; but as success in works of invention is not always
> proportionate to labour, it is not finished at last with the
> happy force of some other of his tragedies nor can be said
> much to affect the passions or enlarge the understanding.*

    How far do you find this an adequate critical assessment of
    the play?

2   '*Richard II* affords a straightforward example of figurative
    language and stage spectacle complementing one another.'
    (*Discovering Shakespeare's Meaning*, Leah Scragg, Longman,
    London, 1988). Show how this is true. How far do the
    images evoked by the language of the play enhance it as a
    dramatic experience?

3   'Shakespeare knew the deposition of *Richard II* to be
    politically right but morally wrong. This is the source of the
    play's tension.' Discuss.

4   Faced with producing *Richard II* with a small, all-male
    acting company, justify your decision to stage the play
    without any female characters. How do you think your
    decision will change the dramatic impact of the play?

5   'O, call back yesterday, bid time return' (Act 3 scene 2 line
    69). Justify the view that the theme of *Richard II* is time,
    and the hopeless human struggle to master it.

6   'The critics have been very much divided on the amount of
    sympathy we should extend to Richard. Some find him
    wholly admirable, and others regard him as wholly
    contemptible.' (*Richard II*, Kenneth Muir, Signet, 1963).
    Where do you stand on this debate, and why?

7   'The only interesting character in *Richard II* is Richard and
    the purpose of all the other characters is to demonstrate
    why Richard deserves our attention?' Discuss.

8   'Thou dost beguile me' says Richard to the mirror before

dashing it to the ground. The question which obsesses Richard, and to which he never provides for himself a satisfactory answer, is 'What is the truth?' How far is his failure to answer the question both the subject of the play and the reason for his downfall?

9 'Bolingbroke ... is granted scarcely any inwardness, and marches inexorably through politics to power, without ever greatly arousing our interest' (*Shakespeare; The Invention of the Human*, Harold Bloom, New York, 1998) In what ways, if any, does the character of Bolingbroke arouse your interest?

10 'Though *Richard II* appears to be about affairs of state, grand events and great political themes, it is at heart a family saga.' Discuss.

11 In *Richard II* characters not only die alone, they live alone. Despite all the talk of family this is a bleak play about human isolation. Discuss this view.

12 Consider the view that *Richard II* is a masterpiece of poetry and heroic language but it gains little from performance since it is not dramatic.

13 *Richard II* is neither humorous nor excitingly dramatic. Our appreciation of it in the theatre is built upon its use of irony, both dramatic and verbal. Discuss, demonstrating why you find the play a satisfying theatrical experience.

14 '*Richard II* is a warning from history of the dangers of absolute government, the horrors of civil conflict and the selfish unreliability of the old aristocracy. Talk of chivalry and honour is no more than a smoke screen. This play is a splendid argument for revolution.' Discuss.

Glossary

Alliteration: A figure of speech in which a number of words close to each other in a piece of writing begin with the same sound:

> *My loving lord, I take my leave of you*
> (Act 1 scene 3 line 63)

Alliteration helps to draw attention to the words and emphasises rhythmical structures.

Antithesis: A figure of speech in which two opposite or contrasting ideas are brought together, often with rhythmical balance:

> *I'll give my jewels for a set of beads ...*
> *And my large kingdom for a little grave*
> (Act 3 scene 3 lines 147–153)

Apostrophe: When a character speaks directly to someone or something who/which is absent. Richard several times apostrophises God, and Salisbury addresses the absent Richard in Act 2 scene 4 lines 18–20:

> *Ah Richard! With the eyes of heavy mind*
> *I see thy glory like a shooting star*
> *Fall to the base earth from the firmament*

Assonance: The repetition of vowel sounds, usually stressed, to reinforce rhythm and mood:

> *We make woe wanton with this fond delay.*
> *Once more, adieu; the rest let sorrow say.*
> (Act 5 scene 1 lines 101–102)

Blank verse: Unrhymed verse in which each line has ten syllables, comprising five 'feet', or measures, of two syllables each. The form of the measures, a short (weak) syllable followed by a long (strong) syllable, is known as an iambus. Thus the main form of the play is unrhymed iambic pentameter:

> *My lords of England, let me tell you this:*
> *I have had feeling of my cousin's wrongs,*
> *And laboured all I could to do him right.*
> *(Act 2 scene 3 lines 139–141)*

To avoid monotony this basic form of blank verse is varied by a change in the pattern of weak and strong syllables, and/or by altering the number of syllables in a line.

Caesura: A pause within a line of verse. Because of the length of the blank verse or heroic couplet line there is often a caesura, which may or may not be marked by punctuation:

> QUEEN ISABEL   *Banish us both, and send the king with me.*
> RICHARD   *That were some love, but little policy*
> (Act 5 scene 1 lines 83–84)

Conceit: An extended metaphor in which several points of comparison are developed:

> *Why should we, in the compass of a pale,*
> *Keep law and form and due proportion,*
> *Showing, as in a model, our firm estate,*
> *When our sea-walled garden, the whole land,*
> *Is full of weeds, her fairest flowers choked up,*
> *Her fruit trees all unpruned, her hedges ruined,*
> *Her knots disordered, and her wholesome herbs*
> *Swarming with caterpillars?*
> (Act 3 scene 4 lines 40–47)

Dramatic irony: A situation in a play when the audience (and possibly some of the characters) know something that one or more of the characters do not. In a pantomime, for example, young children will shout to tell the heroine that the villain is creeping up behind her. In *Richard II* we know by the end of Act 2 that most of Richard's supporters have left him but he does not become aware of this until the end of Act 3 scene 2. The whole play may be considered ironic since, because the plot is historical, the audience may thus know that Bolingbroke will destroy Richard.

Exeunt: A Latin word meaning 'They go away', used for the departure of characters from a scene.

Exit: A Latin word meaning 'S/he goes away', used for the departure of a character from a scene.

Heroic couplet: A pair of rhyming iambic pentameter lines (see *Blank verse,* above):
> *Farewell, my blood; which if to-day thou shed,*
> *Lament we may, but not revenge thee dead.*
> (Act 1 scene 3 lines 57–58)

Homophone: A word which has the same sound as another but a different meaning or origin; for example 'I' and 'ay' in Act 4 scene 1 line 200:
> *Ay, no; no, ay; for I must nothing be*

Hyperbole: Deliberate exaggeration, for dramatic effect. For example Mowbray's address to Richard in Act 1 scene 1 lines 22–24:
> *Each day still betters other's happiness*
> *Until the heavens, envying earth's good hap,*
> *Add an immortal title to your crown.*

Irony: When someone says one thing and means another, sometimes with the intention to make fun of, tease, or satirise someone else. Sometimes irony is unintended by the speaker, as, for example, when Richard reports Bolingbroke's behaviour toward the common people in Act 1:
> *As were our England in reversion his,*
> *And he our subjects' next degree in hope.*
> (Act 1 scene 4 lines 35–36)

Metaphor: A figure of speech in which one person, or thing, or idea is described as if it were another. For example, Richard compares the sun to an eye:
> *When the searching eye of heaven is hid*
> *Behind the globe and lights the lower world,*
> *Then thieves and robbers range abroad unseen*
> (Act 3 scene 2 lines 37–39)

Oxymoron: A figure of speech in which the writer combines two ideas which are opposites:

> *Made glory base and sovereignty a slave;*
> *Proud majesty a subject, state a peasant.*

(Act 4 scene 1 lines 250–251)

Personification: Referring to a thing or an idea as if it were a person, as Richard does to the mirror in Act 4 scene 1 lines 278–280:

> *O flattering glass,*
> *Like to my followers in prosperity,*
> *Thou dost beguile me.*

Play on words: see *Pun*

Pun: A figure of speech in which the writer uses a word that has more than one meaning. Both meanings of the word are used to make a joke. For example, an angel is both a heavenly creature and a coin when Richard says in Act 3 scene 2 lines 60–61:

> *God for his Richard hath in heavenly pay*
> *A glorious angel*

Rhymed verse: Sometimes Shakespeare uses a pattern of rhymed lines. Rhyming couplets round off a scene or incident within a scene, or provide the exit lines for a character. Sometimes the pattern is more complex and is related to the structure of a *Sonnet*. A *Shakespearean Sonnet* rhymes *abab cdcd efef gg*. The fourteen lines of a Petrarchan sonnet are divided into an octave which rhymes *abba*, and a *Sestet* which rhymes *cdcdcd* or *cdecde*. Use of such complex rhyme schemes emphasises the rhetorical 'high' style of the verse:

> *But now the blood of twenty thousand men*
> *Did triumph in my face, and they are fled;*
> *And till so much blood thither come again,*
> *Have I not reason to look pale and dead?*
> *All souls that will be safe fly from my side,*
> *For time hath set a blot upon my pride.*

(Act 3 scene 2 lines 76–81)

Simile: A comparison between two things which the writer makes clear by using words such as 'like' or 'as':
See, see, King Richard doth himself appear,
As doth the blushing discontented sun
From out the fiery portal of the East
(Act 3 scene 3 lines 62–64)

Soliloquy: When a character is alone on stage, or separated from the other characters in some way, and speaks apparently to himself or herself.

Sonnet: see **Rhymed verse**

Stychomythia: Dialogue in which two characters speak single lines of dialogue alternately. The speakers often play with each other's words and echo each other rhythmically, for example in Act 1 scene 3 lines 258–267 and Act 5 scene 1 lines 81–86.

Tetralogy: A series of four connected plays.

Further reading

Students will find it useful to have a knowledge of the sequels to *Richard II* in Shakespeare's second tetralogy: *1 Henry IV, 2 Henry IV* and *Henry V*. The plays of the first tetralogy, the three parts of *Henry VI* and *Richard II*, complete the story of Bolingbroke and Northumberland and demonstrate how the prophecies of the play are fulfilled.

Shakespeare was certainly influenced by Christopher Marlowe's 1592 play, *Edward II*, and a comparison between the two plays offers a fruitful critical exercise.

Anthony Holden's *Shakespeare* (1999) is a very readable biography which places *Richard II* in its historical context, bringing to life the circumstances of its early performances.

Shakespeare: A Bibliographical Guide ed. Stanley Wells (OUP, 1990) includes a review of the critical history of the plays in the second tetralogy. This is the best place to start for a critical reading list. *Appropriating Shakespeare* by Brian Vickers (Yale University Press, 1993) is an entertaining and challenging account of modern critical theories and practices.